Never Again MEANS Never Again

Dismantling hate groups and other musings

By

Michael S. Gutter

Disclaimer and Trigger Warning

You'll see that I wrote this book in the same strong language I would articulate to any member of a hate group. All of us should strive to be honest, and sometimes a topic calls for brutal honesty. The content may offend you; I don't care; refute it. The language may offend you; tough shit. If you are squeamish about the truth and are happy with being ignorant, I suggest you continue reading closed-minded racist pamphlets on the toilet.

You see, the premise of my book targets those who need to know that Jewish people are sick of your unfounded bullshit and lies. Large contingents of Jews are no longer willing to sit back and take it any longer. I assure you; we have the means and capabilities to defend ourselves and be the aggressor. That's what you'll find different about this book. It calls out the haters in the strongest words possible. If we are fortunate, it may resonate. Fingers crossed, it will sway at least a few of our enemies from darkness to light.

Any views, thoughts, and opinions expressed by the author are solely that of the author and do not reflect the views, opinions, policies, or position of SuburbanBuzz.com LLC.

Copyright © 2022 Michael S. Gutter

All rights reserved.

No content of this book may be copied, excerpted, replicated, or shared without the permission of the author.

Published by SuburbanBuzz.com LLC

ISBN: 978-1-959446-04-0

DEDICATION

I dedicate this book to my most significant inspiration, role model, and person of the highest character I've ever met or known — my grandfather, Julius Gutter. The man left his immediate family in Czechoslovakia, consisting of one brother and five sisters (ten children altogether). Two older brothers were married and out of the house, one had already left for America, and one brother passed away at a young age. He opened a successful bakery when he was only 18. My grandfather left Czechoslovakia when he noticed the uptick of antisemitism which included his customer base that no longer came to his bakery.

After the war, he learned that his mother and brother were shot in the back on a march to a concentration camp. Only one sister made it back alive of the seven who were in the house when my grandfather left.

Growing up, my four sisters and I spent a lot of time at our grandparents' home. My grandmother Evelyn was outstanding. She was a chain-smoking Yenta who mainly did the talking for both her and my grandfather.

My grandparents were very active in the Jewish community in Columbus, Ohio. During the High Holidays, they opened their house to the Jewish community and made sure everyone was well fed. They did this on both High Holidays for years, and I'm telling you, their house was always packed. They were both just such beautiful people, honest and fun, and I still remember how much fun my grandmother and I had playing Yahtzee on their kitchen table. Passover is still memorable to me and was always held at my grandparents' house. Besides our large family, if someone else wanted to attend, a chair would be found. My grandfather was always at the head of the table and led the service. He knew I loved him, but he was unaware of how intensely proud I was of him (and still am) as he sat at the Passover table and looked around at his large family.

He was a very intelligent man — quiet, tough, thoughtful, and most of all respectful, and boy, did he love his Evelyn. When we spout the term, "You can't find anyone to say a bad thing about…" it's true of my grandfather in my eyes, but also in the eyes of everyone who knew him. They would always go out of their way to tell me how much they admired and respected him. Loved him.

You can browse online and find information on my grandfather. He did a couple of interviews in print and one videotaped called "Children of the Holocaust." I highly recommend it, and you'll see his intelligence early on while answering some questions about dates and locations from 50 years prior. After watching it for the first time, I kept thinking, "What fucking country on the planet would not want him as a citizen?" Such a beautiful, beautiful person.

I have a word that I rarely give out. I try to bestow it on someone at least once a year, if I tell them or not. It's a word that encompasses everything that I try and strive to be, but I know I'm not there yet. That word is "mensch." My grandfather was unequivocally a mensch. If I was able to gather all the others that I've given that term to over the years, my grandfather, Julius Gutter, would be at the head of the table.

TABLE OF CONTENTS

Introduction 1
Chapter 1: The Rise of Hitler 13
Chapter 2: Feats of Judaism 23
Chapter 3: Let Us Entertain You 39
Chapter 4: Mein Kampf 51
Chapter 5: The Versailles Lie 69
Chapter 6: World War II Allied and Axis Forces 83
Chapter 7: Let's Play a Drinking Game 103
Chapter 8: The Jews Did NOT Kill Jesus. 117
Chapter 9: Monsters in Boots 119
Chapter 10: How To Be and Stay an Asshole 127
Chapter 11: More Assholes 141
Chapter 12: Harvesting the Jews 153
Chapter 13: A Gallery of Thieves 169
Chapter 14: Holocaust Deniers and Hate Groups 193
Chapter 15: The Israeli-Palestinian Conflict 227
Chapter 16: American Jewry 253
Chapter 17: Never Again MEANS Never Again 265
Resources 281

Introduction

"I have not come into this world to make men better, but to make use of their weaknesses."
~ *Adolf Hitler*

I've written this book for those who need it most — the individuals who are involved in any type of hate group. Once they grasp a clear and accurate depiction of the lies they've been told and the lies they are telling others, then perhaps they'll see past the indoctrination and bias. Perhaps they'll shake off the stranglehold of a malignant belief system. They might even transform into the human beings they were meant to be and release their misplaced hate. Maybe they'll finally realize their indoctrination has been based on lies, exaggeration, and falsities.

This book exposes the atrocities, misgivings, and shortcomings that Jews on this planet have had to deal with since the beginning of the twentieth century. It is meant to correct the misconceptions and ridiculous fabrications that society has been spoon-fed and provides the names and timelines of those who instigated the smears, supported by facts. There are times I call out the bigots harshly because of their ignorance, which hopefully dissipates with each fact provided. A lot of the haters have a deeply embedded ignorance that will take longer to address. Hopefully, my research will become the initial spark.

I'm a reluctant subject matter expert on the 20th-century

treatment of Jews. I say "reluctant" because no one in his or her right mind relishes the horrors and utter depravity of the Holocaust. The bloody legacy foisted on the world by Hitler and the terrible atrocities committed by his monstrous minions cannot be justified. The more I study, the more disgusted and outraged I become.

Being an avid historian and researcher, and in the last few years committing my life to expose truth vs. lies, it occurred to me that Jews are still relatively passive regarding modern-day persecution. Despite laws and advocacy groups, we are still accosted on street corners. Our synagogues are defiled. We are continuously targeted online as being either subhuman, or some sort of master race bent on destroying the lives of non-Jews.

I'm sick of it. No more passive tolerance to the antisemites. We must do more than point our fingers and scold the haters. There have to be consequences. The bad guys must be unmasked, publicly called out, and stopped in their tracks. As far as I can see, this is the only way to combat their lies, dangerous rhetoric, and nefarious activities.

Yes, I'm a pissed-off Jew who is forging an initiative to attack this abuse "head-on," so to speak. I've pursued the unvarnished truth of yesteryear and tracked the fallout experienced by Jews today. It's shameful that slander, libel, harassment, discrimination, and hate crimes are still perpetuated against Jews by radical groups and nut jobs. Enough is enough. So, I have looked at various reasonable ways we should address antisemitism going forward, and it all leads back to one inevitable conclusion. We need to go on the offensive.

I'm providing facts with a resource section, and my opinions. Feel free to add to this body of work or refute anything I've written. Disagreements are fine and often lead to more personal education and growth. But refute my musings with rock-solid facts — not conspiracy theories, conjecture, and bullshit. I dare you to let me know what I don't understand about hate groups.

I've always been curious as to why there are people who want to harm Jews. I certainly understand situations where we as individuals can be rude, condescending, mean, or just assholes, but I cannot think of one case where any of that has been displayed by our religion or culture. Not one.

What true, accurate, or real examples could someone provide that Jews, in either culture or religion, want to harm anyone? I'm not talking the bullshit, "make-believe," no proof, irrational lies that we control banking, insurance, the world, etc. I want to know what possible reason — a specific reason — that causes someone to wake up one morning and want to harm us. It's fascinating to me because it's so baffling. We've had issues with some Arab countries and with some small factions of Arabs over the years, but that's overseas, not here. That also fascinates me, as I've met plenty of Arabs over the years, and a few of them became good friends. I don't care if they're Arabs. Why should I? At no point have I ever wanted them to leave this country or for me to pick up a weapon to injure them. Never.

Most people who know me understand that I have no level of prejudice, and I do not judge anyone. I have a very basic and "easy to remember" philosophy when it comes to meeting someone, and it has nothing to do with their race, religion, creed, favorite color, etc. Ready? It's simply, "Are you an asshole" or "Are you not an asshole?" If they are not assholes, then I just made a new friend. I don't waste my time trying to find out what I don't like in a person and just simply rely on them passing or failing my "asshole" test. Once you've passed (99.9% do), then if you're a Black, gay, mentally challenged hermaphrodite who puts ketchup on caviar, my only comment is, pass the ketchup when you're done. If someone doesn't pass my test, then I simply won't hang out with them and LEAVE IT AT THAT.

Please point out anywhere in Judaism or Jewish writings (based on our religious text, not someone who's Jewish and wrote something on his own accord) that goes after you individually or your groups as a whole. If you have something and I agree with you on it, no problem. Let's try and rectify it.

What hate groups either don't understand, or don't care to understand, is that we're Jewish, we're proud to be Jews, and you will not be forcing us to go anywhere. Jews in this country currently make up less than .02% of the U.S. population, yet you somehow think if we're not around, you will gain a louder voice? Enlightenment? Automatically be first in line at the DMV? I'm just guessing, so would you care to share with the rest of the class what it is?

What type of superpowers do you think we have? What type of collusion powers do you think we have? And if we had these powers, why on earth would we target you? Why do you feel important enough that we would spend our time and effort going after you? Most of what I have read and seen about hate groups and their members would put your groups at the bottom of a listing of people that I would be interested in taking advantage of for personal gain. If your goal is to ascend from the bottom, you guys are going about it all wrong. You're way, way off, and by off, I mean you're losing prospective members who would prefer to join a local leprosy club than to be associated with your organizations.

Have you ever thought about where we, as Jews, are located in this country? Think about it. By numbers, we're heavily grouped in only a handful of states and Florida for the entire Southern region. So again, what possible "real world," not made-up crap, have we done to have earned your animosity?

I have never woken up and thought about any of you. Why would I? I have enough of my own issues. You and your groups are so far down my "give-a-shit list" that by the time I may think about you, I'm already asleep. What is so important or lacking in your life that you would risk going to jail for someone you've never met, talked to, exchanged emails with, etc.? I'm confident on day two of being jailed, you will not only be distraught but highly pissed off at yourself over anything senseless you did. You do not need to live like this. Again, we're not harming you or thinking about any of you. You really shouldn't be harming us or thinking about us, either.

The only question you should have right now is, "Why is this author writing about this topic?" You'll soon see the answer to that question and answers to many, many others as you continue reading. It would take me too long to explain, but I have always wanted to write about various Jewish topics, especially about Jews worldwide who have been falsely and incorrectly blamed and targeted. I want to set the record straight. Furthermore, I have world-class OCD, so when I started this book…I couldn't stop. As I dove into more and more research, I became angrier and angrier. The ignorance of Jewish hate is based on such massive farces that I just couldn't stop, and I wanted to address as many issues as possible.

Also, I like to listen to history, military documentaries, Mafia audiotapes, and stuff like that when I go to bed. One night I was listening to something on WWII, and as soon as I started hearing Nazis barking out orders, I got pissed. I've heard them plenty of times before, but something that night set me off. The next day I was reading an article, and near the bottom was a mention of that fucking coward who killed 11 worshipers at a Pittsburgh synagogue. Even though it took place in 2018, I grabbed a pen and started writing.

I have always been very, very proud of my religion, my family, and my friends whom I've been fortunate to meet, know, and love. Early on in my research, I read there have been 4,700 plus anti-semitic incidences in the last 24 months. Let me repeat — 4,700 in two years. That was it. I couldn't take it anymore, and I wanted to see if other Jews felt the same as I do. Also, I wanted to discover how much information these hate groups really have and know about us.

This country, which has given all of us so much, doesn't deserve this vitriol within her borders. Unfounded and untrue lies — we don't deserve it. Misplaced truths and hate — you don't deserve it. If you are continuing lies passed down from previous hate group members, whose lies were passed down from previous hate group members, whose lies were passed down…where does it end? When will it end? I say, why not today?

This book needs to be read with an open mind. If you want to mock or call me out on something you think is untrue, no problem but finish the book first. This book will help clear up a lot of incorrect misnomers and information about Jews and American Jews. My hope is this "kickstarts" your first step in leaving whatever hate group you're in and helps expedite YOU, being welcomed back into society, instead of being outcast by misplaced hate.

I have launched a brand new open forum website, https://www.neveragainmeans.com, in sync with the launch of this book. Everyone is invited to weigh in, as long as it's civil. This growing message board will contain virtually any topic, and we can learn so much about one another. I encourage participation by hate group and non-hate group members, but if you scream, bitch and yell at other members, you will be banned. In other words, don't be an ass. If you want to learn, educate, write your experiences, or whatever,

I truly hope you'll join. Sign up for the newsletter and read the blog posts; I can almost guarantee you will find it illuminating.

In writing this, I was hoping to figure out the thought process of hate group members who want to come after me or any Jew, especially when I don't know them and don't even know anyone who knows them. What contempt could someone have for me when I've never done anything to them and definitely not to the point where they feel the need to form a fucking group to harm me.

To the haters: the irony is that we have more in common than we have in our differences. Yet, this is never brought up in your meetings because you are all too busy consistently blaming others to justify your own misfortunes, predicaments, inequities, etc., etc., etc.

Here's a quick and easy example, as I could go on and on — we're all Americans. Jews are your classmates, teammates, and military mates. We pay taxes; you pay taxes. We chase women; you chase women. We root for certain sports teams; you root for certain sports teams. We help charge your engine battery, cover you if it's raining, and hold your place in line. We sit next to you; we cheer on the USA, together. We want to work and provide; you want to work and provide. I think you get the point, but it still begs one simple question that I want you to ask yourselves as you're reading. What are our differences? Yes, I got it — religion — and?

How does one write down words of passion, frustration, and anger in a way that changes the hearts and minds of antisemites, racists, and all-around hate-filled ignorant dumbasses? This book explores topics of ignorance, lies, deception, and so much more. I've written factually, honestly, and in a way that we all can relate to. My approach is sometimes aggressive because it takes a sledgehammer to tear down the walls of hatred and bigotry.

How do I convince and prove to you that we are not your enemies, and we are not your friends? Again, how could we be, as we don't know one another, and it's another reason why your hate groups are completely unfounded, ridiculous, and baseless? It's time for you to grow up and remove yourselves from your toxic, criminal intolerance.

My mission is to reach the indoctrinated, the misanthropes, and the Kool-Aid drinkers and save them from a life of hatred and intolerance — the antisemites, Aryans, neo-Nazis, White supremacists, White nationalists, skinheads, alt-right, racists, homophobes, etc. My passion is fueled by being on the receiving end of years and years of misinformation, false accusations, and deceptions about Jews and other minorities.

Antisemitic groups directly affect us all. They gather in their meetings to plot ways to threaten us. It seems that we, the recipients of their smear campaigns (or worse), have no recourse. Or do we? In my opinion, we must now deal with hate groups differently than we have in the past. We need to finally be on the offensive and aggressively go after the ones who want to harm us. Don't we, as Jews, have to protect our families and ourselves from horseshit lies and antisemitism right now? Furthermore, we have an obligation to betterment to ensure the next Jewish generation can walk the streets without hesitation. We're not addressing it proactively. We're letting it slide, and shame on us. I want to stop our lazy reactionary way of dealing with various hate groups and punish those who wish to harm us on our terms.

I am a pissed-off and frustrated Jewish man who conveys harsh messages that must be understood if we can ever hope to change the paradigm. I have spent an enormous amount of time researching the Nazis and their atrocities and have become a borderline expert on the topic. This subject-matter expertise brings me no joy, and I won't carry it alone because

I can't do it alone. The truth must be disseminated. The material I share in the chapters below includes historical facts and my opinion and interpretation. If you question any of it, feel free to look it up yourselves. Fact-check me — I dare you.

While writing this book, I wondered how I could reach in and grab every antisemite, racist, and hate group and shake them with words they would understand. How best to persuade them to stop justifying ignorant beliefs and read this with an open mind? My presentation, at times, is as foul as the offenders themselves. If you are an offender, I figure you'll be more receptive if I meet you where you are — in the sewer if need be. This, after all, is where you harvest your harmful beliefs.

In other words, readers will need "thick skin" at times, but overall, my focus is to educate and compel people to immediately get out of whatever antisemitic or racist groups they are in or are considering joining. Clearly, I am not kind to individuals, groups, or organizations that started and now perpetuate Nazism, antisemitism, issues with Israel's rights, uneducated conjecture, incorrect opinions, and more. If you're insulted by this premise, you've earned it. Keep this in mind as you absorb my words.

There are bigots, I assume, who will actually pick up this book for laughs, if nothing else. But then, something miraculous might happen. The information might resonate, and that's the purpose. So, to the persecutors, here's your chance. Here's an opportunity to evolve from a knuckle-dragger into a person of compassion and tolerance. Will you take this opportunity seriously? Yes, if you're not a complete fucking moron or if you're looking for real answers to your highest and most sincere questions.

This book's title — *Never Again MEANS Never Again* — is the hill we'll die on. This isn't hyperbole. I'm not being dramatic, not when we continue to see assaults on Jews, our places of worship, our schools, and other gathering places. I don't think most people truly grasp how small a population we, as Jews, encompass, and this is our line in the sand.

It's time to cut the head off the snake. Remember, it wasn't that long ago, an entire country, Germany, allowed lies to spread with impunity. Those lies led to the "justification" of millions upon millions of innocent deaths. Not to mention, other nations around the world have also let lies run rampant for personal gain or due to agendas. I write not merely to combat complacency and ignorance but to remind every culture and ethnicity that history has a way of repeating itself. Damnable actions escalate if not nipped in the bud. After all, it wasn't so long ago that the Holocaust, Jim Crow, and Apartheid occurred.

What about those who claim they aren't bigoted but do little or nothing to proactively address antisemitism, racism, etc.? They wring their hands as terrible slurs and aspersions poison new generations, but do they speak out? No. The lies perpetuate due to silence and individuals who can't think for themselves. They have no idea that what they're learning is false. I do my best to break the silence and rally the troops because you and I know how wrong it is to sit by as minorities and disenfranchised human beings are abused. We cannot allow ignorant miscreants to verbally and physically assault us for no valid reason.

If antisemitism isn't addressed now in the harshest possible terms, then when? I hope my book also encourages the pacifists to do more than sit by with disapproving expressions. I hope it encourages them to rise up and battle the rhetoric. Perhaps my people, the Jews, will roar. Perhaps they will unleash their outrage instead of bending over and taking it time after time. I address this issue throughout the book and plan to put together a group that will aggressively go after organizations and individuals who want to harm us for our religious and cultural beliefs.

We will no longer sit idly by. We will finally go on the offensive. I'm done holding back. We, as Jews in this country and worldwide, have contributed to every society we've been involved with, and in a very positive way. We will no longer be on defense, as we'll now be leading from the front.

I should add that this book is more than a manifesto that unmasks the crazies. It's a historical account that covers many events over roughly the last 100-plus years encapsulating Jews and Jewish life. I address many aspects of our treatment in various countries, misnomers a lot of people have about Jews, and the outright lies that have been told about us. I cover the daily lives of Europe's Jews from WWI leading to World War II, treaties after the war, and a regime that cost the lives of 70 million people overall in what, six years? This regime consciously put together a systematic program that specifically targeted six million Jews and five million other minorities, leading to gruesome fates.

I also cover the 1933–1945 era in Nazi Germany, including the two largest fallacies that allowed Hitler's rise, *Mein Kampf* and the Treaty of Versailles, and a lot of WWII history from my perspective. Furthermore, it's very important that I correctly describe a psychotic narcissist who took so many lives and had so many tortured, all for a personal agenda. I show you the outrageous amount of lies from Hitler, the Nazis, and others during that time period. Again, if you are in a hate group of any sort, I hope my words inspire you to leave it.

I address topics from Hollywood to The Pulitzer, from the Manhattan Project to Big Tech, and the Academy Awards to the Palestinian conflict. I discuss America Jewry — where we are and where we should be. I expose enemies. All of these topics are important to me, but the greater importance is that you, the bigot, understand the collective words. I want you to understand, learn, and educate yourself.

I hope, I truly hope, you receive these words and make a change for the better. You're wasting your time, money, and reputation by adhering to something evil, destructive, and demonstrably false. In the end, unless you make a change, you'll have the same outcome as every other hate group member before you has received — nothing but regretful shame.

Chapter 1: The Rise of Hitler

"The stronger must dominate and not blend with the weaker, thus sacrificing his own greatness."
~ Adolf Hitler

This book kicks off with World War I, dubbed "the war to end all wars," due to the overwhelming and bloody destruction on multiple continents. History tells us that approximately 8.5 million soldiers and 13 million civilians died, and 20 million additional were wounded as a result. Armistice Day on November 11, 1918, was supposed to bring world peace. But there were skeptics such as David Lloyd George, 1st Earl Lloyd-George of Dwyfor, a British statesman, who said, "The [Great] War, like the next war, is a war to end war."

I suppose the money-making nature of war and the war-mongering nature of mankind ensured there would be more bloodshed, and sure enough, along came Adolf Hitler of World War II notoriety. But first, he rose through the ranks and wrote his infamous *Mein Kampf,* an autobiographical manifesto, which led to the insidious "blame the Jews for our woes" narrative that still plagues us today.

Why discuss *Mein Kampf* (translated as *My Struggle*)? Because it still serves as a popular propaganda tool for antisemites and hate groups ever since its publication in 1925, just seven years after the end of the first world war. It describes Hitler's descent into antisemitism and a warped belief system mixed with Nazi political ideology.

Furthermore, it can't be stressed enough how much this book led to the rise of Hitler and the Nazis. We have the ability now to read this book in retrospect and see the enormous amount of lies and bullshit, yet it somehow still plays such a massive role in current antisemitism, racism, and more.

I took the time and read through *Mein Shit,* and I'm confident in saying it is unequaled in how bad it is. Awful, boring, and inconsistent; let me tell you, I couldn't wait to get to page two. I assure you that you would get much more enjoyment from reading a 700-page book written in Chinese. Obviously, I'm not here to endorse *Mein Crap*, but after reading it, I think you'll get a much better understanding of the rumor of why Hitler killed himself — he was asked to proofread it. Anyway, it wasn't Hitler's antisemitic and racist lies he consistently talked about, no. It's just a "world-class" shitty book. I'd really, really like to meet and discuss this book with someone who liked it.

Note: References to page numbers of *Mein Kampf* in this book apply to a free download of the book found here: http://feineigle.com/static/books/2018/mein_kampf/Mein_Kampf_(1925)_The_Stalag_Edition.pdf.

Oh, how the Jew haters adore *Mein Kampf*. I wonder if they realize that Hitler said, "If you tell a big enough lie and tell it frequently enough, it will be believed." And that, in a nutshell, defines why Hitler became humanity's wrecking ball. The weak-minded, the gullible, and those with low esteem and low confidence believed his lies back then because they so badly wanted someone, anyone, to give them reasons to justify their woes. I know it sounds and seems shocking that his speeches and beliefs still resonate today, but unfortunately, there will always be someone looking and needing to blame others for their inadequacies and perceived inequalities.

Dear Neo-Nazis — Hitler Doesn't Want You

I'd like to point out that Hitler clearly states that *Mein Kampf* wasn't written for those outside of Germany, and I'll add Austria. Let me repeat that for those in the back of the classroom. Hitler's book does NOT apply to you, the American Aryans, at all. Aryans, true Aryans, are only inside the confines of Germany and Austria.

Are YOU racially pure? There is a very, very small chance that you are. America is a big melting pot. So why do you, whom he considered worthless, demean yourselves by chasing after Hitler?

Adolf Hitler stated, "German-Austria must be rejoined to the great German Fatherland and not on economic grounds." He also said: "We do not want any other god than Germany itself. It is essential to have fanatical faith and hope and love in and for Germany." And last but not least, Hitler said, "I don't see much future for the Americans. In my view, it's a decayed country."

He is talking to Germans only. He cared about Germans only, at least those who could carry forward his vision of a perfect, pure race. Oh, by the way, he fucking declared war on America. I would say that's the highest example I can give for his hatred of you and all Americans. His Aryan racist beliefs stopped at Germany and Austria's borders. Anyone born outside of Germany and Austria would NOT be invited to become a Nazi. How could you be invited when the "Aryan blood" he's always babbling about is contained exclusively inside their borders?

If Hitler knew there were people forming groups in the U.S., and basing it off Nazis, *Mein Kampf*, his speeches, etc., he would have sued. If you were the first hate group member from the U.S. to meet Hitler in Germany, you would have been treated as an enemy of the state and summarily executed about five minutes after Goebbels finished ass-fucking you.

Therefore, if you're in the United States, Canada, England, Mexico, Guam, or wherever, and cling to every word in *Mein Kampf*, please understand that your American ancestors who lived outside of the Fatherland meant nothing to Hitler. Nothing. They were not his people. You are not his people. He cared nothing for outsiders, period. As he clearly states it in *Mein GermanandmaybeAustriansonly*.

Note that there are tons of sources that cover Hitler's formative years, and I encourage you to search online and in libraries to learn more. At the end of this book, I share resources that might be helpful as you look for the truth. Below we begin to delve into Hitler's youth, his narcissism, and his evolution as the world's most notorious psychotic, sociopathic, schizophrenic serial killer who ever headed up a country.

Hitler's father (with whom he didn't get along) died when he was 13. Hitler was not a good student — except for P.E. — and dropped out of school at 16. He left for Vienna, hoping to study painting but was rejected at an art academy. Then his mother died of cancer when he was 18, and no relatives were willing to step in (no surprise there).

To encapsulate, basically, hate groups and neo-Nazis are worshiping a rudderless teenage orphan (yes, we know it's not his fault) who pined for direction and attention. He became a failed painter on the streets of Vienna while attempting to sell his paintings for income, and he lived a bohemian lifestyle in homeless shelters and men's dormitories. He was always incredulous about his lack of funds when the obvious response was, "Ugh, you're selling fucking paintings on the street." Nobody bought those back then or now, especially his "finger" paintings. In my opinion, this primed him for indoctrination and someone to blame for his shitty life.

Also, at this time, he started attending various political meetings that were already antisemitic, and slowly, he became interested in politics. He just had to find something, anything, to justify why he wasn't succeeding or blame whoever was holding him back from greatness. So, from his current situation, he decided to sign up for the German military.

After joining the 16th Bavarian Reserve Infantry Regiment, he fought on the Western Front and was awarded the Iron Cross for his bravery in battle. Blinded for a short while from a gas attack, he was removed from the war effort and was upset (and by upset, I mean he was psychotic about it) when Germany lost World War I. He hated the Weimar government for signing the Versailles Treaty (which supposedly financially crippled Germany through demands for war reparations and sanctions) and yearned for the days of the Kaiser.

After the war, Hitler worked for the German Army as a teacher and confidential (snitch) informer. The reason he attended the beer hall initially was to spy on the German Worker's Party. Soon after, he became involved in politics, giving speeches, and writing his horseshit agenda about removing the Jews, blah, blah, blah.

Party leader Anton Drexler tasked him with shaping political ideology and propaganda. In 1920, the party renamed itself the National Socialist Worker's Party — the Nazis — and rolled out its 25-point program. In 1921, Hitler led the party and began spewing his speeches. I'm not sure why his manner of speech was so popular. Have you seen him at the podium? They used to hand out rain gear to everyone in the first two rows of Hitler's speeches to protect them from the massive amount of spit from Hitler's mouth. However, when Hitler got on a roll, the third row was fucked.

Nevertheless, he stirred up a nationalist frenzy. Soon everyone was talking about this "rising star," and to protect himself from objecting views, he launched the Stormtroopers (SA). Despite their protection (the SA was too small at that time to put up a real fight), he was put in prison in March of 1924 for failing to overthrow the Bavarian government. Notice the word "failing." Ultimately, sooner or later, Hitler failed at everything he did.

What came of his incarceration? He wrote *Mein Kampf*, published in 1925 after his release. Fortunately for Hitler, the Great Depression hit, which he exploited to bolster the Nazi party. It worked. Germans were unhappy with the economic downturn and scarcity of food. By 1932, the Nazis were the largest party in the Reichstag, promising solutions for everyone's woes.

However, the Communist Party and other factions prevented the Nazi Party from being a majority. Still, by January 30, 1933, Hitler was appointed Chancellor of Germany under President Hindenburg. A month later, arson struck the Reichstag building (the German parliament) and was blamed on the communists. (It was the Nazis who started the fire.) Hitler banned the Communist Party in Germany, and *voila!* Now the Nazis were the majority. A month later, he was able to concoct one of the most personal political coups in modern history through the passage of the Enabling Act, empowering him to make laws without the consent of the Reichstag. Thus, the doors to dictatorship were opened. He became the architect of the Holocaust and quickly found a group of pussies who would enforce his dictatorial decrees from 1933 to 1945 to purify a master race.

Hitler claimed that Jewish people plotted to weaken Germany and scapegoated them for everything from causing poverty to killing Jesus Christ to dirtying humanity's gene pool. It was always the Jews. I think part of the reason and animosity towards Jews is in part due to Hitler, Himmler, Goebbels, and Goering having very, very small dicks. Rumor has it that they all attended a few bris ceremonies (circumcisions) together out of curiosity, and when they saw that their cocks were smaller than those babies, well, they were outraged.

The Jews and an untold number of other innocent people suffered persecution and unprecedented brutality simply due to their DNA, ethnicity, color, sexual orientation, and religious beliefs.

Ultimately, the Jews were dubbed an inferior race that had to be exterminated before they dominated the globe. Beatings, starvation, torture, and death by gassing became the largest saga of mass murder and genocide the world had ever seen. How quickly the misinformation and smear campaign escalated into persecution, and then to camps, and then to the ovens.

***

Hitler banned trade unions and all opposing political parties, and withdrew Germany from the League of Nations. He pounced on President Hindenburg's death in August 1934 to combine the titles of Chancellor and President and make himself Führer of Germany.

Now, he began building the Third Reich arsenal of manpower and weapons and tossed the Treaty of Versailles out the door. The Nuremberg Race Laws passed in 1935 — the Reich Citizenship Law and the Protection of German Blood and German Honor Law — and now the quest for a pure Aryan German citizenry began in earnest. Where did this leave the Jews? Well, they couldn't hold public office because they weren't Aryan. That was the first sanction against them, quickly followed by the loss of businesses before the Nazis eventually took all Jewish properties away.

Then in March 1936, Hitler re-occupied the Rhineland, which had been taken from Germany by the Versailles Treaty. Britain and France allowed it without force. Then the *Anschluss Österreichs* began in the spring of 1938 to annex the Federal State of Austria into the German Reich, followed by the reclaiming of the Sudetenland area of Czechoslovakia. There was absolutely no opposition to Germany in either land or its money grab.

The Munich Agreement was supposed to prevent Hitler from making further territorial inroads, but did he honor it? Hell, no. In March 1939, he invaded and occupied Czechoslovakia. He did the same with Poland on September 1, 1939, which led to the outbreak of World War II. You may realize by now how much of a psychotic, narcissistic evil fuck Hitler truly was, but he must have had some sort of fetish about signing agreements and pacts that he didn't honor and had no plans to ever honor. Frankly, it's just weird to me. Were his ruses just a short-lived appeasement boner?

Operation Barbarossa

Why did Hitler do it? I mean, why did the head of all military in Germany do it? Because he was a narcissistic, egomaniac, fucking idiot. You really don't need to read more into it than that. The Soviets were caught off guard because of their agreement with Germany, and initially, it was horrific for the Russians. But what came out of it was that the world was able to witness how highly impressive the courage, strength, and toughness the Russians displayed. I will always be indebted to Russia in the sense of how they liberated the concentration camps they entered. Firstly, they liberated a bunch of camps, and secondly, in some of the camps, the Russian soldiers gave Jews weapons and allowed them to go after the guards. Thanks, Russia.

Anyway, there are basically two reasons Germany could take so much land so quickly.

Germany had a three-to-five-year head start on every other country in the world militarily as they circumvented the Treaty of Versailles provision to enhance their military, and outside of Japan, no other country was doing any sizable rearmament.

In the 1920s, German companies generated 40% of the world's market of morphine and 80% of the world's cocaine, which allowed German soldiers a lot less time for sleep or issues of readiness.

Pervitin and amphetamines were given out in chocolate form to all German military troops that were fighting. The Nazis started distributing Pervitin to their soldiers in late 1938. They "rolled it out" for the first time in decent size quantities in the Invasion of Poland in 1939. In Poland, they saw some "benefits." Between April and July 1940, German servicemen received 35 million methamphetamine tablets.

Let me show you a quick example of a lie. Ready? Hitler and all Nazis preached "purity" and "self-discipline" and were not allowed to take any drugs, as it's one of the "backbones" of being an Aryan. Yes, I'm shocked too.

To add to the tough and relentless reputation of the Russians, I present Stalingrad. Facing an overwhelming "coked up" massive military, the Russians never considered surrendering. It would have been easy to justify their victory in Stalingrad by saying that they just continued to send manpower. However, the Russian troops came in staggered waves until Germany could take no more. No one would have blamed the Russians for surrendering early on in Stalingrad, but fortunately, they never even considered it.

Had the Nazis taken Stalingrad, the outcome of the war would've been different. I think the Allies would still win, but at what cost?

We'll cover WWII in greater detail ahead, but for now, I showcase the stark contrast between "the evil" the Jews were accused of perpetrating versus what they actually accomplished on behalf of humanity.

Chapter 2: Feats of Judaism

"If we were forced to choose just one, there would be no way to deny that Judaism is the most important intellectual development in human history."
~ David Gelernter

How utterly disingenuous Hitler was to launch a laundry list of "blame the Jews" slander into the world. Of course, he conveniently left out centuries upon centuries of noble Jewish feats and selfless contributions.

Thus, I'll juxtapose a different pre-WWII narrative. There were many Jewish contributors and champions in the world war efforts, which calls out the stupidity of the hate groups who owe their lives to Jews, even if they don't know it.

The world owes a debt of gratitude to the Jewish men and women whose work has extended and saved lives, entertained us, educated us, and helped our nation rank as a superpower. Isn't it bizarre that the Nazis wanted Jews dead simply because they were Jews? Fucked up, isn't it? Fuck you, Hitler.

Brilliant Jewish scientists and medical pioneers include Dr. Gavriil Illizarov, Jonas Salk, Albert Einstein, etc. How surprising it might be to learn that Ayn Rand, whom many alt groups admire, was Jewish. In fact, the Jews were the "good guys" during the world wars. They stepped up patriotically, as you'll see, and endeavored to be model citizens — hardworking, self-reliant, intelligent, and the world's saviors when it came to science and medicine.

This is the true history of my people as opposed to the bullshit and crazy amount of lies in *Mein Kampf*, which we will cover in much more detail ahead.

We have been blessed to live in the most diverse and ethical country ever — not perfect, but head and shoulder above the rest. Over time, our doctors, lawyers, bankers, politicians, etc., from all backgrounds, have been brought together from first, second, or third generations, and have thrived. What have you guys, the haters, done? What are your astounding accomplishments? Jumping someone correctly in checkers? Did you call "Ball in left corner pocket," AND the ball actually went into the left corner pocket? Did someone in your hate group actually find the one person in the U.S. with Aryan blood?

I'm confident that if any of you were bleeding to death, you would not refuse help from a gay Black doctor, would you? The difference between those doctors and you is that they would honor their oaths and treat your ignorant asses.

What accomplishments would you like to share from any of the esteemed members of your hate groups? So, let's not fuck around; let's start with some "big boy" categories. How about Nobel prizes, Pulitzers, Oscars, National Honor Societies, or maybe Mensa? You can go first and pick whatever organizations you and your buddies belong to. Just pick a couple where you can brag about your members or highlight your achievements. I'm sure you have at least a Kennedy Center award winner. No? Fine. Fulbright scholarship recipient? Maybe a Chucky Cheese birthday medallion? Give us some names so we can all bask in their achievements. No need to feel modest, as we want to highlight your successes to show others. Please, show us how we can finally be accepted by you. You deserve your well-earned recognition to inspire others. Everyone knows how well your various groups and organizations consistently and deservedly sweep the annual Darwin Awards, so we know you have an achievement ability.

Suffice it to say, I have fact-checked Hitler and many, many others, in order to rebut his and their outrageous and spurious misinformation, as you'll see below and throughout this book. Let's start with World War I.

Military Service

If you don't already know about Hitler's disdain for Jews and how he suckered so many others into buying his bullshit, well, keep reading. The easiest and quickest way to understand how he convinced fellow Germans to perpetuate antisemitism was to simply label Jews as "leeches" who only took or stole from their great homeland. Well, the quickest way to demean a group was to isolate their patriotism from the rest of the German citizens. They simply called out the Jews for a "lack of military service" or accused them of not helping in any way with the war effort. In *Mein Kampf*, Hitler mocked the notion of Jews serving. What you're about to read next wasn't shouted until after 1945, but Hitler was certainly never accused of letting lies get in the way of...well, anything.

Herr Dumbshit conveniently ignored the fact that in World War I, over 300,000 Jewish soldiers and 25,000 Jewish reserve officers fought for Austria-Hungary on all fronts of the war. In fact, the Austrian army had 76 rabbis to help with religious matters, kosher foods, as well as military censors of all Hebrew correspondence. I also corrected Hitler, the fucking moron, with the fact that 100,000 Jews fought for Germany in WWI, and not one, not two, not three of those

Jewish soldiers received the Iron Cross. In fact, 18,000 did. Over 400,000 Jews fought on the German, Austrian, and Hungary sides.

The Jews didn't serve, my ass. Obviously, there was no "fact-checking" regarding the Jewish soldiers and their involvement with WWI. The Gold Bravery Medal was given to 79 Jews who were decorated with the highest honor, and there ended up being 20 Jewish generals for Austria-Hungary in WWI.

40,000 Austro-Hungarian Jewish soldiers were killed in action, and 1,000 or more were officers. 12,000 Jews were killed fighting for Germany.

Mocking or denying his fellow citizens in war who were dying and wounded and defending the same country as he was, shows what a shit heel Hitler was. It's utterly disgusting to me. He would end up instigating plenty more horrific atrocities, even early on, but discounting fellow soldiers from the battlefield is shamefully disrespectful and pathetic.

From 1918–1922 there were about 150,000 Jews killed in Russian pogroms. So, Hitler decided that within that three-year span, there must have been some sort of "Jewish domination in Russia." This implies that a tiny subculture of Russian Jews somehow overwhelmed and threatened the status quo, and therefore deserved death.

Bullshit. It wasn't until the 1930s that the Soviet Union opened itself up to Jews. The highest Russian Jewish population percentage was reached in the early 1930s, as high as 1.8% of the total population. At the same time, Jews were 12% to 15% of all university students — promising young lives just like every other promising young life.

By the way, in the 1930s, many Jews held high ranks in the Red Army high command. That included Iona Yakir, Yan Gamarnik, Yakov Smushkevich (Commander of the

Soviet Air Forces), and Grigory Shtern (Commander-in-chief in the war against Japan and Commander at the front in the Winter War).

During World War II, an estimated 500,000 soldiers in the red Army were Jews; about 200,000 were killed in battle. Roughly 160,000 were decorated, and more than 100 received the rank of Red Army General. Over 150 Jews were designated Heroes of the Soviet Union, the highest award in the country. Also, in WWI, there were roughly 600,000 Jewish soldiers fighting in the Russian Army, with 100,000 and up who were killed in battle.

In *Mein Kampf*, Herr Cockbreath wrote he never saw a Jew in battle; they only did clerical work. Why did he write that? Because he didn't just start lying in 1933. He damn well knew that a lot of Jewish soldiers were active in the military, but it wouldn't have played well in *Mein Shit*, his speeches, giving hand jobs, etc. Jews certainly gave back to their countries in the war effort, and, a lot of times, paid the ultimate price. We should honor and venerate all our veterans regardless of ethnicity, culture, or religious views. Anyone who denies the value of military service is a person without honor.

The Nobel Prize

How about this one? Remember, Jews are only .0019% of the world's population. The Nobel Prize started giving out awards in 1901. From 1901 to 2021, they awarded 609 prizes to 975 people. Ready?

These very prestigious awards are given worldwide in five categories: physics, chemistry, physiology or medicine, and literature and peace. Ponder this for a moment—22% (that's right, over 210 Jews) — have been awarded a Nobel Prize. That is a staggering statistic. Just another stat for the White supremacists, who I'm sure had to look up the word "stat" to realize it didn't mean statutory.

Consider, as well, that Jews make up a little under .02% of the United States population. Yet, of all the Nobel prizes awarded to anyone from the United States, Jews have been the recipients of 36%. That's an astounding number. Let me spell that for those sitting in the back row:

THIRTY-SIX PERCENT OF ALL NOBEL PRIZE WINNERS WHO ARE UNITED STATES CITIZENS, SINCE THE NOBEL PRIZE'S INCEPTION IN 1901, HAVE BEEN WON BY JEWS. We understand it's not like winning a monster truck race; nonetheless, we're still very proud.

Honestly, it's just mind-blowing. I mean, for fuck's sake, can you come back at me with one hate group statistic over the same time period that's remotely as impressive? Again, these are Nobel Prizes we are talking about. I know winning the "I'm not the father" on the "Maury Povich Show" (Jew) can be exciting, but it's not impressive. It's just another example of how Jews give back to this great country in ways none of the haters seem to understand.

Worse, Hitler stupidly stated, "Our national policies will not be revoked or modified, even for scientists. If the dismissal of Jewish scientists means the annihilation of contemporary German science, then we shall do without science for a few years."

Hmmm...good call. Ya think this could have been part of the reason he lost the war?

Philanthropy

Jews are taught from an early age about giving — to see the struggles of others and help if possible. This includes giving to Jewish causes and non-Jewish causes. All of us who attend or attended Hebrew School are taught early on about

Tzedakah. Tzedakah can be described in a few ways, but think of it as "charitable giving as a moral obligation." Hebrew School, by the way, is held two to three times a week, beginning at around five or six years of age (or so). Small metal containers are passed around to every class, and students are told where the money goes and to whom it helps. Every Jew I have ever known donates money somewhere. I watched my father, grandfather, uncles, aunts, cousins, and friends all give. I give.

Obviously, it's not a competition, but I always smile a bit when I hear or read about a significant donation made by a Jew. Why? That's how we are raised, and for some reason, I just feel proud of the fact. I'm not here to lecture on giving — if you can, great, and if you can't, no pressure. Give whenever you're able. I just wanted to point out why you see a lot of donations given from Jews to all types of causes.

Hanna Shaul Bar Nissim, writing for *The Conversation*, did an extensive study on Jewish philanthropy, and her findings are as follows.

"Most Jews, regardless of their economic status, heed their religious and cultural obligations to give. In fact, 60% of Jewish households earning less than U.S.$50,000 a year donate, compared with 46% of non-Jewish households in that income bracket."

She goes on to say, "The average annual Jewish Household donates $2,526 to charity yearly, far more than $1,749 their Protestant counterparts give or the $1,142 for Catholics, according to data from Giving U.S.A."

Manhattan Project

The United States had been in the Pacific, African, and European theaters and lost a tremendous number of lives, as well as racking up a high number of wounded. We had finally fortified our positions in the Pacific with just one more thing to do — have Japan surrender unconditionally. A military project that started in New Mexico was put together and made up of the top scientists, mathematicians, chemists, physicists, etc. Their job was to make a weapon so devastating that just one bomb could end a conflict. JUST ONE.

Thus, we have the Manhattan Project. The following are some names and working titles of the men and women who participated in this phenomenal and truly unbelievable project.

For background, like Britain, Japan wasn't backing down as we were bombing the shit out of their cities. Unlike Britain, Japan would have never surrendered, and they weren't going to, even knowing they would be facing a U.S. invasion. The top of the Japanese government and military commanders were psychos (not Nazi psychos but psychos in their own right). I think most historians, in relation to the war in the Pacific, would agree that a U.S. invasion of Japan would have lost more lives than the current number of casualties in the entire war altogether.

However, the U.S. invented a weapon of such mass destruction and a formidable weapon that was so unyielding, that by dropping it, the Japanese would surrender before the Enola Gay had left Japan. Right? However, sadly, Japan still did not surrender. Again, the United States, unfortunately, dropped another nuclear bomb in hopes that it would end the war. Even after the dropping of the second nuclear bomb, Japan's leaders debated for days about surrendering or not surrendering. Finally, cooler heads prevailed, and Emperor Hirohito informed the Japanese government and military of his decision. The U.S. accepted Japan's unconditional surrender, signed on September 2, 1945. By the way, the U.S. had a third nuclear bomb on standby, just in case.

Splitting atoms isn't something you are taught in your 10th-grade science class. Many thought it could not be done. No one knew if THEY could do it. The U.S. assembled the top scientists, mathematicians, physicists, etc., to set up operations in New Mexico, Tennessee, and the state of Washington, and on August 13, 1942, it was officially titled The Manhattan Project.

So, who did the U.S. approach to try and pull off this miraculous undertaking? Let's see if we can put together a list of the men and women involved in this project to save between 600,000 to 1 million U.S. soldiers' lives, according to the military, and leaked to U.S. citizens. This, after a tremendous number of very tough battles and a large number of casualties and wounded in the Pacific theater. The person our government put in charge of this massive undertaking and selected as director of Los Alamos was Robert Oppenheimer, a Jew.

Oppenheimer started with a small crew, but in the end, the Manhattan project employed around 130,000 people and cost around $2 billion. A listing of various individuals who participated in the project highlights their invaluable contributions. Leo Szilard, a Jew, conceived the nuclear chain reaction in 1933 and patented the idea of a nuclear fission reactor in 1934. In 1939, Szilard and Einstein wrote a letter to Franklin D. Roosevelt about a uranium program that the Germans were working on and its nuclear and atomic consequences. Once it finally reached and was explained to FDR, he quickly set up an advisory Uranium Committee, and the U.S. Government shifted from research to the developmental stage.

The Einstein-Szilard letter remains one of the most iconic

documents in American history. In January 2017, Warren Buffet told students at Columbia University, "If you think about it, we are sitting here, in part, because of two Jewish immigrants who in 1939 in August signed the most important letter perhaps in the history of the United States."

Szilard left Germany in 1933, moved to England, and left for the United States in 1936. Here are some other names that Leo worked with at the highest levels. Respect and gratitude should be extolled on them. All these men are Jews born in the U.S. or abroad: Eugene Wigner, Niels Bohr, James Franck, Otto Loewi, Otto Meyerhof, Otto Stern, Alvin Weinberg, David Bohm, Philip Morrison, Frank Oppenheimer, Arnold Kramish, Hans Bethe, Richard Feynman, Victor Weisskopf, Robert Serber, Joseph Rotblat, Felix Bloch, Stanislaw M. Ulam, Isidor I. Rabi, Otto Frisch, Samuel Goudsmit, and theoretical physicist Edward Teller who later became known as the father of the hydrogen bomb, and so many, many, many more.

In this small list of men who gave what they could to expedite the ending of a brutal war, there were 11 Nobel Prize winners.

Because of these men, these brilliant, brilliant men, all of our lives are vastly improved. Is this another group of Jews who are just not good enough for you?

I also want to point out there were very few women who worked directly on the Manhattan Project of any religion, background, color, etc. Yet, a few brilliant Jewish women helped with the effort. From their immense contributions to the Manhattan Project to being at the top of their fields after the war, these lovely, talented, and brilliant women certainly deserve our gratitude. Charlotte Serber, Lilli Horning, Dr. Leona Woods Marshall Libby, Liane Russell, and Elizabeth Rona are among them.

Most White nationalists won't look these heroes up or study their bios, and I certainly understand, as the words are in English. Just note they were all Jewish, and they all saved a tremendous amount of American and Japanese lives.

By the way, Hitler lovers, Germany was somewhat advanced and certainly ahead of everyone, worldwide, in developing the first nuclear weapon. And you know why they weren't first to the finish line? Because a lot of their top scientists and mathematicians were Jewish and had left.

This is not a guess. This is not a probability. This is a fact. After the war, we learned that Germany wasn't even close to developing a nuclear weapon. Between bureaucracy and a shallow talent pool, they basically abandoned it. I mean, how many examples do I need to demonstrate the overwhelming incompetency of Hitler, the dumb-ass leader of hate cults?

Not that any of you antisemites know much about American history, but guess what? It's been invaded by minorities. And despite your feelings, that's a good thing, not a bad thing. The Manhattan Project is proof. It's obvious to me that a collective of Jewish scientists and mathematicians, born here and abroad, officially ended WWII as soon as the U.S. someway, somehow acquired this immense talent. For some of you older antisemites, the Manhattan Project affected your parents. For some of you newer Aryans, it affected your grandparents or great-grandparents. A quick question for any racist, anti-semitic, homophobic Americans — how many of your family members worked on this project?

Technology

I doubt a lot of the racist haters will understand this category, so I will write slowly. Going forward, we are going to out many of you anti-semites and racists. It's not fair that your neighbors, employers, communities, etc., are unaware of your thoughtful and selfless outreach in trying to make their lives better, too. We want to help spread your individual names throughout your communities for deserved recognition. Wouldn't you want to know if you had a neighbor in some type of group that advocates for the expulsion of 35-40% of our country's population? C'mon, it sounds great, and I hate when "great" ideas are overlooked. Anyway, you're welcome.

Your views of us as weak nerds who sit around and try to screw over you, your families, and your cronies are not only patently false but have finally energized us so you may see our real capabilities. In order to "out" you morons, we will need to find individuals who have some pretty good computer skills. Below is a list of some Jews you might be familiar with. None of them have been contacted or have agreed to help us — yet; however, it's safe to say that some brilliant Jewish technicians working for these and many other tech companies will step up.

Here are but a few of a large contingent of current "techies" who have helped advance our way of life through their inventions or advancements. They have helped make it easier for you and your organizations to get your "message out." In other words, if not for them, you would still be writing with #2 pencils. Anyway, let's see if you are familiar with any of them. Facebook founder, Mark Zuckerberg, Jew. Oracle founder, Larry Ellison, Jew. Google founders Sergey Brin and Larry Page, Jews. Dell Computers, Michael Dell, Jew. WhatsApp, Jan Koum, Jew.

Other notable tech innovators are Terry Semel, Andrew Grove, Mitchell Kapor, Mark Cuban, Lawrence Perlman, Benjamin Rosen, Rob Geiser, Amit Yoran, Steve Ballmer, Gil Schwed, Max Levchin, and on and on and on. You don't think we can find some tech talent to, let's say, mess with you guys a bit, ya know, in fun?

Curing Various Diseases

So, Hitler had a penchant for waxing on and on about his favorite topics — Jews, Marxism, and the press — and then, out of nowhere, he stated in *Mein Kampf*: "In large cities particularly, syphilis steadily increased, and tuberculosis kept pace within reaping its harvest of death in almost every part of the country," and "In the case of syphilis especially the attitude of the state and the public authorities was one of absolute capitulation." Well, that's certainly one benefit Hitler had by being a virgin.

Then he babbled about how the nation should suffer because of the "Moral havoc resulting from this prostitution would be sufficient to bring about the destruction of the nation, slowly but surely."

Allegedly, Hitler caught syphilis from a prostitute in his early twenties. I have not been able to corroborate that, and I've spent a lot of time researching. Having said that, perhaps Hitler was never concerned about getting syphilis as he was convinced syphilis couldn't be transferred by anal sex. Again, he would be wrong, and the arguments between Hitler and his "Bavarian boy toys" were legendary.

We know Hitler enjoyed being perpetually pissed about, well, everything, but he hadn't yet blamed this one on the Jews, so what's the beef? "Every possible means should be employed to bring the truth about this savage home to the minds of the people, until the wild nation or notion has been convinced that everything depends on the solution of the problem: that is to say, a healthy future or national decay."

He was all over the board on this topic. Below are two answers he thought of while writing *Mein Syphilis* that would have saved the pain all of us had to endure reading his first chapter. Hitler happily found out six or so months after publishing his shitty book that if a man's penis is two and a half inches or shorter when erect, he couldn't get syphilis. Of course, Hitler told everyone that he had cured himself while his inner circle of friends knew the truth. Duh, it was because of the Jews.

Secondly, Hitler told all the "real" citizens in Germany that they couldn't have syphilis because their Aryan blood would kill any bacterial infection. Sooooooo, with no more testing, Hitler declared Germany syphilis free. That guy could lead.

"What was done to put an end to the contamination and mammonisation of sexual life among us? What was done to fight the resulting spreading of syphilis throughout the whole of our people?" Who the fuck is he talking to? The press? Government? Fine, if he was talking to me, I would have simply introduced him to the brilliant bacteriologist and hygienist August von Wassermann (Jew). Wassermann developed the test for both syphilis and tuberculosis. The Wassermann test allowed for early detection of the disease and, thus, prevention of transmission. It's still used today.

Now, Wassermann probably did not make shitty unsellable paintings like Hitler, but he did help thousands upon thousands upon thousands of Nazis with his life-saving work. No one, I repeat, no one fucks with Jews when it comes to medicine. Jews account for 40% of Nobel Prizes in medicine. Ponder that. When Herr Dumb Fuck came to power, doctors from Berlin and Vienna hospitals alone lost half of their physicians and a MAJORITY of their medical school faculty. I want to make a list of some of these doctors, scientists, and professors, but where would I start? I'll pick a few, but when you hear someone say, "You should go see a

Jewish doctor," they're probably not joking.

Nobel winner Paul Ehrlich was a German physician and scientist in the fields of hematology, immunology, and antimicrobial chemotherapy. Carl Koller invented local anesthesia. Alfred Einhorn invented Novocaine. Karl Landsteiner discovered the A, B, O, and other human blood groups, and the Rh factor. Moritz Romberg was a neurologist.

Sigmund Freud founded psychoanalysis. Ilya Mechnikov pioneered immunology.

Richard Lewisohn developed procedures that made blood storage and transfusion practical — the sodium citrate blood storage technique. Before this invention, blood could not be stored and could only be transfused from one person to another. Waldemar Haffkine became the first microbiologist who developed and used vaccines against cholera and bubonic plague. George Fernand Widal was a serologist and clinician-scientist. I could go on about Dr. Widal; just know his face is on a stamp. Who's next?

Biochemist Edwin Cohn helped develop the methods of blood fractionation, separating blood plasma into its constituent components. Think that had any impact worldwide? Abraham Jacobi was the founder of pediatric medicine and nursing. Ho Hum.

Selman Waksman discovered streptomycin and 15 other antibiotics. This is but a very, very, very small list of Jewish contributions to medicine.

This was a fun chapter, and I feel privileged to recognize but a few and their areas of expertise. Most people don't concern themselves with fission or who invents, diagnoses, and helps cure people, or how someone puts together a motorcycle, injection molds a part onto a piece of equipment that we don't see, or wipes their face on a towel without knowing where it was made. Why is this? Because no one really gives a shit.

However, when you're given a platform to write down names — important names — and then research and laud them for their deserved accolades, it makes others aware of why certain trailblazers deserve the shout-out. Now, at least by reading this chapter, you will appreciate the contributions of these brilliant men and women and how their fields have probably affected and helped you personally.

We hear a lot of, "Well, someone had to do it." Yes, someone did.

Chapter 3: Let Us Entertain You

"Some people like the Jews, and some do not. But no thoughtful man can deny the fact that they are, beyond any question, the most formidable and the most remarkable race which has appeared in the world."
~ *Winston Churchill, Prime Minister of Great Britain*

Okay, let's see if we have any Jewish talent in movies or TV…LOL.

Thanks to thousands of gifted Jews, people at home and around the world have been enthralled with big-screen movies, swept away by TV series, and informed through documentaries. There is no easy way to write down all the Jews that have been involved with Hollywood on the big and small screen, producing, writing, etc. There are just so many, so whomever I list represents a very, very low percentage of the overall number.

Here are some Jewish men you may recognize — Cary Grant, Kirk Douglas, Marx Brothers, Edward G Robinson, Paul Newman, Gene Wilder, Joaquin Phoenix, the great Mel Brooks, Dustin Hoffman, Sean Penn, Sammy Davis Junior, Alan Arkin, Jerry Lewis, Hank Azaria, Leonard Nimoy, James Caan, Elliott Gould, Kevin Kline, Tony Curtis, Harrison Ford, Danny Kaye, Sam Raimi, Harvey Korman, George Burns, Milton Burrell, Jack Benny, Adam Sandler.

With Jews being under .02% of the total U.S. population, it's stunning, and again, this is just a small fraction.

Now, on to our beautiful women. I love me some Jewish women. There are a shitload more Jewish actresses than what I share here, but a few in no particular order are Scarlett Johansson, Natalie Portman, Joan Rivers, Carrie Fisher, Lauren Bacall, Mila Kunis, Sarah Jessica Parker, the great Barbra Streisand, Gwyneth Paltrow, Jennifer Connelly, Sarah Michelle Geller, Kate Hudson, Bette Midler, Nina Mendez, Shelley Winters, and Marilyn Monroe.

What a list of absolute, extremely talented, and beautiful women. In a very cutthroat business, these tough, talented Jewish women have all excelled. And many, many, many, many more.

While I'm sure some Aryans have let loose on their "cum rags" to these lovely ladies, I want to inform you that I'll allow it, and I understand. If you're an Aryan White supremacist and you haven't, you probably have bigger issues than racism, etc. Anyway, do yourself a favor and check out these highly, highly talented, strong, gorgeous Jewish women and plenty of others.

Before I go into the specifics of Jewish influence in Hollywood, you should know that Jews are involved on many, many levels, but I am only going to highlight a few. I think our attraction to Hollywood comes down to three things: our intelligence, creativity…and I think we enjoy the attention. That's certainly not a Jewish phenomenon, but we just might have a Ph.D. in it.

Hollywood Studios

As a backdrop, according to the *Jewish Chronicle*, "Hollywood was invented in 1911 when Shmuel Gelbfisz (a.k.a. Sam Goldfish and later Sam Goldwyn) teamed up with his brother-in-law Jesse L. Lasky to make the first feature film, *The Squaw Man."* This led to an influx of other "dream makers" and the opening of various Hollywood studios in 1911. Shortly thereafter, around 20 or so companies were producing in the area.

In 1913, Cecil B DeMille, Jesse Lasky (Jew), Arthur Friend (Jew), and Samuel Goldwyn (Jew) formed the Jesse L. Laskey Feature Play Company. Adolph Zukor (Jew) and the Frohman Brothers — Daniel (Jew), Gustave (Jew), and Charles (Jew) — owned the Famous Players Company. On June 28th, 1916, the two companies merged, forming The Famous Players-Lasky Corporation. This group ended up evolving into what is now Paramount Pictures. Because of what these men were doing, many filmmakers moved out west by 1915. As more and more filmmakers migrated, other film studios were formed.

Louis B. Mayer (Jew) and Marcus Loew (Jew) founded Metro-Goldwyn-Mayer. Under Mayer's management and direction, MGM was the most prestigious and successful film studio in Hollywood. Everyone involved in filmmaking wanted it to be done by MGM in the '30s and '40s. Mayer grew up poor in St. John, Canada, but through hard work and intelligence, he was able to purchase and renovate a theater to show films in Haverhill, Massachusetts. He quickly grew that business to five theaters and eventually partnered up with Nathan Gordon (Jew) to establish the largest theater chain in New England. Also, a founding member of the Academy of motion pictures and arts and studios. Fun fact: Mayer became the first person in the United States to have a million-dollar salary in 1939.

William Fox (Jew) was born in Tolcsva, Hungary. He sold candy and newspapers and worked a bit in the fur and garment area. He stayed in the Northeast part of the United

States, where he purchased theaters to show films. He started Fox Theater and Fox Film Company in 1915, and between 1915 and 1919, was making millions and millions of dollars.

Warner Brothers was founded by four brothers, Jack (Jew), Harry (Jew), Albert (Jew), and Samuel (Jew).

Darryl Zanuck was not Jewish. He was an intelligent man who left Warner Bros. in 1933 to form 20th Century Pictures with Joseph Shenk (Jew). Later, they bought Fox, which formed what we now know today as 20th Century Fox and the precursor to Fox channel, Fox News, Fox film, etc.

Harry Cohn (Jew), Jack Cohn (Jew), and Joe Brandt (Jew) founded Columbia Pictures. Harry ruled Columbia with an iron fist and eventually bought out Joe Brandt to own the studio with just his brother. He had the longest-running position as head of a major studio, 45 years.

These brilliant, tough, and successful men created a medium that will be around for a long time. The premise and use of directors, actors, and actresses haven't really changed and will be around for a long time. The writers, camera crews, and on and on are still very much involved with making movies, and all of them will be around for a long time.

Look at the accomplishments that followed their wisdom. Someone can tell a story, any story, then find people to play it out while it's being filmed, then put it on a large screen anywhere in America, and it can start changing lives, perspectives, and attitudes on whatever subject is being told.

Can you imagine the wonderment and excitement about surfing in Malibu being watched by a ten-year-old girl in Nebraska? Or a film about gangsters in NYC being watched by a teenager in Texas? There are very few mediums that make the world smaller; radio, television, the internet, phones, airplanes, and movies are some of them, and there aren't many more.

As movie pictures slowly started going international, these men changed the hearts and minds of people throughout the world in how they envisioned Americans. It cannot be overstated how much the world has been impacted by motion pictures and how much those men played such a massive part.

Academy Awards

Let's look at the Academy Awards, one of my personal favorite shows of the year. I like movies, and I appreciate winning talent. So, I tune in, as it allows me to see how the secret society of the Academy ranks some of the best movies and actors that I've seen that year. Anyway, here is a listing of Jewish recipients for Best Actor since its inception.

This award started in 1928, and in that time, a Jewish man won the award a combined 14 times and was nominated in the category 72 times. They are listed in order of acceptance: Paul Muni, Paul Lucas, Richard Dreyfus, Dustin Hoffman, Paul Newman, Michael Douglas, Dustin Hoffman, Daniel Day-Lewis, Adrian Brody, Sean Penn, Daniel Day-Lewis, Sean Penn, Daniel Day-Lewis, Joaquin Phoenix. Jewish nominees for best actor is an astonishing 80%, with 14 winners and a very impressive 15%-win rate since the Academy started awarding them.

Best actresses in the leading role started in 1929. Since then, here are the lovely and talented Jewish women who have won best actress. Norma Shearer, Louise Rayner, Louise Rayner, Judy Holliday, Simone Signoret, Elizabeth Taylor, Barbra Streisand, Marley Matlin, Helen Hunt, Gwyneth Paltrow, and Natalie Portman. Also, very impressive. Roughly 14% of all actresses who won for best actress and 53% of all women who have ever been nominated for best actress are Jewish. Simply outstanding.

I'll throw in one more category from the Academy Awards, Best Director. The Best Director category has been awarded since 1927. Here are the names of all the winners in that category who are Jewish. Lewis Milestone, Lewis Milestone, Norman Taurog, William Wyler, Michael Curtiz, Billy Wilder, William Wyler, Joseph L Mankiewicz, Joseph L Mankiewicz, Fred Zinnemann, William Wyler, Billy Wilder, Jerome Robbins, George Cukor, Fred Zinnemann, Mike Nichols, John Schlesinger, William Friedkin, Milos Forman, Woody Allen, James L Brooks, Sidney Pollack, Oliver Stone, Barry Levinson, Oliver Stone, Steven Spielberg, Steven Spielberg, Sam Mendes, Roman Polanski, Joel Cohen, Ethan Cohen, Michel Hazanavicius. Not sure what to say. Since 1927, Jewish directors of film have won 32 times for a win rate of 35% and have been nominated 130 times. That is not a typo.

So, what would you Aryans say to that? Luck? Favoritism? I assume you guys don't watch any films with Jewish, Black, Gay, Latinos, etc., who either write, direct, or act in any movie. I mean, outside of a few Mel Gibson movies, you're fucked.

The Pulitzer Prize

Now for the more serious arts and a closer look at Jews in media. The Pulitzer Prize is a series of prestigious annual awards given by Columbia University and New York University in the fields of poetry, nonfiction, fiction, music, history, drama, and biography. Non-biography fellowships are also awarded. Founded by Joseph Pulitzer and first awarded in May 1917, the prizes have varied over the years — 14 in the field of journalism and seven awarded in Letters,

Drama, and Music. So, in total, there are 21 categories. Each year, 102 jurors are selected by the Pulitzer Prize Board to serve on 20 separate juries for each category.

Joseph Pulitzer, Jew, came to the United States with his family from Hungary. He immigrated to the U.S. at the age of 17 and went straight into the Union Army, among countless individuals who came to this country without knowing the language and made something of themselves.

In the research I've done on Mr. Pulitzer, I tried to find articles, quotes, or anything about him providing any excuses for not allowing himself to succeed. In fact, a long, long line of people made no excuses even when desolate and poor, including Pulitzer, who, through hard work, determination, and intelligence, helped to build this country.

After the military, Pulitzer found temporary jobs, but nothing stuck. He eventually made his way to St. Louis and became a lawyer and state representative at age 22, which is three years below the legal age of a state representative in Missouri. Oh, and he learned English in three years during and after leaving the military.

Pulitzer bought the *St. Louis Dispatch* and quickly increased the circulation from 4,000 in 1878 to 22,000 in 1882. He ended up buying the *New York World* and took it from a circulation of 15,000 to 600,000, making it the largest newspaper in the country. He was a solid philanthropist, and through him, the Pulitzer Prizes came.

I know a high majority of you won't know this word, even though I have already discussed it. So, I'll type it in bold letters to make it easier for you to google. The word is **PHILANTHROPY**.

Let's look at the stats:

- There have been 101 Pulitzer Prize winners for

Poetry. Jews have won 17 so far.
- There have been 59 Pulitzer Prize winners for Nonfiction. Jews have won 31 so far.
- There have been 97 Pulitzer Prize winners for Fiction. Jews have won 13 so far.
- There have been 89 Pulitzer Prize winners for Drama. Jews have won 34 so far.

I think you get the point. It's a fantastic list of brains, talent, and critical thinkers. I would say that's a very impressive win ratio for .02% of the population.

Also, possibly the greatest influencers of the 20th century were Einstein, Freud, Mart, and Darwin, and three of the four were Jewish.

Writers

I was going to make a list of Jewish screenwriters and TV and radio scriptwriters but realized my pen might not have enough ink. What Jews have brought to cinema, television, and radio is so astounding that I'm not sure where to start. So fuck it, I'll start with an absolute mind-boggling contribution. I hope to encapsulate how impressive and important Jewish writers have been and continue to be at all levels in bringing their talents to entertain us. Here is but a small list.

Again, this is far, far, far away from being a complete list of Jewish Hollywood screenwriters. Also, I suggest you browse online and see their accomplishments. Irving Berlin, Woody Allen, George Axelrod, Stuart Bloomberg, Mark Boll, Irving Brecher, Marshall Brickman…when I see what they wrote, wow, just amazing. Let's keep going. James L Brooks, the outstanding Mel Brooks, Sidney Altman, Lisa Cholodenko, Ethan Evan, Joel Cohen, the first movie ever made with sound Alfred Cohen, Larry David, Helen Deutsch, Henry and Phoebe Ephron, Nora Ephron, Julius Epstein, Philip Epstein, and Carl Foreman.

I'm still only in the Fs.

You are looking at talent, talent, talent. I feel so much pride seeing these names in the movies and on TV. Jules Furthman, William Goldman, Ronald Harwood, Lawrence Albin, Ben Hecht, Lucas Heller, Buck Henry, Samuel Hoffenstein, Ruth Brower, Lawrence Kasten, Charlie Kaufman, Howard Coke, Stanley Kubrick, Ernest Lehman, Alan Jay Lerner, Barry Levinson, Richard Maibaum, Herman J. Mankiewicz, Abby Mann, Elaine May, John Milius, and MANY, MANY, MANY MORE.

A lot, and I mean a lot of you racists are going to be more than surprised when you investigate what these intelligent, witty, and beautiful artistic minds brought to movies and television. Alan Pakula, Norman Nome, Dorothy Pastor, S.J. Perelman, Harold Ramis, Robert Risking, Eric Roth, Alvin Sgt., Budd Schulberg, David Seidler, Rod Serling, the outstanding Neil Simon, Aaron Sorkin, Oliver Stone, Joe Swerling, Billy Wilder.

Movies, televisions, and books "take us away," even if for just a brief period, as we enjoy someone else telling a story. The names I've given obviously aren't remotely close to the number of people who have sat down and put words to paper for our enjoyment. Does it matter one's religion or beliefs when you watch "Breakfast at Tiffany's," "Blazing Saddles," "Mr. Smith Goes to Washington," "One Flew "Over the Cuckoo's Nest," and thousands and thousands more? Did I mention these were written by Jews? Will you not watch them again? Are they worse now that you know who wrote them? Directed them? Acted in them? It's a shame, frankly, if you have to think about your answer.

Do you know why you see so many Jewish screenwriters, TV writers, Broadway writers, etc.? The reason is simple: we're good at it. We're very good at it. I see very little nepotism in Hollywood, but in the writing business, nepotism won't pay the bills and quickly. Why? Talent. It takes a tremendous amount of talent (writing-wise or other) to have a long career in that city.

Hollywood and NYC don't give a shit about who you are, what you look like, etc. You need talent and lots of it, or you just won't be around for too long. We've all seen a famous director or actor get their kid involved in the industry, and we'll watch their performance on screen or television and have a pretty good idea if they'll be returning or if we'll ever see them again. Why? Talent. There are actors I've seen in Hollywood for years that I don't like and would never see their movies, but they're fucking talented.

It's extremely obvious and clear that Jews have a lot of influence in Hollywood; furthermore, there's a shit ton of money to be made in movies, TV, etc., so why the fuck shouldn't Jews stay, try, or expand in the industry? And one more time, we fucking started the studios, so I'm guessing there are a lot of bright minds who grew up in that business and have learned from others living on either Coasts. Hollywood is a business, first and foremost. If movies and TV shows aren't making money, like most businesses, there will be change. The reason it's more obvious about issues in Hollywood is that we see their faces right in front of us one day and gone the next…business.

The Entertainment Industry has been a massive winner for billions upon billions of people, worldwide. And how fortunate for all of us that it's been in our own backyard since inception. We all have our favorite movies, actors, directors, and so on, and we all admire and appreciate the possibilities; the highs, lows, laughter, horror, and thrills films can bring. My point is it's a good thing when we can recognize those men who came to California in the early 1910s and did it.

Ho, Ho, Horowitz?

Have you ever heard the term "holiday ironic?" I know I haven't, as I just made it up, but I think after you look at the songs listed below, you will too. Before I "bust out" this next list, I would like for you to acknowledge that you have sung along to at least one of these Jewish classical hits.

Here is a listing of Christmas songs written by Jews. This is the order that Mattie Albert put them in but feel free to move your favorites to the top. I'm not going to comment on each one because, well, I think it speaks for itself…

1. "Chestnuts roasting on an open fire," Mel Torme
2. "Let it Snow," Sammy Cohen and Jules Stein
3. "Santa Baby," Joan Javits and Phil Springer
4. "It's The Most Wonderful Time of the Year," George Weil and Eddie Poulos
5. "Silver Bells," Ray Evans and Jay Livingston
6. "White Christmas," the outstanding Irving Berlin
7. "Rudolph the Red Nose Reindeer," Johnny Marlys
8. "Rocking around the Christmas Tree," Johnny Marlys
9. "Have a Holly, Jolly Christmas," Johnny Marks
10. "Silver and Gold," Johnny Marks
11. "Walking in a Winter Wonderland," Felix Bernard and Richard Smith's Express

So, when the festive holiday season rolls around, and one of you haters get up a bit early on Christmas morning to give your seven-year-old his or her first high-powered rifle, or your girlfriend or wife a new reversible swastika-embroidered sweatshirt, just crank up your favorite local radio station and enjoy those lovely Christmas songs.

Regardless, great songs should be enjoyed.

I would like to finish this chapter by addressing what I hear and see a lot from various anti-semites, and that is, "Jews control Hollywood." So, if you've read everything in this chapter and after careful and thorough research by me, my answer is this: "Why on earth are the Jews so under-utilized in Hollywood?" I mean, c'mon. With a 1.8% population in this country and what we have produced through films, radio, TV, porn, and Broadway, it couldn't be any clearer — we don't control enough.

Chapter 4: Mein Kampf

"Anyone who does not wish to be the hammer in history will be the anvil."
~ Adolf Hitler

All right, I did something that I thought I would never do — I forced myself to read all of *Mein Kampf* — every single line and lie. Now, taking aside my personal prejudices about Hitler, this was by far the worst book I have ever had the displeasure of reading. I don't think anyone has ever said, "It's an easy read." It is just horrific. I thought it would take me, like, a few days, but it was so bad that I think, overall, it took me, including massive bathroom breaks, two or three weeks.

Hitler mentions early on in *Mein Kampf* that he prides himself on his "oratory skills." I'm guessing he used those skills to charm, dazzle, and control Goering's balls and Heydrich's anus. Those guys always seemed to be willing and smiling. Anyway, it highlights something Hitler was good at — persuasion (like all good mass-murdering cult leaders).

In his first chapter, he talks a bit about his family. I wasn't surprised that it included self-indulgent babbling about himself and the need for his father's approval. The relationship Hitler had with his father was usually contentious and cantankerous, but he tried to work it out amicably through conversations and an understanding of their opposite views.

Boy, that changed. Hitler came a long way from those discussions to 1933, when opposing Hitler's views meant death. Dissension, defiant opinions — tough shit, the outcome was death.

Okay, so far, I've read all the drama between Hitler and his dad that could bore a bullfrog to sleep... until I came across this little nugget. "My lungs became seriously affected that the doctors advised my mother, very strongly, not in any circumstances to allow me to take up a career which would necessitate working in an office. He ordered that I should give up attending the Realschule, for at least a year."

What? Ha, ha, ha! Oh shit, I fell over laughing. Has anyone besides him ever been "doctor banned" from "working in an office?" I think he was just a lazy cunt who wanted to dabble in art. He bitched and whined about not being accepted to the school of painting, but then he claimed he was an "unknown genius" in architecture. I wonder if his professors would be concerned about how Hitler's lungs would stand up in their architectural classes. No matter, he didn't get into the architectural school either.

The self-grandiosity and self-adulation in this chapter are impressive. You would think he wrote the original film in 1911, "The Count of Monte Cristo," and themed it after himself. I mean, how Hitler pulled himself up "by his bootstraps" is inspiring, if you are a naïve, gullible twit who enjoys fairytales. "Star Wars" is more believable than this book.

Remember, you must put *Mein Kampf* in context. Hitler was in jail and 35 to 36 years old when writing this horrible, shitty book on his thoughts and doings in the context of himself in his teen years, as he goes through his upbringing to modern times of his writing age. Hitler was 17 years old in retrospect and didn't once bring up girls or hang out with other young adults. But he found the time and fortitude to concern himself with social democracy, the social democratic movement, German indoctrination, blah, blah, blah ... at 17. Right. Where I grew up, we call that, at minimum, bullshit or, an easier word, a lie.

He claimed to have all the answers by age 20 and vowed to cover every topic, from eliminating all the Jews in Germany to telling his secrets about jerking off with his opposite hand. But did he share his brilliant cures for the world's woes with anyone outside his local pub? No, not until 15 years in the future. Being the selfish, psychotic prick that he was, he kept his "answers" buried deep inside his underdeveloped frontal lobe and waited the equivalent of another lifetime — 14 to 15 years — to write his manifesto from prison. So brilliant, so brave, such foreshadowing. Such a douche.

Hmmm, do you think maybe, possibly, he was fucking lying? Conjuring up bullshit? I mean, yes, Herr Liar was definitely a nerd back in the day, but *Mein Kampf* is filled with anything and everything to try and make himself look good, like a young prodigy or some sort of savant.

Hitler's Ignorance About the Jews

And there it is, finally, near the bottom of page 63 in *Mein Anus*. He writes, "Knowledge of the Jews is the only key to a true understanding of the inner nature and therefore the real aims, of social democracy." That's right, Herr Asshole; that's right.

But further down, he writes about NOT knowing any Jews — "I do not remember ever having heard the word at home during my lifetime." What? So, in the 62 pages of shit I read before this, he claimed knowledge of the inner workings and nuances of every party but the Whigs. And he says up until that point that he'd never heard the word, Jew. Seriously? He constantly talked about the Jews controlling this party and that party, and then he said *that*?

Was his self-esteem that low? I say that because it's so obvious he always sought any means to make himself look smarter, more insightful, and ahead of everyone else. Kind of an inner "Braggadocio" to help offset his real insecurities.

Jews at that time were around 10% of the population in Austria. Jews excelled at being tailors and working in mills, factories, and farms — areas where a young Hitler would obviously have come in contact — yet he actually wrote that he had no idea about Jews until his teenage years, well, except for the one Jew in his school, which he's probably lying about. His audacity is staggering. At this point, if you put *Mein Crap* in the fiction section, the fiction section would ask how Hitler had never heard of a Jew before.

So, this twat was a subject-matter expert on the Jews, except he never met a Jew. Are you getting the picture? Hitler was the emperor of tall tales and whoppers. It's so easy to catch him in his own lies; it's finding the truth that becomes impossible.

The "Genius"

"Genius is a will-o'-the-wisp if it lacks a solid foundation of perseverance and fanatical tenacity. This is the most important thing in all of human life…" Notice how Hitler told on himself in this quote. He believed that fanatical tenacity was the most important thing in life. Yes, he was pathetically, hopelessly, and fanatically mind-locked on an agenda and legacy of annihilation and supremacy. Imagine living with such a high opinion of yourself. If there was a narcissist convention, Hitler would be sitting in every seat.

The advent of the Austrian Jews, of which some were

involved in Zionism, was what pushed Hitler over the edge and into antisemitism. Now that he'd "awoke," everything "Jew" was bad in his mind. Everything. Jewish achievements in the press, in art, in literature, and in the theater were never acceptable. There were a lot of very successful Jewish bankers and business owners who contributed immensely to both Austrian and German societies. However, Hitler felt they should no longer be involved. I said "felt" because he had no fucking idea about banking or running a business. That asshole couldn't run a "pay toilet," yet he espoused condemnation that he was completely clueless about.

Hitler stated, "When the state is composed of homogeneous population, the natural inertia of the latter and the powers of resistance derived from that inertia will preserve it from internal collapse during astonishingly long periods of misgovernment and maladministration. It may often seem as if the life had died out of such a body political; but the time comes when the apparent corpse rises up and gives the rest of the world astonishing proof of its indestructible vitality."

He must've been a blast to hang out with at parties, yelling, spitting, and screaming at everyone while trying to explain "his struggle."

Since I'm basically reading this book now as a comedy, I knew it wouldn't take long to evoke one small grin: "By far the most effective part in political education, which is this connection, is best expressed by the word propaganda." Hitler also stated, "The press is the chief means employed in the process of political enlightenment. It represents a kind of fool for adults. This educational activity, however, is not in the heads of the state, but in the clutches of powers which are partly of a very inferior character."

So, Hitler understood the power of the media and knew

how to exploit it. "It took the press only a few days to transform some ridiculously trivial matter into an issue of national importance, while vital problems were completely ignored or failed and hidden away from public attention," he said.

Ha, ha. Was there a law passed in Germany that anyone caught reading *Mein Kampf* would be arrested? Books, newspapers, radio, those nasty instruments of information — of course, only Hitler knew the real truths as a 20-year-old. If he was the head of Germany, the gatekeeper of "truth," then he would open the press for all citizens. Or so he said.

Well, in 1933, Hitler finally got the chance, and how do you think it went?

Book Burnings and Propaganda

On May 10th, 1933, a nationwide book-burning ceremony occurred in 34 university towns and cities. Anything deemed "un-German" or non-approved literature by these cultural geniuses became illegal. On that date, the largest book-burning ceremony was in Berlin, with an estimated 40,000 people who burned around 25,000 books.

I get that once the Nazis took over, they eliminated the word "fun," but 40,000 people showed up to participate in a fucking book-burning "ceremony." My gosh, this is early in Hitler's reign and before he started scaring the shit out of every young adult in Germany. Seriously 40,000 in one evening to burn books? I always imagined that back then, the guys were at the bars playing various waldzithers (a German plucked string instrument) while German women with blonde pigtails and big tits served them massive beers while singing and laughing. Nah, fuck it, let's go with book burning.

What other example could you possibly need about never, ever, ever living or moving to a totalitarian state?

I mean, he ADDED a fucking Minister of Propaganda just days after taking over in 1933. Who gives someone the title of "Propaganda Minister" in a government? Furthermore, he picked someone who was almost as insane as himself. Again, just spit-balling here, but do you think Goebbels kept a list for Hitler of the number of people who killed themselves after reading his book?

All right, hold up, hold the fuck up. Here's Herr Douche: "During the boisterous years of my youth, nothing used to dampen my wild spirits so much as to think that I was born at a time when the world had manifestly decided not to erect any more temples of fame except in honor of businesspeople and government officials."

How many times do I have to tell the Jew-haters that Hitler, the mother fucker, had no friends? NONE. He didn't have one friend as an adolescent, a teenager, or in his early 20s, 30s, 40s, or after he died. None.

So, statues in honor of businesspeople and government officials were THE biggest things to "dampen the wild spirits of his youth?" WTF. And during the "boisterous years," too? Wow.

Censorship

On page 54 of *Mein Asshole*, Hitler goes off on a mean-spirited rant about newspapers spreading lies and journalistic integrity… ha, ha, ha.

Why am I laughing? From the word go, Hitler did nothing but spread propaganda, bar journalists, and eliminate public radio. Really, like a week after he was made Chancellor. His actions, as opposed to what he writes, ARE NOT in the same stratosphere. The "Do as I say, not as I do" is very typical for sociopaths, so it's not surprising, but it just becomes harder and harder to read because we all know the outcomes of his lies as opposed to what he wrote and said.

It took a little time after he became chancellor, but from 1933 until his death, Herr Douchebag controlled 100% of all news, entertainment, opera, radio, and whatever. Yet there he was, going apeshit that one paper dared to go against his narrative.

He was going to pass a law allowing him to marry himself; however, when he came in for his physical, his doctor noticed that his small arms couldn't reach his very tiny dick. Hitler was informed he wouldn't be able to consummate himself, so the wedding was off.

Oh, and to my female friends, I'd like to hear your thoughts on page 55 in *Mein Misogynist*. Thanks.

Military Career

Now, Hitler finally had his biggest wish come true — he joined the army. Of course, early on, he almost fell into a deep depression, thinking he wouldn't be sent to the front lines and might miss the war. Can you imagine the other guys in his unit? Hitler in the corner of their barracks, crying uncontrollably because he wasn't on the front lines, while the rest of the unit fought each other for umbrellas to keep his spit off of them.

Hitler, so brave, so noble. Anyway, he got his wish and was finally sent to the front. Well, the bullets started flying, and soldiers got shot, and he wrote: "…and while death began to make havoc in our ranks, we passed the song unto those beside us: Deutschland, Deutschland uber Alles uber Alles in der Welt." I've never been in a war but those of you who have, please let me know if singing patriotic songs as a unit while on the front lines is common.

At this point, he immediately explained how difficult war was, how he and his unit had been in a lot of battles, and how war was so much more difficult over time that even he, yes, Hitler, struggled. Yet, someway, somehow, he quickly conquered any personal doubts and responded like a Batman movie. (Pick any one.) "The stronger did resistance become, until finally the internal strife was over and the call of duty was triumphant." Herr Frontlinesinger paused his military-induced internal strife to conquer a diatribe — how the press was lying. Jews and Marxism were to blame for this conflict, and he, while going through his first mustache phase, knew all the answers.

How many "thousands" of examples have I highlighted when he says something like "The reason for this problem for Germans and Austrians is because of the Jewish...whatever," but rarely, if ever, does he give examples. In 1919, in Germany, there were around 500,000 Jews, and overall, these Jews were middle-class. In 1919, 500,000 Jews in Germany equaled less than .09% of the total population.

So, this .09% was the reason for World War I? Did that .09% cause a munitions crisis for Germany? Did it cause Germany to be underfunded during the war? Because whichever political party at the time (Socialist Democratic Party) won the most seats, also won the parliament and controlled the overall government.

It's the Jews' Fault

Anyway, Herr Dickhead *almost*, I mean, it was really close, but *almost* went four paragraphs without bringing up something, anything about a Jew, and then wham: "Eisner's death (Kurt Eisner, Jew) served only to hasten this development and finally led to the dictatorship of the councils, or, to put it more correctly, to a Jewish hegemony, which turned out to be transitory, but which was the original name of those who contrived the revolution."

What appears to be such an innocuous statement is a prime example of him lying, bullshitting, then peeing on himself. He did this all the time, and antisemites just lap it up. What is impressive is how he does it virtually in a couple of paragraphs on every page. Hess must've been like, "Cleanup on aisle five," as Hitler rattled off this crap.

He starts by mentioning the death of Kurt Eisner, who was head of the leading party in Germany, the USPD party. Eisner was shot and killed on February 21, 1919, while on his way to present his resignation to the Bavarian Parliament. By my watch, this puts the party's reign around hundred days. "Eisner's death served only to hasten this development (of a revolution)," Hitler claimed.

Bullshit.

That's just pure nonsense, a blatant lie. Again, he's making up shit. In January 1919, more than one month before February for any simpletons reading this, Eisner's USPD party had been soundly defeated in the elections for both the national assembly and the Bavarian Landtag, coming in sixth place with 3% of the vote.

Eisner's death led to about two months' worth of violence and, finally, to the dictatorships of the Council. From November 1918 to January 1919, Germany was governed by the "Councils of the People's Deputies" under the leadership of Friedrich Ebert (leader of the MSPD) and Hugo Haase of the (USPD) and a Jew. This whole thing was set up as a provisional cabinet of ministers.

This coalition enjoyed mass support among the workers, councils, and people numbering in the millions or so in various political parties in Germany. Hitler, of course, the "pragmatist," "intellectual," "for the working man" kinda guy, shows some fortitude by mocking and dismissing the FOLLOWING LAWS implemented by Ebert and Haase.

They passed:

- The eight-hour workday
- Domestic labor reform
- Work councils
- Agricultural labor reform
- Right of civil service associates
- Local municipality social wealth welfare reliefs (split between the Reich and states) National health insurance
- Reinstatement of demobilized workers
- Protection from arbitrary dismissal with appeal as a right
- Regulated wage agreement
- Universal suffrage from 20 years of age in all types of elections, local and national
- Female and child workers entitled to a 15-minute break if they worked between four to six hours and 30 minutes between six to eight hours, and also one hour extra for longer days
- Committees (composed of the workers' representatives in their relationship with employers) to safeguard the rights of workers
- The right to bargain collectively
- Election of workers on committees
- Establishment of reconciliation committees

Hitler fucking HATED this. All of it. "No one contrived a revolution," he said. Look at those 15 resolutions, and I defy one of you to disagree. For those of you in hate groups, your hero, your champion, and your leader HATED EVERY ONE of those laws supporting everyday workers. What in the fuck are you people thinking, chasing after this loon?

Here are a few reasons why I think he hated them.

He had to be the one in control and the center of attention.

In the first seven chapters of *Mein Kampf*, he doesn't shut the fuck up about socialism and socialists, etc. Then Ebert and Haase "rolled out" socialist types of laws for the ordinary folks in a little over two months, and everyone agreed they "nailed it."

With the overriding mental capacity of one of your Doc Marten boots, I think Hitler disagreed because the former head of the party, Eisner, and current party leader Haase were both Jews.

Even though there weren't many Jewish politicians, Hitler's antisemitism always overrode his sensibilities. I'll just never understand how anyone could believe anything that came out of his mouth. I mean, outside of neo-Nazis (remember, Hitler would have sued your group for using the word Nazi) showing up at his rallies, Hitler wouldn't have spit in your mouth if you were dying of thirst unless you could help keep HIM in power. He was a witless, a-social coward.

Mein Kampf is just so far-fetched, with a litany of lies, untruths, complete mischaracterizations, and a void of facts. This is the first time it really dawned on me that this shitty fiction writing led to so much death and suffering. It led to the systematic murder of my people, our people, and for what? A shitty book with horrific ideologies written by a madman who somehow convinced millions of people he was their answer.

Hofbräuhaus Festival

Hitler's 25-point thesis, the program of his new party, was introduced at the Hofbräuhaus Festival in Munich to an enthusiastic crowd of nearly 2000. Let's go over some of these points, shall we?

Hitler rambled on about all the new changes to be implemented once the Nazis took over. This wasn't just your typical "This is what you will get if you support the Nazi party." Nope, he went all in by telling supporters, "You'll get everything." *Well, shit,* the men must have thought. *Sign us up, and just to confirm, you're saying if we vote to get your party elected to run the government, we will get everything we want? Nothing for the women, right?*

That must be the greatest campaign promise ever. Hitler didn't have to say or utter another word. Drop the mic, walk off, get in his new car and drive over to his new palace. Throughout *Mein Kampf,* Herr Willgetyoueverythingyouwant is constantly bashing and bemoaning countless numbers of "lies" that were spewed by his opponents, yet in one campaign promise, he exceeded them all with that whopper. Let's continue with his paragraph, "The farmer is assured that the interests of agriculture will be safeguarded (lie) and the industrialist is assured of protection for his products (lie), and the consumer is assured that his interests will be protected in regard to market prices (yeah, okay, whatever the fuck that means)."

Germany entered World War I in 1914 as a substantial importer of food and fodder. Blockades and trade embargoes exacerbated shortages. By the end of the war in 1918, Germany's urban population was starving, and 763,000 people were estimated to have died from malnutrition. And the incidence of many serious diseases increased.

The Nazis had a bunch of brilliant plans to help feed their citizens. Basically, in each country it invaded, German farmers would be brought in to work the land and send the products back to Germany. Then, they came up with the "Hunger Plan." Talk about a great idea. This is where, after Germany took over Ukraine and its phenomenal soil, it would severely expedite grains, mainly wheat and oilseeds, back to Germany.

However, there is a downside (or positive to the Nazis). When the Germans were planning the "Hunger Plan," they estimated the starvation of between 20 to 30 million Ukrainians and Soviets. That's it? Only 20 to 30 million deaths by starvation? Look, if the Germans, I mean Nazis, are happy, I don't see a problem, right?

Which part of Hitler's psychotic and evil do today's hate groups admire the most?

Are you okay with 20 to 30 million deaths via starvation, including millions of children? This is the Nazi party. This is your party.

Anyway, the comments of farmers assured the interests of his agricultural initiatives, the industrialists ensured the protection of his products, and the consumer interest would be protected in regard to market prices. But this was, PER USUAL, lies, lies, lies, sprinkled in with a lot of bullshit.

If you were a farmer, you were drafted, and slave labor took over your farm.

If you were an industrialist, the state either took over your business or forced your company to manufacture anything geared towards the war effort.

Unless, of course, you could write Hitler a check every month, then neither of those first two applies to you.

However, you, the industrialist, will SET the market price. The consumer, as usual, always pays market price, but Herr Dumbass, the consumer, ain't setting any price in Nazi Germany. Was there anything Hitler promised that actually happened? Even in his retrospect, writing this "book" at age 36, can you think of one?

The Völkisch Movement

According to historian Nicholas Goodrick-Clarke, Völkisch referred to "National collectivity inspired by a common creative energy, feelings and sense of individuality. These metaphysical qualities were supposed to define the unique cultural essence of the German people." This is the same logic as trying to unite the country under a song. You can't be talked into focus. Hitler spit all over the last ten pages of this nonsense when he could have said something profound, like, "When you're outside walking, remember, other Germans have walked to, so unite, by walking." Fucking idiot.

Weltanschauung

This is simply a person's philosophical belief. The worst thing in the world for people like Hitler is for others to have their own beliefs. In his mind, there was no need for it. He dictated what those beliefs should be, and there was no need to provide a counterargument. If your beliefs were exactly like his, then your beliefs were correct. It kind of makes it easier if you think about it, right? In essence, if you're currently in an antisemitic, racist, homophobic, etc., group that has any ties to Hitler or the Nazis, you are telling the world that you have no free thoughts and you're a conformist. Thanks, it makes it easier for us to spot.

Marxism

I'm ready to start shooting up heroin as Hitler obsesses about Marxism and Jews, Jews and Marxism. Once Hitler brought "Völkisch and Weltanschauung" together, there would be weekly orgies rotating at everyone's mansions on 1000-acre land, which produced rice, shrimp, Cheerios, and scotch. That, or it didn't do a fucking thing because they are all just theoretical ideologies.

Simply put, it's Hitler's opinion and his alone. Over time, he plainly conned and convinced others that these were facts. Which group do you fall into?

If Hitler was alive during the time of Hitler's reign, Hitler would have sent himself to a concentration camp for the mentally disabled, without any doubt.

Mein Kampf is obviously one of, if not the worst, books written in the last few hundred years. I mean, there were better books printed before the Gutenberg Press than this crap. We can all agree that most of what Hitler writes, by a high majority, is written as though he's talking to himself while informing the world of his "brilliance," "ideas," "resolve," and so much more…LOL. This book is fiction, as I've said over and over.

If you had someone read *Mein Kampf* who knew nothing about Hitler and asked them to compare it to how Germany was governed from 1938-1945, the reader would tell you that whoever was in power NEVER, NEVER, NEVER wrote *Mein Kampf*.

I'm guessing early into his reign as German Chancellor, Hitler probably wished he never wrote it, too, as Herr Lying did almost zero of what he typed, and the number of lies is incalculable. I'm not sure there is a sentence that is logically correct. This whole thing is not only filled with a lot of holes, but most of his ridiculous comments are stated as facts when they're clearly not. He talks about the horror if no more Aryans existed in the world: "...yet if the Aryan, who is the creator and custodian of civilization, should disappear, all cultural corresponding to the spiritual needs of the superior nations today would also disappear." Yeah, okay, nut job.

This whole book is garbage. He provided almost zero examples when mentioning Jews and their "misdeeds" throughout the entire book. I didn't realize how fucking stupid and ignorant one must be to think this book has true meaning. I don't care how mentally deficient someone is; to quote even one word of this "book" lets the world know that you're a fucking idiot. You would also have to be ignorant, naive, extremely impressionable, and probably self-loathing to believe anything in the book. You are definitely near or at your end if you try to live by this book. In summary, you have officially given up on being a decent, respectable person.

I'm embarrassed and ashamed that any American, even one, would try to further this fuck's ideologies. I'm not sure I can vocalize how naïve and ignorant one must be to adhere to his words. Shameful.

Well, I finally finished *Mein Kampf* which should have been titled "opposite day." It's truly astounding the number of things Hitler got so, so wrong. I still find it hilarious that he had the German government buy six million copies of this dogshit book.

Furthermore, how incredibly inaccurate this "book" is, boring and dishonest. Why someone, anyone, would try and emulate one sentence could only mean they are alone, without pride, and completely lacking any self-confidence and critical thinking.

What Day Is It? — or — Have We Won Yet?

On January 30, 1933, Hitler took over as chancellor of Germany. Sometime in 1936, Hitler met Dr. Theo Morell, who was called to give Hitler a vitamin injection. Hitler felt like the injections were working well, so the doctor gave him daily vitamin shots for around five years. Sometime in 1941, on a day when Hitler got sick, Dr. Morell gave him a hormone shot and a shot of an opiate. From that day going forward, he became a heavy, heavy drug abuser and addict. By early 1943 he couldn't stop. Depending on the day, drugs would change, but overall, his favorites were heroin, crystal meth, oxycodone, cocaine, and a few others. Starting in 1943 until his death, he was a raging, full-blown addict. We're not talking just in the morning or in the evening; he used anytime he was awake.

Shame he couldn't have made it to the 1980s, as I'm sure he would have loved crack. It is impressive how he could single-handedly run a war, and continue to convince his extremely gullible nation (arguably the most in world history) of his successes, while maintaining Nazi-ism, "stoned" out of his mind 24/7. He started to really ramp up his stealing and looting of art, valuables, cash, gold, etc., in 1943 as well while expediting the process of extermination.

In *Mein Kampf 2, The Return*, the stories of Hitler's parties were legendary. He finally opened up about his love for transvestites, heroin, and Goebbel's porn filming prowess, which really opened up his mind and ass to pleasures he'd only dreamed of.

More on this later.

Chapter 5: The Versailles Lie

"It is not truth that matters, but victory."
~ Adolf Hitler

Let's take a deeper dive into the post-WWI "punishment" for Germany, otherwise known as the Treaty of Versailles. Well, ladies and gentlemen, Hitler and the Nazis concocted another lie, and this was a "world-class" doozy. The Nazis coming to power based on Germany's treatment caused by the Treaty of Versailles is bullshit. Yes, it's been the number one justification in everyone's mind, in every country, for the last hundred years. But it's not, not, not because of the Treaty of Versailles. Teachers and professors around the world can now stop, today, teaching this lie to their students that this Treaty had any REAL reason for Germany starting WWII other than being used as propaganda.

Understanding the Articles

The Treaty contains a series of Articles, with Article 232 stating, "Also, the allies acknowledge Germany's incapability to fulfill the reparations demanded of them. However, the allies required that Germany, nonetheless, undertake the compensation for all civilian damages caused by German aggression by land, sea, or air."

Article 232 "Demands that Germany also be responsible for the complete restoration of Belgium by reimbursement of the monies borrowed by Belgium from the allies with interest at a rate of 5% per year."

Articles 235–244 highlight the specific payments to which countries and for what amounts. This ranges for payments of $20 billion from 1919–1920 to pay for Allied expenses. Furthermore, Germany's paying cash to compensate for the cash taken away, seized or sequestered and "object of nature and securities (heirlooms, fine art and jewelry) that was stolen during the war and found in German territory or that of her allies."

The German government had to recognize the Reparation Commission, release information relative to military operations, and pay for the individual salaries that were on the commission.

Articles 248–263 involved financial clauses. Articles 264–312 involved economic clauses and dealt with commercial relations and custom regulations, duties and restrictions.

Real Outcomes

Okay, now that we have highlighted the articles of substance, let's address the outcome. With the rise of Hitler and the Nazis in the 1920s and 1930s, everyone always points out the Treaty of Versailles and says things like, "If the Treaty of Versailles wasn't so punitive," or "Hitler came to power because of The treaty of Versailles," or "The Treaty of Versailles punished the German people and government way too harshly, giving them no chance, to fulfill its terms."

The Treaty of Versailles is far and away the most consistent attribute worldwide, as the main and some would say ONLY reason Hitler rose to power in World War II. It's just not true. It's not close to being true. It's not in the realm of being true, and the actual facts back up my claims.

France thought the Treaty of Versailles was too lenient, and the U.S. never even ratified it. Accepting the "war guilt" clause and reparations terms probably didn't put too many smiles on the German's faces, but that was far from a knockout blow. Furthermore, and I feel I must explain this like I'm talking to a child, Germany lost the war. And many keep forgetting that 40 million people died.

Of course, there were to be repercussions, but not NEARLY to the level of what the majority believes. Yes, Germany lost a little bit of territory, and yes, German people in government felt that they were having the terms "dictated" to them, but who gives a shit how they were told. Dictated to them or forced down their throats was really their only punishment from this Treaty in Germany at that time.

Are demands and concessions dictated TO winners of wars? I would like any examples, thanks.

Let's look at some specifics and the real outcomes of the Treaty of Versailles. Hopefully, people will stop pushing the bullshit rhetoric that it caused World War II and the rise of the Nazi party. It didn't.

False claim: Germany was unfairly burdened with punitive and costly war reparations that destroyed its postwar economy, caused crippling hyperinflation, and doomed the Democratic Weimar Republic.

Reality: Defeated nations often pay reparations as a part of treaties ending European wars. This penalty was not suddenly invented at the 1919 Paris Peace Conference to punish Germany. It was a long-standing tradition. How hypocritical of Germany to complain when it imposed these types of penalties on countries it defeated.

Penalties imposed by Germany included a demand of billions from Russia, the heavily punitive March 1918 Treaty of Brest-Litovsk, and forcing France to pay billions in "indemnities" after victory in the 1870–1871 Franco–Prussian war. In fact, German forces continued to occupy parts of France until payment was made. The French promptly paid in full, even though the cost was equal to 25% of their national income. Germany's cost for WWI was only between 4% to 7%.

Germany complained about having to pay for civilian damages caused by its invasion and occupation of Belgium in northern France. The allies calculated the amount based on Germany's ability TO pay, NOT on the actual cost of repairing those damages — which was much greater. The claim that the Versailles Treaty required Germany to pay the "entire cost of the war" is completely false, as verified in article 232, which stated that Germany was to pay "compensation for all damaged done to the civilian population of the Allied and the associated powers and to their property during the period of belligerency."

A Slap on the Wrist With a Feather

The following is common knowledge. The initial reparation dollar amount that everyone points to Germany owing was 132 billion marks in reparations. This number was intentionally misleading. The Allies never intended for Germany to pay such a huge sum. It was an effort to fool the general public, but mainly fool the French into thinking that Germany was going to be severely economically punished.

Historian and economist Sally Marx, and others, point out that the actual figure the allies intended Germany to pay, and which they had calculated Germany could pay, was only 50 billion marks. Consider that during treaty negotiations, the Germans OFFERED to pay 51 billion.

By the way, Germany received far more money in U.S. loans (27 billion) than it paid out in cash for reparations and defaulted on the loans in 1932 after paying back only a small percentage. Other than the "in-kind" payments, Germany paid no out-of-pocket war reparations.

Wait? What? That can't be. I'm shocked! It's impossible. I was led to believe that Germany was crippled by war reparations. The truth has to be a myth!

French economist Etienne Mantoux surely was right when he wrote, "Germany was not unable to pay reparations, it was unwilling to pay them."

So, what we hear about the Allies crippling the Germans economically through the Treaty of Versailles, Hitler's subsequent rise to power, and why Germany started World War II — is a ruse? It's bullshit? Yes, sorry to inform all of you of this world-class lie. Lie, lie, lie, lie, lie, lie, lie, lie, lie. Look it up. There are multiple places you can find this information. I mean, Hitler, his henchmen, his butt buddies, and every German who lived in the Fatherland and followed his ideologies could only deny it by outright lying to themselves. Sorry, Hitler DUPED Germany's citizens, and he duped the present-day Jew haters AGAIN.

The overhyped Treaty didn't affect Germany at any level, with the exception of false propaganda. In 1924, The Allies and Germany agreed to implement the Dawes Plan, a great plan that lasted about an hour. It gave Germany back the Ruhr, and it fucked France on the agreed-upon tonnage of coal Germany was supposed to send. And Germany was set up to receive loans from the U.S. to pay back its reparations.

Was there anything else we could have possibly given to help Germany? Think about it. From the day the Treaty of Versailles was signed in June of 1919 until the London Agreement in 1953, the United States banks paid back more of Germany's reparations than Germany. But yeah, it "crippled" Germany's economy. Right. Remember, the Dawes Plan was done in 1924, well before the Nazis came to power. Was there a reason no one brought this up? There is a slight reason it may not have been talked about, and that is...

The Young Plan

The Young Plan further lowered Germany's debt, as did the London Agreement of 1953. But instead of boring you with all the details, just note that none of them did shit, except continually lower the amounts of money Germany owed and increase the time needed for them to start paying it back. I mean, the London Agreement allowed Germany to wait until they were a unified country again, for fuck's sake

The bottom line is Germany was coddled and indulged. By 1933, Germany had made World War 1 reparations of only one-eighth of the sum required under the Treaty of Versailles. The actual effects on Germany were three things.

1. Whatever the travel costs of plane tickets or gas prices for the representatives that attended these three useless conferences.
2. Read what I wrote on the Treaty of Versailles document yourself and tell me what real punishments Germany incurred from it.
3. The Treaty was a fucking joke. A sham. This Treaty was a launching pad "call to arms" from the Nazis even though the treaty wasn't enforced, with only one minuscule exception (France in the Ruhr).

Thus, Germany was never punished for WWI, but we were, us, the rest of the world. WWII was obviously started and caused 100% by Germany, but Allied complacency and constantly letting Germany "slide" didn't help. Trust me; I get it; no one wanted to go back to war due to enforcing a treaty, nor did anyone know how psychotic Hitler would be. It's sometimes frustrating talking about the Treaty of Versailles because, again, most still believe it was a major reason why Germany started the war.

Ironically enough, the biggest gift Hitler ever received was the Treaty of Versailles. He used it to his full advantage any chance he could. Even when he didn't have a chance, he still fucking used it. If a dog had a nasty fart in Berlin, Hitler simply just blamed it on the treaty. Oh, and Jews.

Hyperinflation

I'm not sure where we currently stand on how many times I've used the words bullshit and lies already in this chapter, so let's bring out a new word — myth. It's a complete and utter myth. AGAIN, that the "war reparations clause" had anything to do, at any level, with Germany's horrific hyperinflation of the early 1920s. It simply played no role in Germany's economy.

It's another myth that "crippling and punitive" war reparations caused the disastrous hyperinflation that ruined Germany's economy between 1921 to 1924. The Treaty had 0.00000000 to do with ANYTHING related to Germany's economy. NOTHING, ZERO, NADA, NICHT. Remember, it only paid a small fraction of reparations and used U.S. loans to do so. Germany's economy wasn't ruined.

When Germany was going through its hyperinflation period, and it cost around 4,200,000,000 marks for a loaf of bread, it wasn't because of heavy reparations. But wait, that can't be true! We've all been taught that the Treaty of Versailles was the root cause hourly, the minute after the Treaty was signed.

Pay attention; you'll learn something. Germany's post-World War II hyperinflation stemmed from the Kaiser and his ministers borrowing money rather than imposing taxes. Thus began a steady deduction of the German mark against foreign currencies. So Germany printed more money, causing inflation and then hyperinflation.

Yeah, but what about the Treaty of Versailles? It's the Treaty's fault, right? The Treaty's the real culprit — our trustworthy Nazi leaders told us so! "Hello, this is the Treaty calling, and I've always been told it's my fault too, so kiss my ass."

Can anyone provide information that the Treaty had any part in hampering Germany at all (outside of France's short time in the Ruhr)? What a fucking joke.

In fact, the trigger for post-war inflation was the Weimar government's response to the 1923 French occupation of Germany's Ruhr industrial region after Germany constantly defaulted on its reparation payments. The Weimar government encouraged and abetted "passive resistance" such as work stoppages and strikes to the French occupation. German workers were paid for their cooperation with vast amounts of this printed money. No wonder inflation skyrocketed.

By November 1923, a loaf of bread cost Germans 3 billion marks, a pound of meat cost 3 billion, and a glass of beer was 4 billion. But, but, but...

It's laughable that the Weimar Republic government blamed the hyperinflation crisis on war reparations because Germany wasn't paying reparations at the time. Germany's own economic policies caused the economic catastrophe. In 1924, the German mark stabilized the German economy, and by 1927, years before Hitler came to power, it was one of the world's strongest economies. So again, Germany's post-war decisions crushed the economy. Hitler, of course, would also exploit the Great Depression from 1930 to 1933 as an excuse.

Recapping the Boatload of Lies

So, let me get this straight. From 1920 to 1931, Germany paid $12.5 billion in cash for reparations and $7.5 billion "in-kind" while borrowing $27 billion from U.S. banks over the same time. Furthermore, the next payment Germany made toward reparations was in 1953. From 1953 to 1958, they made interest payments only.

Well, it doesn't take a forensic accountant to see that the Treaty of Versailles played absolutely zero part in any reparations or affected Germany's economy and finances at all. NONE. We've heard for years how difficult and impossible it was for both German citizens and their government. How crippling the sanctions were and how they led to the rise of Hitler and the Nazis, blah, blah, blah. It was all bullshit.

If the Germans knew it or not, it was a boatload of lies spewed by every member of the Nazi Party to get their party elected.

Now, starting World War 1, getting your ass kicked and having 15% of your male population killed will certainly affect your economy. But being given a number of restitutions, having it lowered in half, and still not paying for it, did not and would not affect Germany's economy. IT NEVER DID.

The tens of thousands of lies by Hitler and the Nazis were nothing but horseshit propaganda continually perpetuated because the people that knew it was all lies said nothing.

According to *HistoryNet* (a great resource on this topic), perhaps the most alarming part of the Treaty of Versailles is Article 231, the so-called "War Guilt" clause that mentions neither guilt nor war. Yet German politicians, first in the Weimar Republic and later Hitler and the Nazis, used the term to demonize the treaty and avoid Germany's obligations. German propagandists in the 1920s and 1930s created this fairytale. However, the treaty did not force Germany to accept the humiliating "War Guilt" clause. Blaming this clause for the whole entire war is disingenuous and patently false.

Yet historians continue to parrot this propaganda. It was so successful during the 1920s that many Allied countries

(Britain especially) embraced the notion. This discouraged the Allies from "rigorously enforcing" the treaty.

Standing alone without context, Article 231 does appear to make the German's "war guilt" claim seem credible. *HistoryNet* reminds us that Article 231 is a preamble to reparations and was not solely intended to blame Germany for the war. American Diplomats Norman Davis and John Foster Dulles simply established Germany's acceptance of its responsibilities to pay reparations for civilian damages caused by its military (in article parentheses 233 – 247 and parentheses of part VI II).

Germany started the war and lost. They started it by declaring war on Russia to "defend" Austria/Hungary against Serbia. This declaration of war was justified through mutual alliances. Germany is, without question, culpable. What I don't understand is why Germany feels so slighted admitting to it. This is utterly ridiculous to me, and "how it hurt their pride" is flabbergasting. Does it bother anyone in Germany or on the planet if I say Germany started World War II? Germany started WWI; how could they possibly have been offended by that?

I understand how news was dispersed 100 years ago, but even today, people still bitch about the "War Guilt" clause. Now you know…there wasn't one. How about the "Germany started World War II" clause, if it makes anyone feel better? If anyone is to be blamed, it's unquestionably the German government, as Austria-Hungary wouldn't have done a fucking thing without the backing and urging of Germany.

Germany declared war on Russia and France, and they violated international treaties by invading Luxembourg and Belgium. Hello. Germany started the war, "War Guilt" clause or not, and they simply needed to own it. The German government, at the time before the war and immediately after World War I, through spreading Hitler's charcoal ashes over a Berlin methane plant so it would easily mix in with the same smell. Yes, the lie continued after 1945, as almost every German politician still used it as a battle cry to avoid adhering to the Treaty of Versailles.

Both Davis and Dulles were shocked when German politicians chose to interpret Article 231a as Germany taking full blame for World War I. It was a German ploy for sympathy — war guilt lie. Pay attention to history.net again. "Article 231, when correctly read in conjunction with article 232 immediately following it, actually limits Germany's responsibility for the war by requiring Germany to pay ONLY for civilian damages caused by its invasion and occupation of Belgium in northern France and, as noted, even that was further limited to what the allies calculated Germany COULD pay."

The Real Failure of the Treaty

It's been over 100 years since World War I started and ended. I think that should give most people by now a clear view without having to be dissuaded by bias. Take the war reparations of 132 billion gold marks or equivalent today of $269 billion U.S. — the amount originally agreed upon. That's the only number given when trying to find the actual monetary value.

Germany only made one payment in regard to the Treaty of Versailles (June 28, 1919), and before 1955 that money was borrowed. Germany wasn't paying back anything, so you had a few groups try and help. The Dawes Plan in 1924 did nothing but lower Germany's debt amount. The Young Plan in 1929 did nothing but lower Germany's debt amount. Finally, the London Debt Agreement of 1953, where Germany's repayment number was halved, stipulated that repayment of the remaining debt was linked to Germany's economic growth and exports. The debt service/export revenue ratio could not exceed 3%. Furthermore, the original agreed-upon amount accepted by Germany wasn't even close to the original number, and even that number took Germany 92 years to pay off.

All the bitching, moaning, and whining about how stiff and damaging reparations were for Germany and how it fucked them over was, AGAIN, another lie.

I continue to harp on this as you need to know how Hitler used this document; the Treaty of Versailles was the "calling card" and the perfect opportunity for himself and the Nazis to come to power — for all the wrong reasons.

In the Treaty, Germany lost some territory and all of its colonies. Yea, punishment, my ass; the colonies weren't needed, and fortunately for Germany, it was fewer mouths to feed, and fortunately for everyone else, it allowed fewer Nazi assholes to deal with in WWII. Regarding this part of the Treaty, it was a win/win.

There were a lot of mistakes in drafting the Treaty of Versailles. I'm not sure the authors of it ever thought that it would never be enforced. Although allowing Germany to voluntarily comply is like allowing a drug offender to opt out of a urine test. There's no doubt they all patted one another on the back and toasted with vintage cognac on the completion of this Treaty, but if they had added Cuba as a signee, Germany would have faced more enforcement. I think if the first words of that Treaty started "Dear Abby," it would have garnered more military enforcement.

We've been told by thousands upon thousands of different sources how crushing, demoralizing and unfair the Treaty of Versailles sanctions were. "It will set Germany back a hundred years."

It took Germany 92 years to pay back a fraction of a fraction of what they agreed to pay. But reviewing all the

Articles, I think this may be the only thing, albeit (not even near the agreed-upon number) they agreed to.

The rise of Hitler and the Nazis — blame the Treaty of Versailles. The rise of hyperinflation and the collapse of the German economy — blame the Treaty of Versailles. All of these restitutions on the military that were never adhered to — blame the Treaty of Versailles. It was all bullshit. The Treaty didn't hinder one person for any reason from the day it was signed to today. The citizens of the Weimar Republic of Germany, through Hitler and the Nazis, were NOT hindered by the Treaty of Versailles and actually benefited from it economically and militarily.

Furthermore, and the only reason I give a shit about this treaty is that it led to the world-class propagandist lies which catapulted and gave a platform to the rise of Hitler and the Nazi party. The Treaty of Versailles didn't cause or lead to anything. The lies about it did. The only ones who gave a shit, as they were the only ones affected by it, were the New York bankers and France. The justifications of death, torture, destruction, etc., are really what came out of it, and the Germans bought it hook, line, and sinker.

Germany started World War I, and 40 million casualties later, their "punishment" was to sign an unenforceable treaty after getting their asses kicked, and of course, the Germans didn't adhere to it. Then, the German citizens listened to and elected a sociopath who told them how bad this unenforceable Treaty was. Shockingly, he got elected and started a war that had around 70 million deaths, while systematically murdering six million Jews, that only made up .0075% of the German population at the time. Germans were also killed while perpetrating the largest looting of Europe since, well, no one. Add in the total devastation of property and all other theft. My gosh, what a fucking mess.

The world's largest Ponzi scheme was committed by the

Nazis in a 12-year run, aided by a Treaty that had NO bearing.

You can't make this stuff up. What does this say about those Aryan, White supremacist, racist people? Is naive and ignorant part of the Aryan DNA? What could be so lacking in someone's life that they would gravitate to and endorse an ideology that is all a lie and could easily do their own research to find it out for themselves?

Everything Hitler said he was going to do, didn't happen. The premise of everything he promised never panned out, and now as we check the "box score" on his career, he turned out to be nothing but a psychotic, narcissistic, sociopathic liar. He ended exactly as he started, except he added a tremendous amount of death and theft in between. Even if you could overlook all his personality traits, he's just a murderer with an immense ego. A liar that fooled millions upon millions, but a liar, nonetheless.

Chapter 6: World War II Allied and Axis Forces

"I have been Europe's last hope. She proved incapable of refashioning herself by means of voluntary reform. She showed herself impervious to charm and persuasion. To take her I had to use violence."
~ Adolf Hitler

The quote above is extremely revealing. Hitler either fashioned himself as a savior or justified his reason for war. Regardless, his delusions of grandeur pitted nations against nations in one of the most tragic and preventable global blow-ups in history. If only he had been shot a few times while singing some patriotic songs in his bunker before kicking off WWII, the world would have been a much, much saner place. But I digress.

Perhaps not everyone is familiar with the WWII allied forces — Britain and the British Commonwealth, France (not so much), Poland, etc., and how the "Big Three" then worked together — the U.S., Russia, and the UK. I think it's important to note which countries were reluctant to jump in (the U.S. primarily) and how these supposed "good guys" were already aware of the concentration camps but turned a blind eye. Then we segue to the enemy Axis powers (Mussolini and Japan in cahoots with Germany).

WWII was initially started by a small group of thugs who

may have started out with an ideology for Germany, but it ended up as every other totalitarian dictatorship ends, doing everything for their own personal gains. The devastation they incited led to around 70 million deaths and millions upon millions more wounded.

When discussing WWII, we see a huge number of casualties. We see big numbers. In pointing out the obvious, death is final. That's it. Even with the massive number of casualties in WWII, most could go back to someone, but not the Jews. In many parts of Europe, entire communities were wiped out. We were already a small minority in a lot of those European cities; in some cases, it happened in only a few days.

Here's a casualty breakdown to provide a better understanding of what the unprovoked Nazis started:

WWII — September 1, 1939-May 7, 1945

- The war lasted five years, eight months, and two days
- In that duration and using every second, there were over 25 deaths per minute; 1,507 deaths per hour; 36,168 deaths a day; 253,176 deaths per week in WWII

The fact that the Nation of Israel exists today, and that Jews from all over the world are alive today, is because our surviving ancestors had the intestinal fortitude to carry on.

Our WWII Ally, the British

For our British brothers and sisters in arms, I honestly don't know how Winston Churchill could get out of bed or off a chair with the immense weight of those two huge brass balls he was carrying around. What a leader. The Brits were very, very fortunate; Chamberlain was afraid of his own shadow. From the beginning, Churchill and the British didn't take any shit from the Nazis. The Brits showed how overwhelmingly tough, charismatic, and brave they were.

In the very early part of WWII, the battle of Britain was fought. For two and a half months, Britain was battered by German bombs multiple times daily. Well, the day before it ended, and the day after it ended, the Britons said to Germany, "Fuck you," and something like, "Let us know when the heavy bombing is going to start." Tough people. Don't let their charm and whit fool you.

I have a tremendous amount of respect for the people in the leadership of that great country. Those people, that country, their toughness. They were alone, and I mean all by themselves, until Hitler had the bright idea of invading Russia.

I would like to highlight one more example of the people. I say people because this is the society that raised these soldiers, and they can all hold their heads high.

Battle of St. Nazaire

Whenever a discussion is being held anywhere in the world about toughness, resolve, and character, the Battle of St. Nazaire might be mentioned. Why? There were obviously many, many battles, conflicts, and missions in WWII, but the one I found most impressive was the Battle of St. Nazaire.

The St. Nazaire Raid or "Operation Chariot" was a British amphibious attack involving both the Royal Navy and British Commandos on the very heavily guarded Normandy dry dock at St. Nazaire in German-occupied France. If the British could somehow eliminate that dock, the Germans would have nowhere to repair, refuel or resupply their larger ships outside of Germany. I can't highlight enough how extremely important and vital a military location this was, as proven by their fortification of it.

Most knew the overwhelming odds against this mission. So, before they left for St. Nazaire, the commanding officer did something that's rarely, rarely done in war. He told all 611 of his men that if they wanted to, they could recuse themselves from this mission. "There would be no punishment, mocking, or reprisals of any kind." This was a one-way mission, after all. When they were in formation, he barked out, "Two steps forward if you're in this mission." Amazingly, 1222 steps were taken.

A lot of people don't know this, but the Brits started Special Operations, commonly referred to as "Special Ops." The Special Air Services (SAS) was formed in July 1941 from an idea and plan from a world-class badass named David Stirling in June 1940. In essence, Great Britain revolutionized warfare for the rest of the 20th century and beyond.

Those soldiers, along with the rest of Britain's military, were brave, tough, and intelligent. We were fortunate to have them as allies.

Our So-Called Ally, France

First off, I don't think France gets near enough credit for helping the U.S. in the Revolutionary war. They did an outstanding job by helping us with supplies, arms, ammunition, troops, and naval support. We should never forget that. World War II, however, could be the most inept use of military, possibly, in world history. The French did nothing. Nothing. One can only surmise that the French, and I would guess a high percentage of French, supported the Nazis and that most of the population sat by and watched. That is really the only logical answer I can come up with.

France came out of World War I as a world tiger, but 20 years later, it came out of World War II as a flourless croissant.

Look, I get that the French were going through economic and political issues, but everyone was. I just find it very hard to believe that as soon as Germany crossed into Austria, they didn't know that they would soon be at war. Furthermore, at a minimum, there was one year of mandatory service in France. I don't think that France's leaders were naïve or were lacking intel that Germany was building massive amounts of armament, especially at their borders.

The Maginot line did help; however, it was fortified in fixed positions only, and Germany just went around them. There were just way, way too many holes. How is it remotely possible for France to claim that no one thought the Germans could go through the Ardennes? Like there was a big secret in France about Germany's military equipment? I mean, there just had to be more at play here; French incompetency was so high that when Hitler, Hess, and Goebbels heard the news about Germany's easy march through the Ardennes, they immediately postponed their game of "Truth or Dare" (well, after they pulled the 14" ribbed black dildo out of Himmler's ass). Those guys knew how to party.

The French had more troops, more supplies, and more equipment than the Germans. The French Air Force had a 2-to-1 kill advantage over the Germans. I mean, it just doesn't make sense. Germany took over France in what, six weeks? The French needed help in the battle of Bir Hakeim, where their men certainly fought hard, but they couldn't finish it without the Brits who were needed elsewhere.

The French kicked ass in Elba, but what the fuck were they doing in Elba? Frenchmen fought bravely in the Colmar Pocket, but again with help from the United States. They came up short on this one, and those soldiers are why I wonder and question France's defense of their home front.

Furthermore, what was the percentage of the population that supported the Vichy regime? You had the Legion Imperiale fighting against the Allies. You had the fucking French Volunteers against Bolshevism fighting alongside the Nazis in Russia. I mean, WTF? And then these assholes later worked with the Waffen-SS. Eventually and unbelievably, the Legion Imperiale fought alongside the 754th Germans panzer grenadier regiment in the Battle of Tunisia.

I'm sure by now we're confident that all of you White supremacists can't keep your long-awaited orgasms wishing you could have volunteered for the SS. However, I am highly confident that you would have the same ending as most of them. Are you trying to tell people or show someone that you could at least say you were brave enough (or rather dumb enough) to give up your life for a psychotic, megalomaniac meth user and his weak lying underlings consisting of various assholes like Napoleonic asshole (Goebbels), loudmouth assholes (all of them), fugly asshole (Himmler), wannabee asshole (Hess), and arrogant asshole (Goering)? Congrats, I believe you.

In 1939 the French had 900,000 soldiers in service, and also roughly five million men who could have been called up. I really, truly don't get why it was such a mismatch. They were receiving plenty of arms from the U.S. France had 5,800 tanks, almost double the number of guns in Germany, and roughly the same number of troops. Yet, in six weeks, Germany took over your country. I'd get it if this were Luxembourg, but France?

And lest we forget, from France alone, 72,500 Jews were murdered in the Holocaust.

Our Enemy in Italy

Never fear; I haven't left out the asshole Benito Mussolini. Now it's his time to shine, so let me introduce you. If we had a category for the most overrated dictator of all time, it would easily be Mussolini. If Hitler wasn't so fucking hard up for a friend, we would probably have never heard of Mussolini.

I think because of Hitler's "infectious" and "lovely personality," along with Mussolini's beautiful, flowing Italian accent and the fact the Italians were in desperate need of protection from somebody, anybody, this beautiful relationship was struck.

Another horrible decision by Hitler was to join Italy for military support. Germany went from babysitting Italy to defending it. Italy brought nothing, I repeat nothing, to the table for Germany.

Italy's military had two victories, one prior to WWII. That illustrious initial victory was over Ethiopia. Yes, Italy invaded the military juggernaut of Ethiopia in 1935-1936, which will become Il Donkey's most successful military campaign ever. Congrats.

That campaign was followed by the massive military opponent, Albania. Italy had to somehow overcome the Albanian forces, which consisted of 8,000 troops, five aircraft, and three boats. Impressive. I probably could've walked over to the local bar in my hometown, found 20 guys to join me, and we would have taken over Albania in a week. However, let's not take this monumental achievement away from the Italians.

Full disclosure — I'm not counting their victory against the partisans (*partigiano*, meaning civilian party supporters) in Yugoslavia for two reasons. 1. They had help from Germany (coordination) of Croatian and Chetnik forces. 2. Because they were partisans. Moving along.

Daniel Boustead stated, "The conflicts of the '30s between Italy and their smaller opponents combined with their Spanish Civil War debt became too much for them to overcome. By the time they invaded Poland in 1939, they had run out of gold. And by the time they declared war on France, their military was so inept various units were spying on one another. By 1940, the Italians couldn't supply uniforms or equipment to its troops."

Hitler is both literally and figuratively up Mussolini's ass about the "help" Germany needed from Italy, while Mussolini continued to tell him he needed more time to build up his forces. Fine, we get it; it happens. However, the arrogance and bolstering that Mussolini continually displayed while basically overseeing the Boy Scouts is just another example of a dictator "running wild." Furthermore, Mussolini is THE case study on why fascism is shit.

Anyway, as bad as that was, here are Italy's other results in WWII:

- Egypt... lost.
- Palestine dropped some bombs, then hurried out... lost.
- Greece... lost.
- Sicily... lost.
- Italian East Africa... lost.
- North Africa... lost.
- Tunisian Campaign... lost and ass kicked.

Mussolini couldn't get to a phone fast enough to beg his "Ben Wa balls buddy" for help. Hitler sent in his Africa corps, led by a very good general, Erwin Rommel, who was beloved by his troops and German citizens. Later in the war, Hitler was kind enough to give Rommel the option of being killed or killing himself.

Montenegro... tie. The Italians claim victory, but you can decide. Italy sent in ten units which consisted of around 70,000 soldiers. This victory was against, ready for it, partisans, again. They weren't fighting a country or an allied territory. As mentioned, partisans are made up of civilians who are pissed off or fed up, and this group had few partisans with any military background. Anyway, these partisans went up against 70,000 Italian soldiers and fought to a draw.

At this point, Hitler was probably thinking about going back to Himmler or even Goebbels to play "hide das wiener schnitzel" — not really hide, but it worked for them.

On July 25, 1943, Il Duce was voted out of office and shortly thereafter was imprisoned. Guess which country joined the Allies after that?

So, Il Dummy is eventually rescued by a German unit and brought back to Germany. Hitler tells him he looks like shit and asks Il Duce, "Why aren't you going after the Italians who put you in this predicament?" Hitler is adamant that Mussolini start some type of Italian movement/government while in exile.

Mussolini agreed to take up a new government and called it Duce of the Italian Social Republic. Of course, it was a German puppet state, but, you know, details. Anyhow, for all intents and purposes, this was basically German-controlled. It lasted about 19 months while Il Drama Queen was on house arrest by the SS.

Near the end, Mussolini wrote his memoirs, like anyone would give a shit. Surprisingly though, it seems he finally got honest with himself. He wrote, "Seven years ago, I was an interesting person, now I'm a little more than a corpse." Shortly thereafter, Mussolini didn't know what to do, and it wasn't long until he and his mistress were caught by some partisans trying to flee to Switzerland.

The next day, Mussolini and his mistress were shot, along with the others from his ministry department. The bodies were brought to Milan and, after being kicked and spit on, were hung upside down in Piazza Square and stoned and pissed on by civilians. He was eventually buried in an unmarked grave. His corpse was later dug up by some obvious morons, who buried him in his hometown.

So, there you have it. Mussolini was Hitler's main ally and only friend of the Axis coalition. Let that sink in. Mussolini was just another narcissistic psychopath whose decisions did only one thing — enrich himself and other high-ranking officials. I can somewhat understand how Hitler got to power; however, I will never fully understand how Mussolini did. The Italian people have always been genial, nice, caring, passionate, etc. Yet, this clown somehow meandered his way into ruling them and then entering the Axis "party."

Who we surround ourselves with has always been a reflection of us as individuals. Hitler with Mussolini and Mussolini with Hitler could be considered one of the highest-ranking narcissistic friendships in political history. That's saying something and worthy of recognition, but to me, it was like an incestuous ideology of narcissism, and in the end, at least they went out with their real personalities intact. Cowards.

How early into 1944 did Hitler or his generals realize it was probably a bad idea to have killed all his Jewish scientists and mathematicians?

Invasion of Russia (End of WWII)

"The fight against Jewish world Bolshevization requires a clear attitude toward Soviet Russia. You cannot drive out the Devil with Beelzebub." Yes, this is another quote by Hitler. "The war against Russia will be such that it cannot be conducted in a knightly fashion. This struggle is one of ideologies and racial differences and will have to be conducted with unprecedented, unmerciful, and unrelenting harshness. All officers will have to rid themselves of obsolete ideologies. I know that the necessity for such means of waging war is beyond the comprehension of you generals, but... I insist absolutely that my orders be executed without contradiction." Again, I'm quoting Hitler.

Add megalomaniac to his long list of psychoses.

This madman, the hero of today's racists and neo-Nazis, was just starting up his experimentations with various drugs while contemplating invading Russia. The horrific decision begs the question, "What was Hitler addicted to?" as it takes a while to get the correct timing down going from heroin to meth, meth to heroin, and he could have been trying to adjust the right cycle. I get it.

Think about decisions we make stoned; maybe stealing some M&Ms, driving while high, fecal impaction, all serious issues with consequences; however, I'm confident no one has ever decided to invade a country with over 200 million people.

Despite the outbreak of war, Hitler continued his policy of aggression. By May of 1940, Britain was the only western European country that had not been overrun by the Nazis. Hitler lost the Battle of Britain and pivoted to an invasion of Russia.

By now, there was a long list of undesirables who endured terrible fates under Hitler. Jews, homosexuals, gypsies, communists, the handicapped (both physically and mentally), and others were forced to wear identification badges. Jews were just starting to be sent to concentration camps to either be exterminated in gas chambers or forced into labor. In January 1942, plans were approved to exterminate the entire Jewish population, known as the

"Final Solution."

I'll be covering World War II in depth later in the book; suffice it to say here that WWII pitted the U.S.-led Allies (U.K., France, and the Soviet Union) against the German-led Axis (Italy and Japan). Germany invaded Poland on September 1, 1939, and marked the start of WWII. It lasted until Germany unconditionally surrendered on May 7, 1945.

So, we have taken a quick look at how bat-shit crazy Hitler was and have highlighted the fluffers under him. However, I think the biggest example of how fucking stupid, ignorant, and world-class narcissistic Hitler was would be the command he gave to attack the Soviet Union on June 22, 1941.

Hitler had very successfully occupied Poland, Austria, Czechoslovakia, Norway, and France. They had a signed pact with Russia, and there was no indication that Russia was using this time to aggressively build up its armaments. Outside of Hitler's psychosis and fevered ravings about communism, there were zero reasons to invade Russia at that time.

And if he was going to attack Russia, all the dumbfuck had to do was simply wait until winter was over to invade, that's all. I mean, the dumbass crossed into Russia in late June. Did he think he was going to take Russia in four months? In that time, soldiers could have healed, another round of Hitler youth would be ready, and they could've obviously had time to repair equipment and receive new planes, artillery, and other weapons. But the biggest advantage would have been to keep their soldiers out of Russia during winter. Zero reasons for him not to wait until March, April, or early May for the invasion.

Winter or not, if there is any sound, somewhat intelligent Aryan, White supremacist, or antisemite reading this, tell me why this wasn't arguably one of the dumbest military decisions in modern warfare, by a mile. The only sliver of an argument was that the Germans were trying to take the Soviet oil fields, but it was way too far inland for the German military and borderline impossible during winter.

Furthermore, when they attacked the Soviet Union, they had NO long-term supply chain. Let's say one of you racists was fighting for this asshole and blitzkrieged your way to Stalingrad in a tank. You and your unit finally get there, and there is no food, ammunition, or even blankets. Remember, your hero sent you out there, your leader. This extremely premature conflict cost 830,000 German soldiers their lives. I'm just baffled at how naïve you White supremacists are.

But it's just as bad as the clown show of Hitler's subordinates. Your opinions may somewhat matter in your plans, chat rooms, and meetings, but your opinions would have slowly dissipated into an ass-kissing show of affection under Nazism.

Germany starved to death or killed 3.3 million Soviets. Germany's excuse was that they didn't think they would capture so many so quickly. Who gives two shits? That's your reason? That's bullshit. You think Hitler or any Nazis lifted a finger to help one Russian? Hitler didn't care and was probably disappointed at such a low number. And why did Germany attack in the first place? Because the Russians were communists? It's going to be a long, long time until we see someone as psychotic, selfish, ignorant, and mentally deranged as Hitler running a country in Europe.

Finally, if you're going to "bum rush" the country, you may want to consider whom you are attacking. After all the shit Joseph Stalin had done to his own people, did Hitler really think they were just going to "moonwalk" into Moscow? The Russian people are tough, really tough, and by the time Stalingrad became an issue, Stalin would have forced 12-year-old transgender twins to aim and fire. He already had women sharpshooters fucking up the Nazis. I bring this up to show you the mentality of your hero, Hitler, and how this was such an idiotic and extremely toxic move for the German Army. In my opinion, the day the first German soldier put his foot into Russia, WWII was over.

Stalingrad

Now, let's discuss Stalingrad to further unveil the Russian's tough and relentless reputation. It's easy to justify their victory in Stalingrad by saying that they simply continued to send manpower. However, these troops came in staggered waves, and it would have been very easy for them to give up. Fortunately, they never wavered.

Had the Nazis taken Stalingrad, the outcome of the war would've been different. I think the Allies would have still won, but at what cost?

I will be highlighting Hitler's psychotic consistent tendencies, and I just need you antisemitic, Aryan, White supremacists to understand that I lump all of you together with Hitler. If you believe in him and his philosophies and are trying to finish whatever the fuck he stood for, then to me, you're the same.

Hitler should have never, ever, ever invaded Russia.

By the middle of April 1945, the Russians were bombing, bombing, and more bombing of Berlin. Around this time, Hitler had taken his last breath of fresh air outside. There's a tradition that a soldier is honored by being shot to death. Hangings and beheadings were for everyone else. So, and not to be outdone, for the first time in history, before or since, Hitler became the first head of a country to kill himself by cyanide, shooting, and fire. I'm confident he'll hold that record for a long time. Congrats, asshole, you hit the death trifecta. Even HE wanted to make sure he was dead.

Wait, I said What?

More lies, I mean quotes, from Herr Horseshit. "Humanitarianism is the expression of stupidity and cowardice." WOW. I wonder how many other countries were vying for Hitler's leadership.

This might be my favorite quote from Hitler, the lying coward: "Anyone can deal with victory, only the mighty can bear defeat." Ha, ha, ha. If by mighty you mean turning yourself into a human charcoal pit, then yes, you bore defeat. Reality-wise, it turned out that Hitler wasn't such a gracious loser in the end and refused to take responsibility for his defeat. He blamed his followers. "It is not I who lost the war, it was the German people," he said. "I await my death as a release from a hard life of difficulties." What a psychotic pussy. He ran a country, became a multi-billionaire, and he was awaiting death from a hard life of difficulties? He had millions of babies and little children intentionally murdered among thousands of atrocities, and in the end, he could still ONLY think about himself.

Here's another reason why Hitler was full of *scheiße* (shit). In *Mein Kampf*, he talks about how he was sympathetic to the people who were being hurt or intimidated. "The more I understood the methods of physical intimidation that were employed, the more sympathy I had for the multitude that had to succumb to it." LOL. You must be joking. This, from the fucking guy who just couldn't intimidate, torture, and kill enough people.

For those who say, "Yay, I follow Hitler and his doctrines. He's brilliant and tough and so great for the White race. White power, White power," what dramatic pussies you are. You are idolizing a coward with mental illness. A mental illness that he sent millions to the gas chamber for. What does this say about you?

You know that thing about shooting himself? My guess is it took him three tries. Oh, wait. Here's a good one. Now mind you, I have no idea what did or didn't qualify as comedy in Germany around the mid-1940s, but this is just comic genius. Guy Liddell, a British intelligence officer, wrote in his diaries about a letter from Jokinen von Ribbentrop, German Foreign Minister, and I quote: "He said that neither he nor Hitler had ever wanted a war with England and that he himself had always regarded England as his second home. He was sure the future lay in close collaboration between England and Germany." I truly don't know what to say about that, but I really, really, really hope that Churchill got to read it.

While we're here, let's just throw out some more quotes from the favorite leader of today's neo-Nazis, Herr Douchebag. You Aryans can see for yourselves why nobody respects your organizations. You are being led by a theoretical ideology that's only proven outcome so far is that it doesn't work. By now, you know Hitler is just a psychotic murderer who took the idea of Nazism to its highest level and let the world witness how it failed miserably.

When you add Hitler's stealing and looting billions upon billions of dollars for himself, his shocking number of atrocities, and how he started a war that ended 70 million lives, perhaps you'll update your ideology to something saner. Why would you and your antisemitic, racist friends want to continue to pursue this? What can you show us in his 12-year reign of disasters that you want to emulate? What were the positives?

"When diplomacy ends, war begins." That's your boy, Adolf.

How about this? Now, this is a government we can all get behind. "The great strength of the totalitarian state is that it forces those who fear it to imitate it."

Here's one I've never seen. "Conscience is a Jewish invention." Well, he finally admits it. My gosh, is there anything we Jews can't do?

Near the end of the war, the Germans were training and using young boys and the elderly as soldiers. For the millionth time, clearly, this war was way over, but it at least shows that Hitler didn't discriminate and was kind enough to include all ages in the killing. Also, around this time, Hitler got to unleash his last few brilliant edicts for his beloved German citizens. Ready?

Hitler demanded that the battle he started "be conducted without consideration of our own population." So, what did he do? He ordered the destruction of all industrial plants, the main electricity works, the main waterworks, and the main gasworks. He ordered that all food and clothing stores create a desert for the advancing Allies. Herr Selfish declared, "If the war is lost, the German nation shall also perish. There is no need to consider what the people required for continued existence." What a guy. What a leader. What an asshole.

You, the Aryan nation, neo-Nazis, White supremacists, etc., need to see and understand what most of us have already seen in his nature, attitude, and outlook. Why would you advance his bloody cause? Is he the Pied Piper, even in death, and you the mesmerized little boys and girls who follow him? To all the racist military types, is this a guy you would have wanted to go to war for?

He is just one big fucking lie. Whatever thoughts he had for Germany and Austria at one time, or even some early horseshit ideas he once wrote in *Mein Kampf*, went away soon as he came into power. GONE. He immediately switched to "power and me, me, me" mode. All dictators do. From Idi Amin to Saddam Hussein, pick one, any dictator you like. Furthermore, his entire rule over Germany came so quickly and easily that I suspect his thoughts turned to: "Why not the rest of the world?"

Can you imagine him speaking to the Germans at this point? "Hi, this is the Führer of Shit. Ugh, sorry, I caused a little damage to our city, but I only cost the lives of about five million soldiers and five point seven million civilians from air raids. Anyway, we're not going to surrender, so just go back to bed. Ugh, if a bomb is dropped on you, no sweat; I'll already be asleep. Just because I'm 50 feet underground, under 20 feet of concrete, and taking 2,000 mg of Seroquel before bed, it's important for all of you to understand that I must get my sleep. Hope this clears it up."

Still slinging saliva, I can envision him spitting out, "Also, look what I've given to all of you over the last 12 years. You should be way more grateful. Just go back to bed, as there is nothing you can do, and you won't see them coming anyway. More importantly, and you better not forget, make sure you're getting in your 150 Heil Hitler salutes a day.

German deaths from air raids totaled 126,000 after January 31, 1945. Ironically enough, when Hitler got up from his 13 hours of sleep, he was heard saying, "I figured, you know, I'm still alive, so I must be doing something right and just to shut all of you Germans up, here is my 'more important than yours" schedule. I wake up at noon and take a nap. I get up in the afternoon, snort meth, and play with my dogs. Man, are they cute. I haven't had much food in the last couple of years as I've been diligently writing a book that I'm calling *Mein Meth Diet*. It's another gift I'm giving my fiefdom. Early evening, coke or PCP, followed by more coke late at night because that's when I'm working. Work, work, work. You know, for Germany, and the Nazis. Goodnight, going to bed."

Jews, racists, homosexuals, political and religious persecution, and 200,000 German people with disabilities — all were sent to concentration camps and died through the

T4 program or euthanasia. I imagine these thoughts were rolling around in Hitler's brain: "Listen, they were disabled. I obviously did them a favor, so again, you're welcome. I really enjoyed bringing up the murders of the disabled at parties."

As we inch closer to Hitler's one-alarm personal fire drill to put out his black-on-black-on-black charred body, he somehow made the time to get with Goebbels to celebrate FDR's death. That's a fucking laugh. FDR spearheaded helping to avenge Pearl Harbor and kick the shit out of Germany. He died comfortably, and his funeral was attended by hundreds of thousands.

Hitler, however, ended up dead after swallowing cyanide and then using a pistol on his diseased brain, and then ended up with 20-degree burns, laying on the street with his mouth wide open as his ashes littered and dirtied the pavement, which is now a site of a fucking parking garage, so people run over and pee on him too. Those two sociopaths, Hitler and Goebbels, laughing about FDR kind of sums it up.

Chapter 7: Let's Play a Drinking Game

> *"You ask me what I have done for the women of Germany? My answer is this: in my new army, I have provided you with the finest fathers of children in the whole world."*
>
> ~ *Adolf Hitler*

Outside of a few staged videos, does anyone know if Hitler ever told a joke? Laughed? Smiled? I mean, in 800 of the most boring and ludicrous pages ever written (theoretically while he was young), not one fucking joke. Not one. Hitler, the socialist turned fascist, initially called for "all hands on deck" so Germany could spread the wealth around and everyone would work for the common good. Well, how'd the National Socialist German Workers Party turn out for German citizens in that respect?

I think it's time we all took a little break to digest what you've read so far. I was thinking about making this chapter into a drinking game. Invite some friends over, pass the book around to read out loud, and just have fun. The problem is that every chapter will get you "blackout drunk," with the game premise being one simple question: "Was this the truth or a lie that came out of Hitler's mouth?" If it's a lie, you have to drink.

So, if Hitler says something and it's the truth, just sit back, relax, maybe get up from the couch, and stretch. If he's lying, take a shot.

Now, drinking game rules are varied throughout the country, so I am not going to suggest how you do yours. HOWEVER, I highly suggest you have an ambulance parked in your driveway before starting. You'll never get off the couch.

There is plenty of documentation on Hitler's beliefs, mainly because he never shut the fuck up about them. Here are his views on various items that most either don't know or think about since his atrocities "trump" any topics, and deservedly so. He was a fucking nut job, and I assure you nothing on this list takes away from that. It does highlight different groups and topics of interest that most would be interested in knowing his position on, if only they cared enough to research on their own.

How about his view on Christianity or Catholicism? And if you happen to be a female racist, then you'll just love his views on women. He bet against American women twice in WWII, and I really wanted to highlight when American women were called upon, they answered. We know that already; just another example of how he was consistently wrong.

Yes, if you ascribe to Hitler's ideology, you are following a deluded, dark, and dangerous path. When you read more and more of Hitler's own words, it's utterly shocking that someone would even follow him to the bathroom. As he aged, it seems he swirled further down the toilet, which was no doubt helped by a shitload of drugs. Perhaps this explains his "about face" on religion, depending on whatever political situation he found himself in. Rest assured, he was really, really mentally fucked up starting in his early to mid-thirties onward and, by any metric, should have been institutionalized.

I have never professed any intelligence on religions, although religions have always fascinated me. By the way, I have yet to find one religion that states anywhere in its literature to kill, maim, or hurt anyone, especially someone from another religion or race. No, it's ALWAYS some asshole who interprets something in a religion to justify harming others and then somehow finds followers. Please, someone, let me know what religion and in what text endorses or states murder of the innocent. Anyway, even though Hitler's only religion was Hitler, I decided to "throw in" a few of his quotes on Christianity.

By now, you should know that in some form or fashion, Hitler hated everyone, with the exception of himself and Goering's lips. Here is a varying "smorgasbord of shit" (S.O.S.) into Hitler's life — his religious views and the disgust and vitriol that you may not know.

Christianity

You might be surprised at Hitler's flip-flops on Christianity. First, he claimed to be a Christian and continued this subterfuge when convenient, although he actually despised Christianity. How two-faced, but are you surprised? Enjoy a drink every time he lies about his beliefs, and you'll probably wake up in handcuffs.

> ***Christianity is a rebellion against natural law, a protest against nature.*** *Taken to its logical extreme, Christianity would mean the systematic cultivation of the human failure.*
>
> *You see, it's been our misfortune to have the wrong religion. Why didn't we have the religion of the Japanese, who regard sacrifice for the Fatherland as the highest good? The Mohammedan religion too would have been more compatible to us than Christianity.*

Why did it have to be Christianity with its meekness and flabbiness?

We do not want any other god than Germany itself. It is essential to have fanatical faith and hope and love in and for Germany.

But Christianity is an invention of sick brains: one could imagine nothing more senseless, nor any more indecent way of turning the idea of the Godhead into a mockery.

The Catholic Conundrum

Hitler, despite turning on Christianity, was a supposed life-long Catholic and used this affiliation to reel in the Vatican. How strange that the Nazis imprisoned over 2,700 Protestant, Orthodox, and Catholic clergy and sent them to the Dachau Concentration Camp, and yet the Vatican still played ball with him.

The Vatican? Bullshit, you say. It's shocking, but yep, the Vatican, as you'll soon see.

As it relates to WWII and the Nazis, I have a problem with the involvement of the Catholic Church. I don't have a problem at all with everyday Catholics or their parishes; however, I do take exception to the "ratlines." Yes, you heard that right — ratlines.

This system of tunnels and escape routes was created for Nazis and other fascists fleeing Europe after World War II, all done in secrecy. They extended mainly to South America but were also used in Europe to ship these assholes to the United States, Spain, Switzerland, Mexico, and more.

These passageways out of Germany and into the various destinations sent criminals and their families into the world with new documents and paperwork for each person. The ratlines also provided money, housing, new jobs, etc.

There were two primary routes. The first went from Germany to Spain, then Argentina. The second was Germany to Rome to Genoa, and then South America. It started in 1942 when Monsignor, or Luigi Maglione, asked if Argentina would take in Europeans in order to encourage European migration, land ownership, and capital. Great idea — let's bring in a bunch of psychotic murderers, torturers, and rapists who hadn't been told no in five to ten years to "encourage European migration." Shouldn't they have been interested in trying, I dunno, a different area in Europe? "Encourage European migration" — did that actually come out of someone's fucking mouth? How about just saying this… "We were all paid off."

Shortly after, a German priest traveled to Portugal and then Argentina, laying the groundwork for future immigration. Okay, the war had just ended, and now murderers and evil Nazis were either in encampments, jailed, hiding, or on the run — through the ratlines. Now, there were plenty of Nazis who only fought in the war and whose conduct didn't circumvent the Geneva convention. (Those five guys get a pass.) Anyone who fits under that simple description should have been allowed to go home or migrate elsewhere. But OBVIOUSLY NOT war criminals.

How did thousands of Nazis who committed such heinous acts of torture, starvation, and mass murder … simply escape?

The Vatican.

From Gustav Wagner to Franz Stangl, former commanders of Sobibor and Treblinka, these fucks were responsible for the deaths of one million Jews and helped heinous animals like Adolph Eichman, Josef Mengele, Klaus Barbie, and thousands and thousands to "escape repercussions" with the help of the Catholic Church.

The Pope at the time was Pope Pius XII. Many debates have erupted over the years involving "Did he know" or "Did he not know?" Just a few years back, his archives were opened with a lot of anticipation, as many believed the answers were somewhere on those pages.

My take — of course, he fucking knew. The Nazis were rounding up Jews all over Europe, putting them on trains, and sending them to concentration camps over the last five or six years, while the Pope lived in Rome. In 1943 the German occupiers in Italy rounded up 1,100 Jews who lived in a ghetto in Rome. There's a fucking plaque about 800 yards from St. Peter's square that reads: "On 16 October 1943, entire Jewish Roman families ripped from their homes by the Nazis were brought here and then deported to concentration camps. Of more than 1,000 persons, only 16 survived."

Pope Pius XII, it is now confirmed by documentation, knew about Warsaw. Read the *Vanity Fair* article titled "Hitler's Pope." He knew about the 150,000 Jews killed in concentration camps in 1942, and when asked by the United States government to confirm, he lied to the Americans and said, "I cannot confirm."

The Pope knew they were slated for deportation to a concentration camp. I mean, really. This is even a question? We now know that this Pope was introduced to the Nazis when he was a Cardinal in 1933. Furthermore, he spearheaded an agreement between the German Holy See and the Third Reich. By never coming out against the Nazis, psycho Hitler took it as an affirmation by the Catholic church. We'll never know the total number, but a tremendous amount of Catholic leaders helped the Nazis.

In other words, Hitler killed Catholics, yet the Catholic hierarchy was running interference for the killers. The irony. And people waited 80 years to confirm what was obvious.

Pathetic.

There's been a lot of great popes, but Pius XII just ain't on that list. Nazis numbering 9,000 made it to South America alone. That's 9,000 murderers, rapists, and war criminals who made it out unscathed and unpunished, thanks to the Vatican. Why? Was it for financial gain? Hatred of the Soviets? Antisemitism? Did they just love fascism? Were they just cowards? Did they get a big lift from Hitler's pseudo-Catholicism? I could spend a lot of time going over each guess, but it's pointless now. Priests, bishops, cardinals, archbishops, and a pope. Why?

By the way, have you heard the name, Edith Stein? Well, here you go. Edith Stein was a Jewish woman who converted to Christianity. She became agnostic in her teenage years and converted due to what she saw in WWI. Later, she was baptized into the Catholic Church. She was a writer and taught at a Catholic school. In August 1942, Edith and 243 other Nuns of Jewish converts were sent to Auschwitz and murdered. Edith Stein is canonized as a Martyr and Saint of the Catholic Church; she is also one of six patron Saints of Europe.

How deluded and fucked up could all of those involved be? From picking the victims up at their residences, putting them on a train, offloading them from the train, and putting them in line, there are just no words to describe the mentality of those evil fucks. I mean, 244 nuns, really? What, were they afraid that the nuns were going to set up ambushes? Put grenades in flowerpots? I'm speechless on this one. I hope all you Aryans and Aryan wannabes enjoy being affiliated with the murder of innocent nuns. "Great bunch of guys, those Nazis." Wow.

Hitler's Views on Women

You know the old saying, "I'm not prejudiced; I hate

everyone." Take the "female" version of that from 1933-1945. At least Hitler was consistent, and here are his demeaning views on women. If he wasn't trapping them in the kitchen and demanding they bear Aryan children, he was gaslighting men into military action in order to defend the frail female.

I was fortunate enough to grow up with four outstanding sisters — beautiful, smart, tough, sensitive, and hard workers. They never held back on their thoughts and feelings, and you could depend on them for anything. In our house, growing up in general, we were all taught to respect ourselves and each other. It's one of the main things I pride myself on, and it seems that it is becoming a somewhat lost art as everyone thinks their opinions are beyond reproach.

As my sisters turned from girls to teens to women, these qualities never left them. Had they been born in the time of Hitler, such character traits would have been discouraged and diminished, if not snuffed out altogether in the concentration camps.

Hitler had no problem devaluing the amazing spectrum of women's abilities, diminishing their role in society, and curbing their freedoms. To him, they were breeding stock and useful idiots. Think "Handmaid's Tale" and consider modern-day Afghanistan. We had every right to go into Afghanistan to get Bin Laden (but unfortunately stayed too long). As soon as we arrived, women and girls (who are all grown up today) received an education and were running for office. They could stay out after 8:00 p.m., dress fashionably, etc.

A week after we left, it was full burkas and no schooling. In one fucking week.

Certainly, people in this country have no idea what it's like to live under that kind of rule. None. Most people in the free world have no clue. But the women in Germany under Nazi rule certainly did.

I assume even Hitler wannabes love their wives, mothers, daughters, aunts, and other women in their lives. So how can you justify following a misogynistic pig named Hitler? Even if you agree with his views on traditional gender roles, how can you turn a blind eye to the control he exerted over women while stripping them of free will?

What about rape? Do you have any idea the amount of rape and "encouraged rape" the Nazis committed? I mean, they had fucking military units set up for it. It's utterly shocking to me that you, as hate groups, encourage rape. That's certainly a stigma I wouldn't want to put my name behind for others to see.

> *The goal of female education must invariably be the future mother.*
>
> *Woman's world is her husband, her family, her children, and her home. We do not find it right when she presses into the world of men.*
>
> *A woman must be a cute, cuddly, naïve little thing — tender, sweet, and stupid.*
>
> *The woman has her own battlefield with every child she brings into the world she fights a battle for the nation.*
>
> *If the man's world is said to be the State, his struggle, his readiness to devote his powers to the service of the community, then it may perhaps be said that the woman's is a smaller world. For her world is her husband, her family, her children, and her home.*

The Hidden Army

If you're still ready to "Heil Hitler" after reading the

dumpster fire above, then you deserve a cast iron skillet over the noggin, courtesy of "your woman." And if your woman agrees with any of it, then she deserves whatever you dish out.

It's true that most American women in the '30s and '40s were also confined to gender roles and studies (think home economics and typing) ... but not upon pain of death. And unlike Germany, exceptions were made in times of war.

Consider our "Rosie the Riveter" female defense industry workforce during World War II, courtesy of Pearl Harbor, our declaration of war on Japan, and soon thereafter, Germany. This "hidden army" of American women filled the gap when men left the factories to become soldiers overseas.

These women hit the ground running. The Japanese and Germans were well aware of the potential and technological know-how of the U.S. However, when assessing our troops and armaments, they assumed the war would be over before we were at full capacity as they "knew" our women would not be able to fill the manufacturing needs of war. It just never occurred to them that American women could step up and replace men in factories.

Really? Through the extremely hard work of our tough and beautiful women, they were able to help supply the U.S. military with 17 aircraft carriers. Wow — and 297,000 aircraft and 193,000 artillery pieces, plus 86,000 tanks and two million trucks in only four years. American industrial production, already the world's largest, doubled in size.

From the film "The War," directed by Ken Burns and Lynn Novick: "War production profoundly changed American industry. Companies already engaged in defense work expanded. Others, like the automobile industry, were transformed completely. In 1941 there were over three million cars made in the U.S. Only 139 were made the rest of the war. Chrysler made fuselages. General Motors made airplane engines, guns, trucks and tanks. Packard made Rolls-Royce engines for the British Air Force."

I really want to highlight this paragraph. Hitler bet against American women, and AGAIN, he was wrong. Also, see the film: "At the Ford plant in Ypsilanti, Michigan." "The Ford Motor Company did something like a miracle every 24 hours. The average Ford car had some 15,000 parts. The B-24 Liberator long-range Bomber had 1,550,000 parts. One Bomber came off the line every 63 minutes." Again, who were the mind-numbing dumbfucks that called us out and wanted to face us in battle? Hitler and Hirohito, you insult the letter H.

So, while the Axis commanders, generals, and leaders were convinced, completely convinced, that there was no chance, no way, that our munitions supply could be maintained, the "hidden army" proved them wrong, again.

Female employment and defense industries grew by 462% from 1940 to 1944. Between 1940 and 1945, the overall female workforce again grew by 50%. At the height of the war, 19,170,000 women were skilled laborers.

How stupid that the Axis douchebags thought our women, when called upon, would just sit around. Have Hitler or his henchman ever gotten anything right?

Nurses

Here in the U.S., we celebrate National Nurses Day and National Nurses month, and by extension, show gratitude to the nurses in World War II, abroad and domestically. Again, the Axis countries didn't think our women could handle anything above applying bandages, let alone the blood and gore of being field nurses.

Abroad, these brave nurses were put in precarious locations and, in most cases, had to help build and set up field hospitals. In a normal hospital setting at the time, one nurse tended to three or four patients. In the field, one nurse tended to eight to ten patients with a violent mortality rate and a high number of wounded. Despite long shifts and few breaks, they were outstanding and demonstrated grace under pressure. The nurses back home had it very rough, too, as soldiers who needed more attention came home.

I read a lot of tragic stories these nurses had to deal with, but there was one extremely important assignment they always had to carry out. I doubt I could have handled it as well. It was doing everything possible to make sure no patients ever saw them cry. Can you imagine all of the horrific shit they saw and stories they heard, and people who died in front of them? Without tears?

Our nurses were indoctrinated to keep morale as high as possible, and they did. It didn't get easier for any of them over time, but they knew what the effects on the wounded soldiers would be, so they didn't.

Of course, when they finally got off their long shifts, they would go back to their bunks and let it out, but these women, American women, were kind, tender, sensitive, and very fucking tough. We were fortunate, and that psycho in Germany who bet against them lost, AGAIN.

It's a prime distinction between dictatorships and democracies. Can you think of any dictatorships that treat their women as equals? I just have to grin when I think about the dumbshit in Germany who had to write up reports regarding the U.S. re-armament production when it was being done by our women and then hand the report to Hitler.

Our women wouldn't step up? If I may, Hitler, fuck you.

I'll add a bit more about the resolve of our men and women. The United States, like all countries, has its ups and downs — disagreements, dissension, socio-economic divisions, and more. However, we collectively come together when called upon. This is true going back to the American Revolution. Our country was founded by kicking England's overwhelming force out of our country.

In World War I, Germany antagonized their enemies as it released U-boats onto civilian ships. But when WWI ended on November 11, 1918, we had kicked the shit out of anything put in front of us. When victory was announced, the U.S. had 4.7 million soldiers in total and 2.8 million overseas.

You would think the Germans would have learned from WWI, but nooooooooooooooo. They made the same fatal misjudgments about our men and women once again in WWII. Same song, second verse. Are you convinced now that Hitler was a dummkopf who mismanaged everything in his path, or do you need to see more lies, deception, and murders? Now that I've had the time to think about it, you may not want to make this into a drinking game. I had a friend come over to test it out, and he got expedited cirrhosis, and I don't want that on my conscience. I would like to highlight: he did make it to the fourth paragraph on the Introduction page.

From any logical or strategic military viewpoint, how could anyone discount the effectiveness of women rearming the U.S. military, to any level? I think the Nazis assumed American women could supply or re-supply our soldiers at a 10% or maybe up to a 20% rate. Our nurses not being able to stomach war? STFU.

I got to hand it to Hitler and the Nazis about being consistent. No matter the topic, issue, or opinion, they were always wrong; frankly, it's quite impressive.

Chapter 8: The Jews Did NOT Kill Jesus.

Chapter 9: Monsters in Boots

"The greater the crime perpetrated by the leadership, the less likely it is that the people will ever believe their leaders to be capable of perpetrating such an event."
~ Adolf Hitler

We've discussed the mind fuckery that influenced the Germans to carry out the atrocities — the carrot-and-stick approach to bending the people to Hitler's will. Stand with him, and you'll be able to feed your children and keep a roof over your head. Stand against him and die. Still, it boggles the mind that German soldiers or officers could stomach their duties. Imagine these recruits monitoring and interacting with imprisoned men and women daily, while those poor souls were under 80 pounds or freezing to death right in front of them.

It must have taken some mighty brainwashing to compel soldiers to inflict constant beatings as Jews, and other prisoners slaved and labored in the camps. How could the soldiers tolerate the smell? The odor must've been indescribable. Surely the gore, oozing wounds, blood, shit, piss, sweat, and vomit got to them. Or maybe they relished it, delighting in the sights, sounds, and odor of innocent men, women, and children meeting their demise. Other soldiers of a more decent variety were probably on the verge of a moral crisis and mental breakdown. Anyone with a scrap of honor would have developed PTSD from working in the camps.

Remember, these weren't small rogue units who went out on their own and attempted vigilante justice or Black Ops. Nope, these groups were formed under and given instructions from the top guys of the Nazi party. Shit, they encouraged these enlisted units and always looked for ways to expand them.

If you're in some type of hate group (don't answer yet) after you've read this chapter and the following few chapters, I wonder if that's how you want your top military advisors to lead and soldiers to implement such heinous atrocities.

After coming to power, Hitler had the uncanny ability to find other psychos who recruited new psychos who ended up finding more psychos. Why were their recruitment tactics so successful on such a large scale? How could the term "Stockholm Syndrome" be coined before the words "Nazi Syndrome?"

We know those sick fucking cowards in Germany killed over six million Jews, and I've already mentioned that we weren't the only minority. The Nazis believed that Aryans were a master race, and German children learned this in school. Grownups were re-educated about their role in the world and their superiority — as long as they looked the part. Well, with the exception of ugly-ass Hitler and his posse of killers, who weren't exactly blond and blue-eyed.

Who on earth would EVER consider Hitler, Himmler, Goebbels, Hess, Goering, and Eichmann of "Aryan" descent? Those are some of the ugliest, nonathletic, dark-haired, small dick, knuckle draggers and have about as much Aryan in them as a toad. And these guys were running the "white bread" show.

In order to explain the various levels of atrocities committed by the Nazis, I categorize them to hopefully explain their levels of horror against their own civilians to the levels of horror committed against other countries' civilians and militaries.

I use an international unit of measures that will not be needed for translations in foreign languages — the "cocksucker" scale. Now, the "cocksucker" scale is from 1-10. Like North Korea is a 1 (all bark, no bite), and Hitler, who holds the highest number that cannot be superseded, is a 10. For perspective, Genghis Khan is an 8.

I had to cut back on military units that I was going to highlight, as this chapter could have been a thousand pages. Here, I focus on the "Big Three" and cover the fun-loving, congenial, and friendly units of the Nazis that were used to guard Hitler and his top henchmen. These Nazi actions of torturing, raping, false imprisonment, looting, and murder were not only allowed but encouraged by Hitler. Their edicts, roles, and jobs came from the top and were carried out by all to protect him. So, without further ado, let me present the "monsters in boots" — better known as the Gestapo, the SS, and the SA — whose jobs were to murder and carry out any order given to them by Hitler and his henchmen by any means necessary. This is but a sample.

Neo-Nazis, feel free to look this up for your own fucked-up purposes, as there are plenty.

It sickens me to make mention of these groups, but unfortunately, most members of hate groups acknowledge that Nazis killed Jews and other civilians, but I'm not so sure they understand how. I hope you antisemites read every word in the next few chapters. When finished, ask yourself if you're sure that being a Nazi is what you truly identify with. Could you have been in any of these units and carried out direct orders? I fucking hope not.

The Gestapo, SS, and SA all played different roles and were each instrumental in Hitler's rise to power and keeping power. These three units were mainly an internal force, for example, like your local police, state police, and federal.

The Sturmabteilung or SA

The SA was formed in 1921 by Adolf Hitler himself and a couple of other psychos as the initial paramilitary wing of the Nazi Party. Also referred to as Storm Troopers or Brownshirts, they protected Nazi rallies, roughed up citizens, and assaulted political foes. Eventually, they were organized into a pseudo-type army. In 1933, the SA had around 3,000,000 soldiers and was growing at a rapid pace. Eventually, Hitler became extremely nervous that the SA could easily stage a coup, so he began using the SS and felt they were better suited to carry out his psychotic policies and criminal acts.

Internal fighting from the top leaders erupted about what to do with the SA, and some of the leaders didn't want to absorb them into the German military. With ongoing internal strife, a solution needed to be made. So, what do you think the solution would be for the men who were with the Nazi Party from the beginning or very early on? Demotion? Transfer? Dismissal?

Hitler called a meeting for the top 200 or so leaders of the SA and placed them all under arrest. Mind you, and it needs repeating, but a lot of the top guys of the SA had been with Hitler from the beginning, extremely loyal, and did what was needed to protect Hitler and others. The 200 were simply shot and killed. Ernst Rohm was with the SA from the start and later became head of the SA. He was supposedly Hitler's good friend, but so what? Ernst was the start of a long list of soon-to-be Hitler's EX-good friends. Hitler had him murdered too.

The SA was the unit directly involved in the Night of the Long Knives in 1934 and Kristallnacht, showing outright contempt, destruction, looting, and murder of Germany's

Jewish citizens. Soon after, the SA was overshadowed and gave rise to the SS.

It was well known that Rohm was gay, and he and Hitler spent a lot of time together. Point being, I think both of them would have loved this rating system.

Cocksucker rating: 4.

The Schutzstaffel or SS

The SS was created in 1925 to serve as Hitler's personal bodyguards. These dudes were rabidly antisemite Germans, which is why the SS was so feared throughout Germany. These SS psychos were led by another fucking whack job Heinrich Himmler. Himmler was a goofy, real goofy-looking motherfucker.

The SS consisted of two main units, the Allgemeine-SS and Waffen-SS. The Allgemeine-SS was responsible for enforcing the racial policy of Nazi Germany and general policing. The Waffen-SS consisted of combat units within the Nazi military. And, of course, the SS wouldn't be complete until they had the Totenkopfverbande SS, in English, the "Death's-Head Units." This unit was responsible for running concentration camps and extermination camps.

There were also two subdivisions of the SS, the Gestapo and the SD.

Every one of these assholes would've been more than happy to take Hitler's little dick in any hole of their bodies, and fortunately for Himmler, it easily fit. That was the first known saying of "It's a win/win."

The SS was the organization most responsible for the deaths of Jews and other innocent victims.

By the way, when Himmler took over the SS, he instituted strict Aryan policies in order to join the SS as spelled out in the Nuremberg laws and tried to implement physical criteria based on height and appearance. Good idea, coming from the ugliest motherfucker in Europe. Anyway, more than half were admitted who didn't meet Himmler's criteria that he personally, never, ever, ever, would have passed.

The SS was chosen to implement the final solution, and they were the main group responsible for the institutional murder and democide (murder by government) of more than 20 million people. They murdered anyone who simply disagreed with them ideologically. They murdered Jews, Slavs, Romani, and plenty of other racial or ethnic groups. They murdered mentally or physically handicapped, homosexuals, political dissidents, members of trade unions, clergy of all faiths, Jehovah's Witnesses, Freemasons, Communists, and Rotary Club members, as well as obtaining for themselves an absolute shitload of war crimes.

Outside of Herr Fuck Face, the SS is most responsible for carrying out the actions of the Holocaust.

Cocksucker ranking: 9.

The Geheime Staatspolizei or Gestapo

The Gestapo was the Secret State Police created by Hermann Goering in 1933. Basically, it combined Prussia's political police forces into one group. Oh, you Aryans would have loved these guys. One of their main roles was to protect the regime from racial and political enemies, but their main responsibilities were coordinating the deportation of Jews to ghettos, concentration camps, killing sites, and killing centers. They were the official Secret Police in Germany and in any occupied lands Germany invaded. In 1936, a law was passed that the Gestapo could operate without judicial review, meaning they were above the law. So, what do you think they did?

They could kick your ass, torture you, or even murder you without any recourse. They could imprison anyone without cause, they could steal your dog, they could walk in your house and use your toilet, etc. Nice way for the citizens of Germany to live.

Let me sum up these cocksuckers. This is another group of low-esteem assholes who were granted 100% immunity to carry out orders from other sick, psychotic assholes. These "officers" found out that the only way for them to advance in rank was to do their own sick, psychotic confrontations. This "police force" became Hitler's "wet dream" and was used to carry out many atrocities.

I cannot and will never be able to wrap my head around the atrocities these three terrorist organizations committed. But it does explain the position ordinary Germans found themselves in. After the Treaty of Versailles, Hitler held "sway" over the German people due to a mix of charming words and promises made. Then he surrounded them with a scary, violent, and authoritarian regime. In this manner, Hitler and his minions bull-dozed a country (an educated country) into either looking the other way or participating, as an entire race was systematically exterminated. Fear, intimidation, brutality, and lies — that was Hitler's control mechanism.

Just another nightmare in a long line of psychotic institutions that murdered, tortured, raped, etc., etc., etc., all in the name of Nazism. Whatever the fuck that means.

Cocksucker ranking: 8.

Chapter 10: How To Be and Stay an Asshole

> *"To attain our aim we should stop at nothing even if we must join forces with the devil."*
> ~ *Adolf Hitler*

The Dirlewanger Brigade deserves a chapter unto itself. These assholes are also known as the "SS Storm Brigade Dirlewanger," a.k.a. "36th Waffen Grenadier Division," an offshoot of the SS, also known as the Black Hunters. The unit was created in 1940 and named after its psychotic commander, Oskar Dirlewanger.

I should add a "sensitive content" label here. This is grim reading (well, if you're human) — fair warning.

The Dirlewanger Brigade consisted of convicted criminals who were not expected by Nazi Germany to survive their service with the unit. The unit's main occupation was in Poland, Eastern Russia, and Slavic regions during national uprisings.

It gained a reputation among the Wehrmacht and Waffen-SS officers for its brutality. Wait, hold up. Do you know how fucking nuts and sociopathic a unit in the German Army during World War II must have been if the Wehrmacht and the Waffen-SS pointed out another unit's brutality? No biggie, Hitler and top commanders have already endorsed them. Moving on.

Before we get into some of the details of your soon-to-be favorite unit of World War II, let's meet the person in charge of this unit, better known as your soon-to-be favorite commander.

The person put in charge of this unit was Oskar Dirlewanger. Convicted criminal Oskar Dingleberry was considered an amoral violent alcoholic with a sadistic sexual orientation and a barbaric nature — described as the most "evil man in the SS."

Now, I know what you're thinking, being called the most evil man in the SS is a compliment and a goal for most Nazis. Unfortunately for our modern-day Aryans, that title has already been locked up by Hitler, but it does give you a small sample size of Oskar Dirlewanger.

Dinglewanger joined the Nazi Party in 1923 and was sentenced to two years imprisonment for the statutory rape of a 13-year-old girl and stealing government property in 1934. You must be joking. Statutory rape was a two-year sentence, along with stealing government property? Sorry, you can get the fuck out here with that. Yeah, your utopia.

Apparently, Dirlewanger could not get enough rape under his belt and was rearrested for sexual assault and sent to a concentration camp at Welzheim. In desperation, he called his old-World War I buddy, Gottlob Berger, who was now a senior Nazi working with Himmler. Burger used his influence to help Dingleberry join the Condor Legion.

So, if you're keeping score at home, as the future head of an entire brigade, Dirlewanger had one statutory rape, one sexual assault, and one theft of government property with a total jail time of two to three years. I will never forget that these cock suckers murdered, maimed, and decimated my family, my Jewish family, and are now known as the dog shit on the bottom of history's shoes.

I guess I can put this question here: Why did so many, so fucking many people have to be tortured? What compels that amount of people to torture children, the handicapped, and the elderly? What on earth happened to the German civilians? Nice, kind, genteel Germans who would go on to torture and murder at rates that can't be comprehended? Again, I get the somewhat brainwashing aspect of a good portion of Germans, but most people cannot and will not torture someone, and certainly nowhere near the levels that the Nazis were doing. Do the hate groups in the U.S. really approve of this? If so, wouldn't you agree that Jews and other minorities have the right to protect their families by any means necessary if you're going to continue to promote this and your horseshit? I mean, you couldn't possibly argue with that, could you?

Gottlob Berger was an SS-Obergruppenführer und General der Waffen-SS (lieutenant general) responsible for Schutzstaffel (SS) recruiting during World War II. After the invasion of Poland in the mid-1940s, he arranged for Dirlewanger to command and train a military unit of convicted poachers for partisan hunting. You read that right. You see, the Ministry of Justice received a telephone call from Himmler's headquarters informing them that Hitler had decided to give "suspended sentences to so-called honorable poachers and depending on their behavior at the front to pardon them."

Now, this is something I have no problem with. I'm certainly not absolving Nazis, but to let convicted poachers out to fight in a war is a "nothing burger." The real problem was that Germany was run by a psychopath, and I think we can all guess how this would play out.

Dirlewanger was sent to the Oranienburg Concentration Camp in 1940 to take charge of 80 poaching convicts who were temporarily released from their sentences. After two months of training, 55 were selected, and the rest were sent back to the camp. The 25 guys who didn't make it must have been world-class, and I mean world-class, fuckups. Like next level, unless Dirlewanger initially thought he was putting together a tier 1 elite fighting unit.

Regardless, if anyone could ever find out what happened to one of those 25 "geniuses," you've got yourself a movie deal.

Dirlewanger was then promoted to SS-Obersturmfuhrer by Himmler, overseeing 300 men. In came an influx of criminals and the criminally insane. Shocking, impossible, a lie, I tell you. There's no way Hitler would agree with this…unless he said to his fellow Germans, "I told you I would get rid of all the crime. Look, our jails, prisons and psych wards are all empty." Thanks, Herr Asshole.

Hitler, Himmler, Goering, etc., had to have been thinking, "Why just kill and murder soldiers or civilians when you can torture or rape them first? Duh. Those poachers were way too congenial for combat, so bring on the sociopaths."

Within a couple of years, the unit had grown into a band of common criminals. (Really?) Accordingly, the unit's name was changed to Sonderkommando Dirlewanger (special unit Dirlewanger). Or, as Hitler liked to call it, "The psycho who picks up young boys from all over Europe for Himmler and me to play with." As unit strength grew, the name was again changed to SS Totenkopfverbande and re-designated as the SS Sonderbataillon Dirlewanger. It eventually grew into a brigade.

Well, where could this unit be getting all these new, young, gung-ho men for them to grow so quickly?

Other Strafbataillons were penal battalions but operated "normally" — meaning they were understaffed with a low arsenal for detaining soldiers who had committed minor offenses. Also, in Germany, all the Strafbataillons operated under the German military police, except one. Any guesses?

Recruits convicted of major crimes such as premeditated murder, rape, arson, and burglary were sent to the

Dirlewanger Brigade and committed atrocities on such a scale that even the brutal SS complained.

NFW (no fucking way) someone from the SS complained about this unit's brutality. Hitler and his psycho friends encouraged this behavior.

I wonder what cabinet position Hitler had picked for Dirlewanger. Or what kind of medals he couldn't wait to give to Dirlewanger and his soldiers. Do you think a lot of the guys in this unit qualified for the Knight's Cross? Since hate groups obviously support Nazis, their philosophies, military strategies, and war crime achievements, can you think of a U.S. medal equivalent that you would have awarded those guys?

Let's look at the operational history of your Nazi brothers-in-arms. During his time in the Soviet Union, Dirlewanger and his demons burned women and children alive, let starved packs of dogs feed on them, and injected Jews with strychnine.

How about Poland? In August of 1940, Dirlewanger guarded the region of German-occupied Lublin, Poland (site of a Nazi-established "Jew reservation" under the Nisko Plan). According to journalist and author Matthew Cooper, "Wherever the Dirlewanger group operated, corruption and rape formed an everyday part of life and indiscriminate slaughter, beatings and lootings were rife."

Even war criminal Friedrich-Wilhelm Krüger, a paramilitary commander and high-ranking member of the SA and the SS during the Third Reich, complained about Dirlewanger. Thus, in February 1942, the Dirlewanger unit was transferred to Byelorussia (Belarus).

Wow. Quick question. Of the thousands and thousands of various units the Nazis put together, and all the atrocities that the Nazis committed, how many units do you think were transferred for unlawful behavior? Of course, they didn't disband these cocksuckers; nope, they just moved them somewhere else. Nice job, Friedrich. Oh, and Friedrich, this might surprise you, BUT THERE ARE PEOPLE IN BELARUS, TOO, you fucking nitwit.

I mean, if Attila the Hun had a group of cannibals available to fight, the Nazis would have found a place to send them. And the Dingleberry unit was doing a lot more than just "unlawful behavior." If that unit got transferred, at a minimum, those soldiers got caught fucking holes in trees.

In Byelorussia, the unit was overseen by Eric von dem Bach-Zelewski and cooperated with the Kaminski Brigade, a militia force comprised of Soviet nationals under the command of Bronislaw Kaminski. There, the Dirlewanger unit's typical mode of operation was to lock civilians in a barn, set it on fire, and machine gun those who tried to escape.

Historian Timothy Snyder notes in his book Bloodlands: Europe Between Hitler and Stalin, "As it inflicted its first 15,000 mortal casualties, the special commando Dirlewanger lost only 92 men, many of them, no doubt, to friendly fire and alcoholic accidents. A ratio such as that was possible only when the victims were unarmed civilians."

Ugh, Timothy, these morbid jackasses lost 92 "soldiers" in their own unit, while murdering 15,000 unarmed civilians. That's 92 soldiers. These antisemitic and racist assholes lost 92 of their brothers while killing unarmed people. How is that possible? Were they playing various games, like how many live grenades they could fit in their asses? Were they excessively drunk and trying to shoot apples off each other's heads…from a German tank? Has anybody found out any information yet on the 25 guys who were left out of this unit? Did they line up their firing squad in a circle? How the fuck do you lose 92 "soldiers" against unarmed civilians?

In September 1942, the unit murdered 8,350 Jews in the

Baranovichi ghetto and then a further 389 people labeled "bandits." According to historian Martin Kitchen, "The unit committed such shocking atrocities in the Soviet Union, in the pursuit of partisans, that even an SS court was called upon to investigate."

With all due respect to Mr. Kitchen, I'm calling bullshit on an "SS court" being called upon to investigate. More likely, they awarded medals for what this unit had been doing. And even today, you get applause, accolades, and pats on the back from people who support Nazis. Of course, none of the neo-Nazi "fanboys" has seen mutilation, torture, and experimental surgeries up close. But no need, their Nazi heroes in the field did it for them.

An SS court investigating an SS unit… give me a fucking break. Before the end of World War II, this "unit" became a brigade. That's right, only Hitler and his underlings and the Nazi Party would expand a unit of clinically diagnosed psychopaths, sociopaths, schizophrenics, delusional pedophiles, rapists, whatever, to eventually almost 5,000 soldiers.

I will ask again, what on earth did Hitler say or do that makes today's neo-Nazis want to emulate him and the Nazi party? You must know by now he wouldn't have given a shit about you, your family, your friends, no one. I mean, what is it? There must be something that draws you into this horror.

A raving, extremely selfish, "over the top" embezzler and multi-year drug addict, who systematically murdered 11 million-plus civilians while killing millions of his own civilians and soldiers, had no care or sympathy for others, and that would include the haters today. So why? What's the attraction for Nazi war crimes, murder, and mayhem?

Hitler killed his own friends, generals, and anyone — and I mean anyone — who disagreed with him. I can go on and on. All of it, every part of his reign in Germany, was always,

always, always about him, especially as the war raged on. If you can't see it by now, his use of the military and especially Nazis was to further HIS agenda and HIS alone. If you can't distinguish between these obvious examples of good and evil, then you have problems much larger than attending hate groups.

Let's move onward to 1943. In May, ALL criminals became eligible to volunteer for service in the Regiment, and 500 men convicted of the most severe crimes joined. In August, a third Battalion was authorized. In November, the regiment was sent to the frontline to halt the Soviet advance and suffered extreme casualties due to Dirlewanger's ineptitude. Yet, he received the German Gold Cross in December in recognition of his EARNESTNESS, but by then, the unit was comprised of only 259 men. More "amnesty criminals" were sent to rebuild the regiment, and by late February 1944, it was back at full strength.

First off, this unit must've been the easiest unit to refill in the history of refilling units. Dirlewanger should have been able to have that unit replaced by the weekend just from camp guards. I understand the definition of criminal, but I certainly don't know the definition of a criminal as the Nazis knew it. My guess is as the war dragged on, the ability to sneeze would get you in a Nazi unit somewhere.

Dirlewanger's unit eventually became brigade size (roughly 4,500 – 5,000 men) because there were so many Nazi "sick fucks" at that time. I'm guessing they had to turn some of the criminals, sorry, soldiers, away.

Quick question. How many Nazis in Dirlewanger's unit do you think accepted the German G.I. bill?

By the way, bravery, valor, and sacrifice are all very valid and deserving of whichever medals a government or military unit bestows upon a worthy soldier. We applaud those men and women, and they have an automatic and earned respect from their country's citizens. Having said that, who the fuck gets a medal based on earnestness? Was that a joke?

Can you imagine the medal ceremony and another soldier receiving a German Gold Cross at the same time as Dirlewanger? Dirlewanger looks over to the soldier and asks what he did to receive his medal. The soldier replies, "Well, I was in this battle where I lost a kidney, blew up my knee, received shrapnel in my skull but saved three of my men." The soldier then returns the question to Dirlewanger. He responds, "Ugh, well, I commanded a unit where we raped, pillaged, and buried alive thousands upon thousands of people. I will say, though, "I'm getting this sweet-looking medal because of my great earnestness."

Anyway, let's see where your heroes were in 1944. When the Armia Krajowa began the Warsaw uprising on the 1st of August 1944, the Dirledouches were sent in and given a free hand to rape, loot, torture, and butcher.

Excuse me for a well-placed tangent. You really must be a special kind of fucking loser to admire Himmler. That pussy had never been in a fight in his whole miserable life. What do you think Himmler would have done if it weren't for the Nazis? In my opinion, best case is by the time he reached his fifties, he would've been working at a public park, in the "pooper scooper" division, and would have picked up shit all day until his early retirement from a finger blister.

Heinrich Himmler, you must be fucking joking. The head of the SS informs a battalion commander to rape, loot, and torture. WTF. You racist Aryans have sworn allegiance to this fucking guy, and you want people to "leave your country."

Back to your hero's unit. In what became known as the Wola massacre, Dirlewanger's unit indiscriminately massacred 40,000 Polish combatants along with innocent men, women, and children in less than two weeks. Also, since they were already hanging out in Wola, they murdered all hospital patients and staff.

Many otherwise unknown crimes committed by Dirlewanger at Wola were later revealed by Mattias Shank, a Belgian national who was serving in the area as a German Army Sapper (combat engineer). Regarding an incident in which 500 small children were murdered, Shank stated:

"After the door of the building was blown off we saw a daycare full of small children, around 500; all with small hands in the air, even Dirlewanger's own people called him a butcher, he ordered to kill them all. The shots were fired, but he requested his men to save the ammo and finish them off with rifle butts and bayonets. Blood and brain matter flowed in stream, down the stairs."

Well, at least Himmler, Dirlewanger, and you hate groups are happy. More killed, right? So, under the Nazis, what does the unit get after performing that task on civilians?

The Regiment arrived in Warsaw with only 865 enlisted personnel and 16 officers, but it soon received 2,500 replacements. These included 1,900 German convicts from the SS military camp at Danzig-Matzkau. Yet extremely high casualties were inflicted on Dirlewanger during fighting in Warsaw by the Polish resistance, where Dirlewanger's unit lost more than the 2,500 replacements they were just given. I don't think Germany was the first nation to coin the phrase "shit floats uphill," but the Nazis may have, as Dingleberry was actually recommended for the Knights Cross and promotion to SS-Ober Führer der Reserve ... well, of course, he was.

Is anyone with half a brain remotely surprised? They'd already shown, multiple times, that they were the worst military unit in World War II. The Italians would have massacred this unit. It wasn't put together to fight; it was put together to inflict pain and suffering in the most brutal ways possible to satiate the sickest appetites of the sickest of men, Hitler, Himmler, Goebbels, Goering, etc. They could have pulled this unit out of the war at any time, but they didn't. Why?

What other possible explanation could there be for keeping this unit around when they proved on countless occasions they couldn't fight? And since we all know it came from the top of the Nazi party, I just have to ask the hate groups or whomever, why do you endorse this? Why do you endorse killing babies and children? You see Himmler giving direct orders. You're good with rape? Raping children? Bashing in children's skulls? That's now your hands, your fists, your kicks, your deaths. This, apparently, is what you want to carry on and teach your children.

Let's recap.

So, what do one's competent government and military do with a unit that can't fight, take land, or figure out how to get into their own sleeping bags, but excels at raping and pillaging? You make them a brigade…duh. Oh, and certainly reward and name the unit SS-Sonderbrigade Dirlewanger after its illustrious leader. But wait, why stop there? Before Dirlewanger could even get the cum off his mouth, the unit was promoted again to the Waffen-SS combat brigade. Finally, all of you sick, psycho fuckers, can now rejoice that the Dirlewangers unit is officially a full 4,000-plus-man brigade.

UNFUCKINGBELIEVABLE.

Who would've thought at the time that once this war was over, people would try to revive Hitler's ideology, government, and possibly military? I bet there definitely wasn't one German.

You've been had, bamboozled, suckered by someone who DEFINITELY cared more about personal ambitions than he ever cared about Nazis, Germany, and YOU.

Dirlewanger's unit hung around in some fashion until the end of the war. He was captured by the French in Germany and allegedly killed by Polish soldiers in Alts Haven.

What else could I comment about this unit and Hitler's direct henchmen who ordered it? Worse, they followed through with this unit until it became brigade-sized, a military pariah. Hitler and the rest of those jerk-offs knew that not only were they extremely incompetent, but they could not help militarily at any level. They formed that unit for one reason, and by now, you know, to loot, rape, torture, and murder.

Hitler, your hero, was directly responsible for baby killings, pedophiles, rapes, murders, burning families alive, and more. Those are the legacy of your heroes, Hitler, Goebbels, Himmler, et al. These are the people you admire, revere, and brag about. What happens when you begin to full-on emulate Hitler's actions? Are you going to murder the innocent? Are you going to lock people in barns and burn them alive too?

It would be one thing if a bunch of psychos found each other and started a rogue group that committed atrocities (disgusting and not acceptable), but there is absolutely no justification, none, that the heads of the Nazi Party formed this group and others. You hate groups need to explain why you endorse this kind of horseshit.

As a reminder to the men and women of the U.S. military involved in some of these hate groups... those of you who chose to join the United States military swore to uphold the Constitution and to protect and serve ALL citizens of the United States. If you did not faithfully agree to your sworn oath to protect ALL, fine, it's your choice. However, you need to immediately relinquish your service (either currently serving or a vet) and re-classify and accept an immediate

dishonorable discharge.
   Cocksucker ranking: 9.

Chapter 11: More Assholes

"Those who can make you believe absurdities can make you commit atrocities."
~ *Voltaire*

Another sick fuck unit put together for the murdering of civilians was the Einsatzgruppen. These assholes were a legitimate military unit who could play soldiers when called upon, unlike Dirlewhacko's. This unit has so many atrocities attached to its name that it would take years for me to write down 10% of them.

They were called death squads. Not the death squads you think of off the top of your head, like a small group of mercenaries who go out to kill a select target. NOPE. Their roles were to find and round up innocent civilians and murder them by the "truckload." The closest these fucks got to the Geneva Convention was a Geneva watch they stole from their victims.

The Einsatzgruppen was the unit founded for the destruction and annihilation of whomever their orders were for. Initially, as part of their unit's first missions with about 3,000 soldiers, they were ordered to go into the Soviet Union for Operation Barbarossa. Again, this unit wasn't there to capture territory. They were sent to kill soldiers, civilians, pets, snowmen, whatever, while also providing the services of maiming, hanging, torturing, and any other heinous act they wanted.

Initially, the Einsatzgruppen were divided into four groups and sent into the Soviet Union at four different coordinates. The unit advanced in the wake of the Wehrmacht. Each Einsatzgruppen was attached to one or more military units. Again, these units were assigned to track down and eliminate the foes of Nazis, Communists, Partisans, and Jews. They were basically in charge of eliminating all potential enemies and potential dangers. Point being, they were given a lot of leeway to murder, torture, rape, etc. Be it politicians, saboteurs, anyone. If they didn't like a person's beard, no problem, just murder them. Eventually, Hitler realized they could also be effective in looting and stealing for him, so they took that up when asked. I mean, why try and win a war when you can have troops steal for you?

This unit was responsible for murdering, in total, around two million people, of which 1.3 million were Jews. It's a shame when you look back because Hitler could have put a lot of those "soldiers" in Dirlewanger's brigade.

If the Allies had gone after more German people and German soldiers after WWII to bring them to justice, this unit would have had about 90% hung from a "long rope rate" or LRR. Though the Einsatzgruppen should be comforted knowing Dirlepsycho's unit had an LRR of 99.99%.

The Einsatzgruppen's preferred method of death was shooting. Of course, when they were low on bullets, they would just bury alive their victims if one bullet didn't do the trick. Einsatzgruppen had seven groups and, in total, 4,250 "soldiers" at full force and all with the same goal — gather up Jews and other minorities, then murder them before or after stealing anything of value, bolted down or not.

There are so many disgusting, fucked-up atrocities I could mention about this "unit," but I picked only a few. They carried out the murders of many, many innocent civilians, but their main responsibility was to carry out "The Final Solution." Truly, only evil men could exist in the Einsatzgruppen.

Babi Yar

On September 29 and 30, 1941, the Nazi's largest massacre, Babi Yar, was carried out during the Germans' campaign against the Soviet Union. Around 150,000 men, women, and children were murdered there. Jews, Russians, communists, Roma, P.O.W.s, and more.

You know, I've looked, but I can't find a group or military unit that was taught how to pull the trigger on four and five-year-old children. I mean, was there a special ops group formed in Germany to handle 13-year-olds? We know they were ordered to do it by a bunch of dickless, cocksucking cowards, but how do you carry it out?

The fucking Nazis. Unreal. How many armies in the last 500 years, from the top down, were ORDERED to murder civilians throughout the entire conflict? We're not talking a dozen or two. Millions upon millions upon millions were murdered by the Nazis and their collaborators. I understand it's war, and bad things happen. I also understand, to a certain extent, how Germans became Nazis. But what I just can't comprehend is how those Germans could murder civilians in the volume and in the ways they did.

I mean, how do you distribute these orders?

Commander: "Here's your order, soldier. You go to that house right there, you murder the eight-year-old, you rape the nine-year-old, and you tie up the rest of the family and burn their house down. And you better make sure their dog's inside."

Commander: "I just want to let you know that order comes directly from Hitler."

Soldier: "Are you serious? Thank you, thank you. May I please have the piece of paper that the order was written on? I want to frame it and will cherish this souvenir from Hitler forever."

I mean, where do you find this many sick, deranged lunatics?

On September 26, 1941, a couple of Nazi fucks, Jeckeln and Eberhard (more about them in the next section), along with the SS and local police chief, had just finished their four-man orgy when they all agreed to exterminate the Jews of Kiev. It was agreed that they would use Einsatzgruppen C to carry out the murders. They posted signs around the city for Jews to bring documents, money, valuables, warm clothing, jewelry, etc. The sign also stated, "Any Yids who do not follow this order and are found elsewhere will be shot. Any civilians who enter the dwellings left by Yids and appropriate the things in them will be shot."

On September 29–30, 1941, the Nazis and their collaborators murdered 33,771 Jewish civilians and, per usual, by shootings only. What words should I type here? I have none. To order and carry out shooting innocent people in front of their own family members who are watching them get shot, then falling into a pit and, if they're not dead, hearing their screams. WTF. 33,771. Give me a couple of words stronger than barbaric.

The commander of the Einsatzkommando reported two days later (noted in the Nuremberg Military Tribunal, Einsatzgruppen trial, Judgement, quoting exhibit NO-3157): "The difficulties from such a large-scale…"

You fucking pussies. What, not enough bullets? Difficulties? You were ordered to shoot defenseless civilians, and you did. I imagine Himmler had an inner orgasm when he gave the order. "Oh, the difficulties…" Fuck you. And yes, a very "clever" article was written for the Jewish people of Kiev who already knew their options, dumbass. They came that morning in hopes that maybe, just maybe, there was a chance you Nazi fucks would send them to a concentration camp instead of individually shooting 33,771 people.

Michael Berenbaum (an American scholar, professor, rabbi, writer, and filmmaker) wrote in his book *Witness to the Holocaust* that, according to the testimony of a truck driver named Hofer who was at Babi Yar watching the massacres, "I watched what happened when the Jews — men, women and children — arrived. Ukrainians led them past a number of different places where one after the other had to give up their luggage, then their coats, shoes and over-garments and underwear. They also had to leave their valuables in a designated place." What on earth could the Germans want with all their belongings and valuables?

The driver continued, "Once undressed they were led into the ravine which was about 150 meters long and 30 meters wide and a good 15 meters deep... When they reached the bottom of the ravine, they were seized by members of the Schutzpolizei and made to lie down on top of Jews who had already been shot... The corpses were literally in layers. A police marksman came along and shot each Jew in the neck with a submachine gun... I saw these marksmen stand on layers of corpses and shoot one after the other... The marksman would walk across the bodies of the executed Jews to the next Jew, who had meanwhile lain down, and shoot him. Wounded victims were buried alive in the ravine along with the rest of the bodies. In the months that followed, thousands more were seized and taken to Babi Yar, where they were shot. It is estimated that more than 100,000 residents of Kiev, of all ethnic groups and mostly civilians, were murdered by the Nazis there during World War II."

Now, I'm sure some of you are disappointed that only 33,771 Jews were shot in 48 hours, but... the Nazis were neatly stacking up the bodies, and that takes time. I bet a lot of you assholes wish you were out there murdering defenseless civilians right now. I bet you imagine yourselves coming back from war, regaling to your family and friends how proud you were to serve in an army with such high ethics and moral standards. These were formed units. They were ordered to do it. You still don't have a problem with this?

Rumbula

The asshole known as Himmler was dissatisfied with the pace of the exterminations, so he assigned SS Oberfuckface Jeckeln, one of the perpetrators of the Babi Yar massacre, to liquidate the Riga ghetto. On the first day of executions, November 30, 1941, Jews had to bring all their possessions and walk roughly 300 yards into a forest. They were ordered to strip and lie down and were shot either in the head or in the back of their necks. 25,000 Jews were murdered in two days. Jeckeln was promoted to Leader of the SS Upper Section Ostland for doing such an expeditious job of murdering his victims.

Only from the sickest man in history to the sickest generals in history, to the sickest commanders in history, to the sickest unit commanders in history, could one get promoted for killing unarmed civilians. What a country and military Germany offered the world at that time.

Also, personally, I would never step foot in Estonia, Latvia, Belarus, Ukraine, or Lithuania. I understand decisions being made for self-preservation, but active participation in the rounding up and murdering of Jews by civilians is obviously unacceptable. Look, it certainly doesn't take away from what the Nazis did. But the large active participation by the police and citizens from those countries was so far over the top that I feel they need to know we haven't forgotten.

Einsatzgruppen D participated along with citizens in the murder of more than 30,000 Jews which took the Jewish population from 30,000 to 702 in Dnepropetrovsk, Belarus, in four days.

As the Soviets were kicking Germany's ass back into Germany, along with the advent of Zyklon-B for mass killings in concentration camps, the Einsatzgruppen was no longer needed. The soldiers were melted back into various units. It must have sucked for those guys in those units, knowing the Nazis found something quicker and cheaper to kill civilians than their own unit. I know they all tried hard, but...

Cocksucker rating: 9

As usual, most of the perpetrators of this group were never found. It boggles the mind how a military unit could be founded for the sole purpose of killing civilians. As mentioned earlier, we've heard of small units (10 to 20 troops) here or there, set up to kill a few "bad apples," but a unit of 3000+? And given full amnesty to murder? Your multi-billionaire hero was very, very proud of those units.

Between the Einsatzgruppen and the Dirlewanger brigade, more than 10,000-plus soldiers received and carried out orders to murder civilians. Do none of you see how fucking crazy, psychotic, and mentally deranged these "soldiers" had to be? These units were raping their way through Poland and Russia and then burning and murdering on their way back. How do today's hate group members have any respect for themselves?

These topics were acted out on real people in real time with real consequences. I would hope our United States soldiers never, ever carry out any such heinous acts.

Overall, how mind-boggling that the Nazis killed 16,315,000 by genocide. Jews, Gypsies, Slavs, and homosexuals. And really, most of this was done in less than three years, from 1942 to 1945, when the Nazis basically wiped out Europe's Jews. Furthermore, there was an additional 11,283,000 people killed by the Nazis through euthanasia, forced labor, prisons, and death camps.

20,946,000 civilians were murdered in democide alone in what, a little over four years? You must be one sick, sick fuck to be giving these types of orders and one sick, sick fuck to implement these heinous acts. Who in their right mind would try to "rekindle" the Nazi Party and emulate Hitler and his staff today? Especially knowing what we know. It's, well, just as sick and almost worse because we know the outcome.

The vast and various volumes of the German population and others were murdered for Hitler's imperialism, greed, disagreements, and obvious **WORLD-CLASS INSECURITIES**, which led to so many millions of civilian deaths too. Not just the groups he initially focused on, NOPE, these murders started happening as soon they crossed into Czechoslovakia and never stopped.

I bring this up for two reasons. 1) it's true, and 2) it got to the point that if a three-year-old was aimlessly crawling on the floor and started a path toward Hitler, the baby would have been hanged. His political opponents, ugh, yeah, I think after the first ten political opponents who opened their mouths to yawn were summarily executed, the word political opponent from 1933-1945 in Germany was not only never said, but it was almost said less than someone saying Goebbel was well hung.

Staying within his own borders, he certainly murdered more than just his political opponents. He murdered anyone who opposed him for anything. If you parked in his spot, you and your family were gone. If you held up the line at the grocery store for him, it was death in the frozen food section, and I don't want to tell you the punishment if you tried to jump him in line at the pharmacy.

A contingent of Nazis tried to assassinate Shitler, and as we all know, he survived. Now, at some point, every Nazi had a secret about something, anything, that they would never tell anyone as they never knew what would get them imprisoned or killed. Hitler had 5,000 Germans executed for trying to kill him. Read that again — 5,000. Now, knowing something like an assassination attempt meant automatic death, especially in an environment where secrets are very hard to keep, could there have been more than 50 or 100 Nazis participating? Quite a few reports say around 200, but I find that extremely hard to believe. Anyway, using Hitler's math, 200 conspirators equal FIVE THOUSAND deaths.

Furthermore, this is 1944 while Germany was getting its ass kicked everywhere, and you want to use large amounts of resources to find out who tried to kill you? A fucking genius, ladies and gentlemen.

The Nazis also killed their own dissidents and critics during lulls of murders being done elsewhere to stay focused, or when they couldn't find a book to read. (Ugh, they forgot they burned them.) The Nazis came up with reasons, either logical or illogical, to kill hundreds of thousands of their own. Hitler's philosophies were very simple — you either agreed with him 100% or expected to be killed... actually, you could agree with him and still be killed. Germany, internationally and domestically, was just a fucking mess. We can't wait until you hate groups bring that type of government here. Are we sticking with English, or are we going with German?

Insane numbers started by an insane psychopath, followed by insane military leaders, and carried out by a lot of insane soldiers. Genocide is not a new phenomenon, nor is murder, but in a civilized country, on a civilized continent with civilized people and culture (prior to 1933 Germany), the Nazis will go down in history as having the most atrocities performed by one country, likely ever to be seen and it wasn't that long ago.

Whatever the definitions for the words despicable, reprehensible, sadistic, and incomprehensible, feel free to let those words guide you through a few more examples.

Also, what in these readings sounds like something anyone would want to participate in? From 1933 to 1945, what on earth do you see as a positive in the life of a Nazi? What accomplishments could you point to as an affirmation that confirms why you want to be a Nazi? Most of you are better than this; you must be, as I refuse to believe anyone born in this country would want anything, at any level, to do with a totalitarian dictatorial government and a psychotic sociopath being the head of the government and military. I just can't, can I?

Who writes a chapter on atrocities? In wars, there are certainly atrocities, but they are isolated and very low in occurrence. WWII for Germany was "open season" for atrocities. My words won't do it justice. I am trying, but how could I? I wasn't there. The screams, the stench, the hunger, I can't replicate that. I want these words to sting, I want to insult the haters, and I want to hurt those who somehow replicate and glorify the pain and suffering of all of those civilians, but I can't. What's it going to take for you people to STOP identifying with fucking Nazis? The definition of atrocity, as I write this, will never, EVER be the same definition for those murdered not so long ago.

What Germany did from 1938-1945 will not be replicated. Today, with technology, information, weapons, etc., I just don't see any scenario where the world would let a country get anywhere close, but who knows? Those people, those beautiful people, suffered so much for an outcome that a madman and a country had no chance of winning. Yet, here we are, trying to convince another batch of people not only how insanely despicable they are viewed in our society but how they have a much, much less chance than Hitler to succeed.

Bombings of hospitals, schools, retirement homes, etc., happen in war, but it's usually isolated incidents. It's war, it sucks, but most countries in this world don't target them specifically or continually.

What Hitler, his asshole buddies, and a shitload of Germans did are incomparable in modern warfare. Feel free to espouse your Nazi beliefs; I don't give a shit. Brag about your new understanding of *Mein Kampf*; great, I don't care. But trying to justify any physical harm, defacing of property, or intimidation of Jews and any other minority groups in this country WILL NO LONGER BE ALLOWED WITHOUT RECOURSE. It's cowardice, reprehensible, and frankly, never helps with your agendas anyways.

Writing some of these chapters was not easy. Frankly, it really pisses me off, and in the future, if I feel that I am "wavering about my resolve," I will open up this book and read these chapters again.

Chapter 12: Harvesting the Jews

"Never forget that everything Hitler did in Germany was legal."
~ *Martin Luther King Jr.*

Read the quote above, then read it again. The Jews, a peaceful and industrious people, were never a threat to anyone. Not to Hitler. Not to their fellow Germans. They were harmless men, women, and children and a credit to their country. The Jews did nothing to Hitler to deserve the suffering and torment he inflicted on them. It was they who needed a defense against Hitler — and none was forthcoming in that police state.

Yes, he simply targeted a group, scapegoated them for every problem, and decided to eliminate them. I'm sure he did this to strike terror in the hearts of anyone who opposed him but also had many mental disorders, none higher than "Jew derangement syndrome."

It didn't take long after 1933 for the German press to stop asking questions and just succumb to Hitler's "What I say goes, period," and his "Next question?" mantra.

It's actually bizarre. Hitler admired the Muslims and hated the Jews, yet he only had one religion — Hitler, and he never missed a day to pray to himself. Without the Holocaust, would there ever have been lampshades made of human skin? The mere thought is so sick and twisted that I wonder why antisemites align themselves with such behavior. I cannot stress this point enough, but if you align with Hitler, then you are ignoring unspeakable atrocities. This makes YOU an unspeakable atrocity.

AND, for the hundredth time, we do NOT separate any hate group member from Third Reich Nazis, and as such, you must be dealt with accordingly. By the way, you, your family, and your friends must be so proud, just so, so proud of you. Have you always been a problem solver?

If you or your groups want to make light of political policies, politicians, and political parties — no problem. Political debate, along with voting, is the cornerstone of democracies. Unfortunately, this chapter is not about that. I'd like to give my opinion of the Nazi Party solely based on policy; however, it can't be done. The Nazis, as individuals and a party, became one and the same. Eventually, they had no equal when it came to death, destruction, torture, looting, and any other form of violence. I've come to the conclusion that the ONLY thing the Nazis were never prejudiced about was murder.

If something or anything could benefit Hitler, he would simply have someone take it. That goes for every other officer and soldier who put on a Nazi uniform. Obviously, Hitler got first dibs, but as orders trickled down, no big deal; there was always something for the lowest-ranking soldier to take too.

As the 1930s was coming to a close and the Nazis, Gestapo, SA, and SS wanted more, so did their means of collection. Killing in war sucks, but was and is acceptable. Killing when someone breaks into your home, acceptable. Killing someone who's trying to kill you or others, acceptable. Gassing, starving, mutilating, shooting, drowning, torturing, and murdering by medical experimentation ... well, I know my answer. The scary part is, what's yours?

The Great "Utopia"

Try to imagine yourself as being the 1 out of 100 or so that would qualify as an Aryan in Germany's late 1920s or early 1930s time frame. You get up, go to work, provide for your family and participate in community yodeling contests twice a month, but you're just not happy. You think, *Wait, I deserve so much more. Maybe, becoming a soldier could provide fulfillment. Or an officer. Yeah, an officer who tells others what to do. That could be it.*

While daydreaming, various scenarios wander your mind — *having the power to eliminate that damn Treaty of Versailles which is holding Germany back ... and those Jews. Those Jews who keep taking all of our good-paying jobs. Man, there has to be someone who can come along and facilitate these "meager" requests and be our "beacon of light" that every country in the world will want to imitate and travel to. There just has to be a government that does all the talking for me and my neighbors and also provides for us, the deserving, proud, and patriotic. I wonder how that would work in Germany.*

It took only a few years to get this great so-called "utopia" up and going. Hitler went from theoretical socialism straight to a hellish totalitarian dictatorship. You hate groups love that, don't you? You crave neo-Nazi dictatorship because you need to be told what to do. Right? You are followers. You want the government and military to run everything, just like in Hitler's days.

From his own mouth: "The [Nazi party] should not become a constable of public opinion, but must dominate it. It must not become a servant of the masses, but their master!" I guess today's Jew-haters and terror groups need a master too. After all, Hitler was the head of the sanitation department, the head of the local chess club, and the head dog catcher. I mean, he had his fingers in everything. (If you don't believe me, just ask Himmler's anus.) I suppose hate groups and their members value the "Shut up and do as I say" approach to life.

Furthermore, this utopia that Hitler envisioned and never shut the fuck up about was only off by 988 years of his "1000-year Reich." Let's see what was closer to Hitler's 1000-year Reich than he was:

- European Jews
- My toaster
- SpongeBob SquarePants

Doctors Turned "Medical Soldiers"

How do you get normal people to do these kinds of acts? How do you find doctors who are this evil? Performing surgeries without anesthesia and medical experimentation on younger twins is a fucking horrific concept. Only a monster would think it up. I don't have words to describe people who actually performed these crimes against humanity. How do you look a child in the eye and medically experiment in the cruelest manner on such innocent beings?

Prepare for some sleepless nights if you ever read Edwin Black's *War Against the Weak: Eugenics and America's Campaign to Create a Master Race*. Prepare for nightmares if you ever read *Children of the Flames: Dr. Josef Mengele and the Untold Story of the Twins of Auschwitz* by Lucette Matalon Lagnado and Sheila Cohn Dekel. Or watch "Science and the Swastika: The Deadly Experiment" directed by Saskia Baron. It used to be available on Amazon. Now you can find the series on the World at War YouTube channel.

"Brilliant" and psychotic doctors who believed in eugenics stepped up to find and eliminate impurities in the bloodline. Aside from the shits and giggles of watching children suffers, the doctors in concentration camps had a mission. They especially targeted twins to find ways to improve the Aryan race. From 1943 to 1944, Josef Mengele experimented on almost 1,500 sets of twins in Auschwitz, killing about 1,300 by amputations, infectious diseases, injecting dyes to change eye color, conjoining twins by sewing them together, or using one twin as a control subject while experimenting on the other. Oh, and dissections.

To all the Hitler advocates and Mengele fans — are you parents? Do you have an ounce of love for your own children? Do you remember what event took place in your life that made it acceptable for you to endorse medical experimentation on children? Even if you have German ancestry, the chance of your children being "purebloods" is slim to impossible. Hitler's definition of "Aryan" disqualifies your kiddos. To him, your little ones are nothing but unworthy mongrels. Well, not totally unworthy. They'd be fit for medical experimentation, right?

And you support this. You support this even though it's beyond sinful. Your loyalty to serial killers and child abusers is just jaw-dropping. What is wrong with you?

The experiments on adults were also heinous. Bone, muscle, and nerve transplants, organ transplants (oh goodie, let's see if a kidney can replace a liver), head injuries, freezing, malaria, immunizations, hepatitis, mustard gas, sulfonamide, seawater, poison, high altitude, incendiary bombs, blood coagulation, electroshock — what a gruesome list. It's like Germany turned into a house of horrors ... or one ginormous laboratory filled with evil scientists, and yet, in this day and age, we have hate groups all throughout this country who still support these horrific atrocities. I truly hope your children pass the impassable Aryan test, or they may be next on the doctor's "examination table."

Sterilization and Fertility Experiments

Hitler enacted "The Law for the Prevention of

Genetically Defective Progeny" in July 1933, and thus came involuntary sterilizations for hereditary diseases, disabilities, birth defects, alcoholism, mental illness, blindness, deafness, and other less than Aryan qualities. Nothing but perfection for the Master Race, right?

Well Duh. If you want that purest of pure whiteness, it's simple. Make sure your citizens who aren't pure can't procreate. Smart huh? Well, who's going to mow your fucking yard in ten or so years?

So, of course, there were sterilization experiments on live humans in the concentration camps. Although Mengele gets the lion's share of attention for medical torture, other doctors were just as complicit. Carl Clauberg, a German gynecologist, was tasked with sterilization and fertility experimentation. The goal was to develop a method to sterilize millions of people in the most efficient way. Jewish and Roma women between 20 and 40 who had already given birth were exposed to X-rays, surgeries, and drugs. From 1941 to 1945, 300,000 women were experimented on in Auschwitz and Ravensbrück, mostly geared toward their cervixes and fallopian tubes.

Also, a compulsory sterilization program victimized 400,000 males and females to block ova and sperm through iodine, silver nitrate, and radiation. Again, if you weren't white enough or German enough, then you were unwanted and disposable.

Euthanasia

Between 1934 and 1941, about 100,000 physically and mentally disabled Germans were killed, without, of course, consent from their families. Do you White supremacists believe that you are superior enough to kill the less fortunate? I have no other comment except you are sickening.

Along with Jews being murdered, we can add Jehovah's Witnesses, homosexuals, alcoholics, pacifists, beggars, hooligans, criminals, Gypsies, Blacks, and pretty much anyone whom Hitler felt was taller or stronger than him. So, every minority.

What an absolute fucking monstrosity he turned Germany into, and you must be some kind of special fucked up serial killer to literally target someone as a pacifist and then send them to the gas chamber. His own citizens. I cannot even fathom how much of a traitor Hitler was to his people.

Lest We Forget

Here's a look at the concentration camps — the names and locations of mass genocide. The early Nazi camps were: Breitenau, Breslau-Dürrgoy, Esterwegen, Kemna, Lichtenburg, Nohra, Oranienburg, Osthofen, Sonnenburg, and Vulkanwerft. Imagine the plight of those who perished, either by being worked to death or smitten with disease, or shot for fun.

You are likely more familiar with the notorious, more well-known camps. But I bet you have no clue just how many hundreds of camps existed. It will shock you. Hundreds upon hundreds upon hundreds — almost endless when you consider the subcamps and satellite camps.

May they be burned into your memory, just as the Jews were burned in the ovens. There were so many, just so fucking many death camps. A lot of these former death camps are still around and opened up as memorials. When walking into one, what would your thoughts be? Maybe a slight giggle? A laugh? I sincerely hope not, as you're walking on sacred ground.

Each step you take is walking on or over a dead body. With complete and indiscriminate murders everywhere in those camps, you probably just walked over a 5-year-old who got lost and was bayoneted right where you are standing. As you move on to the next place you want to see, you know it covered 50 steps or 50 bodies.

I cannot replicate the horrors of those places to you in my writings. Movies and television cannot replicate those places for us. How could you possibly replicate being freezing cold, starving, and having some type of disease or virus, 24 HOURS A DAY? EVERY DAY? HOW? HOW? I WANT YOU TO FUCKING FEEL IT AS THEY DID.

I hate to even provide a list of concentration camps, and I wasn't going to because it's important, very important to me when someone reads anything on the Holocaust, that they must show complete and total respect. I doubt you will, but maybe, just maybe, someone in your group will. When I look at those names, all I see is death. Not one positive thing came out of those camps. Not one.

Here's a listing of some of the camps. Skip it if you're going to laugh or mock. And remember, there were a tremendous number of non-Jews whose deaths you are stepping on too.

- Arbeitsdorf
- Auschwitz (and the Auschwitz I, Auschwitz II, and Birkenau satellite camps)
- Bergen-Belsen (and the Bomlitz-Benefeld, Hambühren-Ovelgönne, Lager III, Waldeslust, Unterlüß-Altensothrieth/Tannenberglager satellites)
- Buchenwald (and pages of satellites — see the List of Subcamps of Buchenwald on Wikipedia)
- Dachau (same thing — see the List of Subcamps of Dachau on Wikipedia)
- Flossenbürg (and more of the same — see the List

of Subcamps of Flossenbürg on Wikipedia)
- Gross-Rosen (again, I point you to the extensive list of Subcamps of Gross-Rosen on Wikipedia)
- Herzogenbusch (yes, and more satellites on the List of Subcamps of Herzogenbusch on Wikipedia)
- Hinzert
- Kaiserwald
- Kauen
- Kraków-Płaszów (more satellites at the List of Subcamps of Kraków-Płaszów on Wikipedia)
- Majdanek (see the List of Subcamps of Majdanek on Wikipedia)
- Mauthausen (see the List of Subcamps of Mauthausen on Wikipedia)
- Mittelbau-Dora (see the List of Subcamps of Mittelbau on Wikipedia)
- Natzweiler-Struthof (See the List of Subcamps of Natzweiler-Struthof on Wikipedia)
- Neuengamme (see the List of Subcamps of Neuengamme on Wikipedia)
- Niederhagen
- Ravensbrück (see the List of Subcamps of Ravensbrück on Wikipedia)
- Sachsenhausen (see the List of Subcamps of Sachsenhausen on Wikipedia)
- Stutthof (see the List of Subcamps of Stutthof on Wikipedia)
- Vaivara (see the List of Subcamps of Vaivara on Wikipedia)
- Warsaw

Gassing Vans

Oh, woe is me. Problems, problems, problems. Hitler and his "circle jerk" crew just could not find enough ways to kill Jews and other minorities. I assure you it was not from a lack of effort. Anyway, some fuck head came up with the idea of sealing off vans and either redirecting the exhaust into the vans or just dropping in some lethal gas.

It became so effective that they decided to use it on Jews, prisoners, Poles, asylum inmates, the mentally ill, or whoever was on the current German "bus line."

I wonder what medal or commendation that guy got. They can now just bring the gas chambers around like a traveling circus. Well, a death circus, but you know what I mean.

You know what else would help with this program? Make the vans look like regular passenger vans. Brilliant. You could tell your "passengers" that they don't need to put on a seatbelt, and they'll be driven around for about 30 minutes and then dropped off individually.

From May to June of 1940, Sonderkommando Lange, another sick fuck in the Dirlewanger mold and in charge of all the vans, killed 1,588 sick people from Soldau camp.

In August of 1941, SS Chief Heinrich Uglymotherfucker threw up after watching a mass shooting and ordered (that order lasted about an hour) a "kinder and gentler way" to kill innocent, unarmed civilians.

Can you imagine the awful, gut-wrenching screams coming from those vans? And the time it took for passengers to finally die? I mean, just when you think these assholes can't get any more barbaric.

Eventually, the gas vans were turned over to and run by the Einsatzgruppe, who ended up gassing hundreds of thousands of civilians.

I wondered if the Nazis had barbaric contests where the winner got, like, a stolen bracelet or a couple of gold teeth. I have no idea what was in the water in Germany back then to consistently conjure up such cruel and inhumane ideas, then follow through with them.

Gassing vans… Fuck You.

The Hunger Plan

Here's a tidbit you may not have heard about. Herbert Backe, an SS-*Obergruppenführer*, state secretary, and minister in the Reich Ministry of Food and Agriculture, thought up a plan where he was positive Hitler would actually kiss him after blowing a load in Hitler's mouth. He called it the "Hunger Plan." This was to reduce the population in conquered territories, especially in Slavic regions. Food supplies were diverted to the German Army and German civilians, and the rest could starve. Another bright idea was razing cities and allowing the area to return to forest or be resettled by Germans.

An astounding 4.2 million Soviet citizens were starved to death from 1941-1944 due to Backe's handiwork. Hitler could quite possibly be the only leader in world history to have actually implemented a war plan to create famine as an act of policy to kill millions upon millions of people. Only in Hitler's sick, psychotic, schizoid mind would you have famine listed as a worthy method of exterminating others.

Have any of you ever gone three or four days without eating? How about a month of no more than 200 calories a day? It is so barbaric I had to double and triple-check it. This is the fucking guy that some of you are willing to go to jail for? Starving 30 million people? How about 30 million White people?

Here's a crazy idea that never entered the Nazis' minds. Instead of planning to starve 30 million people, maybe you could try and figure out a way to FEED 30 million people. Maybe "slow the roll" on your imperialism quest and find a trading partner for food. That's your leader, your hero, someone who knowingly and deliberately tried to starve 30,000,000 people. Is that how you guys think too?

You morons who wear Nazi clothing and have Nazi tats, do you feel that you are great role models? Do you brag about this failed way of life to your kids? Have you seen this Backe character? Look him up. He looks just like all the other Nazi bureaucrats. I looked at his high school yearbook, and he won a couple of awards:

- Most likely to stay a pussy.
- Most likely to get caught fucking a goat.

This bitch hasn't peed standing up since he was five, yet he writes a "brilliant" plan to feed Germany by starving 30 million people. THIS NEEDS TO SINK INTO YOUR BRAINS, A PLAN TO STARVE TO DEATH 30 MILLION PEOPLE. How insanely fucked up were the Nazis. How fucked up do you have to be to endorse this policy?

I doubt most German citizens knew about this policy, but when hearing about it after the war, I'm highly confident it came as no surprise. My point is, this policy has to be known by every hate group in this country. Why would you endorse arguably the worst type of torture on such a massive scale? This was a military edict to starve 30 million people, and yet you continue to espouse Nazism? Why? WHY? How does one endorse starving newborns, toddlers, and children? The elderly? Teenagers? Women and men?

Stealing Gold Teeth

Think about this for a moment. You're an SS guard or SS dentist or SS Doctor and your one job, your only job, is to extract teeth from dead victims. I would be remiss if I didn't mention the number of civilian German dentists who volunteered to steal; sorry, I meant "help." The Nazis retrieved gold teeth from everyone and everywhere after Heinrich Dickhead in September of 1940 ordered it.

Okay, next time you look at a mirror, open up and take a look at one of your fillings. If you just have silver, that's fine too. If you don't have any fillings, just go over to your neighbor's house and ask to see one of theirs. Look at it; they're very small, light, and may even be a little off-color.

A gold crown typically uses about one-tenth of an ounce of 16-karat gold. Ready? "About 1,320 pounds of gold bars held by Germany's largest bank, Deutsche Bank AG, during World War II probably came from melted-down teeth fillings of Holocaust victims." You can now eliminate the word "probably," as this article was written in 1998 by *Deseret News*, and I have found no other outcome.

And the Swiss, my gosh, who knows how many billions of looted dollars the Swiss bought from the Nazis and how many tons of gold teeth they purchased. Eventually, the Nazis stole crowns and dentures. Why not? I mean, they're already in the area. The number of teeth that had to be pulled in order to add up to the tons and tons and tons of gold is incalculable. It's staggering. They couldn't have missed one fucking tooth in Europe. I mean, were they fighting for land, an ideology, the Fatherland? Fuck no, they were fighting for teeth. My gosh, those cocksuckers.

Here's a 1987 article in the *Associated Press* by Kevin Costelloe titled "Files Say Nazi Victims' Gold Teeth Yanked; Bodies Thrown into Bonfire" regarding Nazi war criminal Josef Schwammberger. I excerpt from his article:

FRANKFURT, West Germany (AP) Accused Nazi war criminal Josef Schwammberger used pliers to rip out Jews' gold teeth and forced concentration camp prisoners to strip before having them killed and cremated, witnesses said in accounts released Wednesday...

... The 75-year-old Schwammberger, arrested this month in Argentina, is awaiting possible extradition to West Germany to stand trial in Stuttgart. Prosecutors have accused the former commander of two concentration camps in east Poland of killing about 1,000 people, most of them Jews.

One account was from Siegfried Kellermann, who spoke to Innsbruck police in 1946 about the roundup three years earlier of Jews from the southeastern Polish town of Przemysl.

"There was a huge wood pile, which was set on fire and all people had to strip naked and give up any gold, money and jewelry," Kellermann said in describing Schwammberger's treatment of the prisoners.

"Schwammberger and two or three other men killed the people, and their bodies were immediately thrown into the fire."

Kellermann added that children's heads "were beaten against a wall, and then they were thrown into the fire." He said 900 people died in the roundup, which he watched from a hiding place.

Heinrich Kirschenbaum, a former inmate in the camp at Mielec near Krakow, told investigators Schwammberger checked to see if inmates had gold teeth and told those who did to report to him at night.

> *"After they showed up, Schwammberger personally ripped out their gold teeth with a pliers,"* according to the file report.
>
> *Loew Chiel, another camp inmate, told Austrian police: "Schwammberger had a universally feared dog that he sicked on Jewish prisoners at every opportunity."*

Back to the Lampshades

Do a bit of online browsing and see for yourself that making lampshades from human skin was an actual Nazi occurrence. Who in their right mind would condone it? Oh, wait — modern-day Aryans condone it, right? I mean, you can't really cherry-pick your ideology when your hero is Hitler. You can't really say, "Oh, I agree with all of Hitler's tenets except turning people into lampshades."

You sick fucks. Wake up. What do you find when you browse "Karl-Otto Koch" and his wife "Ilse Koch." By the way, the English translation for her name is Cunt Cunt for anyone who doesn't speak German. What kind of people could have a little pillow talk before going to bed, a quick kiss, lean over and turn off the light covered by a lampshade made of human skin?

Read Sylvia Plath's 1965 poem, "Lady Lazarus," and her description of her skin as "Bright as a Nazi lampshade." Read about the sale of a Holocaust victim's skin (via lampshade) for $28,000 in the *Times of Israel* and in author Mark Jacobson's book, *The Lampshade: A Holocaust Detective Story from Buchenwald to New Orleans*.

While you're at it, search *National Geographic's* "Human Lampshade: A Holocaust Mystery." Oh, and look up "WAR 'WITCHES' — Female Nazi guards tortured and killed thousands, beat naked women to death & 'made lampshades from human skin'" in the *U.S. Sun*.

With all of the inhumane, vile, horrific events you haters just read and endorse, I will still discuss, debate, talk, and try to help any antisemitic group or individuals who will act like gentlemen. However, I will not have a discussion with anyone who won't listen, is closed-minded, or can't grasp reason. For example: if anyone states the Holocaust didn't happen (I consider that small group to be the top of the heap, dumbass), or anyone who wants to justify to me their "rationale" on why it's okay to starve 30 million people.

A lot of you are as brainwashed as those early Germans. The big difference is most of them didn't have a choice. You do.

Chapter 13: A Gallery of Thieves

"The petty thief is imprisoned but the big thief becomes a feudal lord."
~ Zhuangzi

Well, you've just read a litany of brutality against your fellow human beings, the Jews. But Hitler had very personal accomplices in his inner circle, and all of them were thieves. You would think that stealing from the Jews would be anathema. I mean, if the Jews were dirty scum destined for the death chambers, wouldn't their artwork and valuables be equally dirty and undesirable?

So riddle me this. Why did the Nazis steal and steal and steal from the Jews?

Well, when it came to wealth, the Nazis were suddenly less picky. They accumulated bloody fortunes and paid for roughly a third of the entire war by stealing Jewish treasure.

If Hitler and his cronies weren't so fucking greedy, with the amount they stole from Jews alone, they could have paid for their entire war plus Italy's, Britain's, the U.S.'s, and others and had enough money left over to send everyone to Poodle Island in Delaware, where someone could have taught the Nazis how to dress and…

I guess the love of money overwhelmed their sense of indignity and distaste for anything Jewish. Again, these were soulless diabolical maniacs without consciences. The sick, greedy bastards simply looked the other way when pillaging and plundering the "dirty Jews" possessions in a quest to make them their possessions.

Eeny, Meeny, Miny, Moe

There are many themes regarding the Nazis, Hitler, the German Army, etc., and we must first acknowledge that Hitler surrounded himself with the dumbest, weak-minded, ignorant "yes-men" since the Roman Empire. They were probably racist before they joined the party, but once they saw that antisemitism could help their own standing in the Nazi Party, they immediately tried to make various audiobooks of *Mein Kampf*.

But first, here are the "extremely qualified" and "self-made" assholes whom Hitler surrounded himself with and a quick snapshot of their craven, worthless lives before they joined the Nazi Party. I was kind enough to write down all of their "highlights" to impress…ugh, well, maybe, ugh, maybe impress *someone* about their previous governmental and military history.

Hitler wanted these men and entrusted them with all of Germany's government and military. If I had to guess, Hitler was at a male brothel one day and hanging out with Hess, Goebbels, Goering, Himmler, and Heydrich. At some point, he put their names in a hat to decide their roles within the Nazi Party. After the pain in Hitler's ass subsided, he called them back to his office and gave them their positions, one more time. The rest is history.

Here is a quick breakdown of Hitler's highest underlings, the guys you hate groups follow, admire, and look up to. You laugh at their brilliant and witty humor. You admire their tactical achievements in battle. You marvel at how they ran an economy so flawlessly. You're proud and amazed at how secure and safe all German citizens felt. But most importantly, you trusted Hitler's judgment and knew he would never put anyone in prominent roles who couldn't facilitate his vision. You hate groups must be awfully proud of these men and their many "accomplishments."

Including Hitler, how many children born after 1945 do you think are named after any of these fucks? These will be brief synopsis, as I want to puke just typing their names.

Hermann Goering

World War I, Pilot. Joined the Nazis in 1922, age 29. Pretty solid pilot in WWI and climbed the ranks to the top of the Nazi hierarchy quickly. He had a lot of responsibilities in the party and was head of multiple ministries in the Nazi government. He eventually became Germany's 16th President and commander of the Luftwaffe. As commander of the Luftwaffe, he did an absolutely horrific, lackluster, and, well, shitty job.

After he got his ass kicked in the "Beer Hall Putsch" in 1923, he was given morphine from an injury he sustained, and it turned into a lifelong addiction. By 1941 he started losing favor with Hitler and others. As the Luftwaffe quickly turned into a useless division, Goering was rarely available as he was always hunting for more art, gold, etc., in the countries they captured that he could loot for Hitler and himself.

Though it did not happen, the only accomplishment he ALMOST had was in late 1945. Before getting in the shower, he looked down and almost, I repeat almost, saw his dick for the first time in 30 years. That, ladies and gentlemen, would have been a legitimate accomplishment for him. Committed suicide.

Joseph Goebbels

As a child, Goebbels had polio which left him with a

deformed foot and one leg two inches shorter than the other. His head was the size of almost two watermelons; his walking style would later form the future basis of "break dancing." World War 1, no service club foot. He earned a Ph.D. in 1921. His thesis was "18th-century romantic drama." He wrote a novel that no one bought. He wrote two plays that no one saw. Became a bank teller and caller on the stock exchange, and was fired in less than a year. Joined the Nazis at age 27 in 1924. Became Germany's Minister of Propaganda. Committed suicide.

Heinrich Himmler

Worked less than a year at a manure processing plant. Age 23. Army—one year, however, did not serve. Himmler saw no action in World War I. He studied agronomy in college and soon thereafter joined the Nazi Party in 1923 and the SS in 1925. From 1929, he grew the SS from a few hundred people to over a million, and eventually, was the German Chief of Police, Minister of the Interior, and head of the Gestapo, and controlled the Waffen SS. I guess to Germans in the 1920s, agronomy must've really been a badass major. A true cock sucker who helped with forming the Einsatzgruppen Unit that we discussed earlier. The good news for Himmler is that this finally gave him a chance to spend more time tickling the taint of Reinhard Heydrich. Their love couldn't be bound by borders, even though Reinhard always insisted that Himmler wear a bag over his head.

He was a coward and would have never been further than a parking maid in any other government in the history of militaries. Committed suicide.

Reinhard Heydrich

Left home at 18 and joined the German Navy. He was an officer who was summarily discharged because he left a senior Navy officer's daughter for some other woman. He was forced to resign at a hearing in front of the "Military Court of Honor." Can you blame him? This new gal was a FANATICAL Nationalist Socialist.

Eventually, Heydrich was introduced to another FANATICAL Nationalist Socialist, Himmler, and let me tell you, it was love at first sight. Once Himmler confirmed that Heydrich kept Hitler's unwashed anal beads in his mouth for 24 hours, Himmler immediately promoted Heydrich to head of the Gestapo. Heydrich was eventually Chief of Security Police, SD, and was the person authorized by the Nazis to plan for the Jewish "final solution."

The cocksucker was killed by a couple of Jews who threw a bomb in his car. Didn't die initially, but a few days later expired from an infection caused by the blast. Would have preferred suicide.

Rudolf Hess

This demon served four years in the military before joining the Nazis in 1920 at the age of 26. He's the guy that had to listen to Hitler shouting and spitting every day while jotting down and dictating *Mein Kampf.* In his memoirs, it seemed like he really enjoyed jerking Hitler off and watching Hitler fist him. (Relax, people, they used mirrors so Hess could see.) Hess was an idiot. He had some clout initially within the Nazi ranks, but it was tough for him long-term to hide his "idiotness." In 1941, he flew a plane to Scotland to try and negotiate a peace treaty with Great Britain while telling no one in Germany.

Now you see why I had to come up with the word

idiotness. I mean, what else can I say about this dolt. He really just did nothing of note outside of typing or dictating Mein Crap and had a high position within the Nazi ranks because of his early relationship with Hitler. Fun Fact. Hess was not given the death penalty at the Nuremberg Trials and passed away in a prison where he was the only prisoner for his last 20-plus years. Committed suicide.

Hi, My Name is Gullible. Can You Tell Me Who to Support?

Including Hitler, ya got five suicides and one murder. These are from the top guys, your guys, the heads of the party, the heads of government, and the heads of the military. What, and I mean WHAT, could possibly motivate a person on this planet to emulate them? Here's a piece of advice — if you really want to mimic any of those douchebags, I suggest you don't run for any office positions at your local hate group unless your life insurance policy is current. Five top Nazi officials killed themselves. Has that happened anywhere at any time?

These assholes accomplished not one positive outcome for Germany, ZERO. NOTHING. Nothing but death, destruction, lies, and thievery. Why the fuck would anyone look up to any of these clowns? They did nothing, they were nothing, they accomplished nothing, yet, for a brief moment in time, they somehow found the ability to destroy tens upon tens of millions of people's lives and, surprisingly, find an "audience" somewhere, ever since.

Those guys weren't great. They're not heroes. They were a bunch of psychotic, extremely insecure geeks led by a schizophrenic sociopath. No one ever woke up and said, "I can't wait to play or hang out with Himmler, Goebbels, Goering, Hitler, Hess, etc."

Yet, they were able to climb to the pinnacle of German

politics. Once there, they became untouchable and could rubber stamp with a smile, a way to systematically kill an entire race. A race that was .0075% of the entire country's population, yet they somehow convinced an entire country to believe they were 99% of the problem. I guess THAT was their "gift."

These cocksuckers are obviously STILL fooling people. Anyone who believes one sentence in *Mein Kampf* is a fucking idiot. Anyone who agrees with any laws they passed is fucking stupid. And anyone, and I mean anyone who doesn't think that Hitler was anything but a failure in life, who became a narcissist, self-indulgent, drug addicted, multi, multi, multibillionaire on the backs of his rhetoric and timing, is simply a willful, ignorant, no esteemed failure too.

Would you want those guys running our government in the United States? They couldn't run a fucking PTA meeting, yet they somehow managed to place themselves in a position to kick people out of their homes, steal their possessions, steal their businesses, rape, torture, and murder them, and when it was their turn to bolster and brag to the world all of their "accomplishments," they chose the coward way out by killing themselves. Shocking.

Pay attention. Here is how sarcasm or propaganda can be used in one paragraph. These brilliant world-traveled statesmen, thankfully, were all able to come together to form this beautiful ideology under one government. Their vast experiences, covering a multitude of governmental necessities, somehow all came along at the same point to ensure and exceed Germany's need for change. Hitting the Powerball lottery twice would have had better odds than being fortunate enough to have these specific men all available at one time.

Personally, I wouldn't let them put together a Lego set, let alone a government. But hey, Hitler's wisdom should rise over anyone else's sensibilities, right? They knew little to nothing and had no experience, yet somehow worked their way up to run an entire military and government. Soon they realized that the more power they exerted, the easier it was for them to stay in power. In most towns, guys like Himmler, Goebbels, and Hess wouldn't be allowed to run a pay phone. With Goering and Hitler's insatiable looting, stealing, and murdering appetites, there was no way they would give up power. They had nothing else, and frankly, they didn't want to take a chance of someone being able to tell them NO.

As for their jaw-dropping acts of thievery, let's start with…

Looting and Hitler's Wealth

Early into Hitler's reign as Chancellor, he received a letter from the tax office in Munich informing him that in 1934 his taxes (*Mein Kampf* sales) was around 10 million dollars (the equivalent of today's value). He knew the need to give back to his beloved Germany as he spoke about it time and time again. Germany still hadn't recovered from WWI and was dealing with its own massive inflation and hyperinflation. The point is that the country needed any and all funds it could get. A few days after he received his tax bill, he ordered the Ministry of Finance to intervene, which resulted in Hitler being declared 100% tax-exempt. The head of Munich's tax office declared all tax obligations by the Führers were annulled from the start. Hitler was now 100% tax-exempt.

And he had the tax office write it down and put on record that he was exempt from paying taxes for life.

Hitler set up a company called "The Adolph Hitler Donation of German Industry." Not kidding. Yes, even ignorant antisemites like you guys know this is a slush fund, and it starts the "pay to play" atmosphere if you want to make deals in Germany.

Apart from killing Jews, the handicapped, and all other minorities, Hitler somehow found the time to implement three of his favorite things in order: personal gain, dictatorship, imperialism, and giving blow jobs. Oh, sorry, that's four. Anyway, Hitler became a billionaire around the age of 41 and a multi, multi, multi, multi, multi-billionaire until his death. "His struggle" …LOL. His struggle was where to hide his vast wealth, and yet you Aryans continue to keep his lies alive.

After Hitler came to power, he focused a lot, personally, on German industry, theft, and looting to achieve his ultimate true goal, simply making Adolph Hitler the wealthiest person in the world (in my opinion). Many suckers find it hard to believe since he ran on a socialist platform. Plus, in all his speeches and throughout *Mein Kampf*, he would never dare lie or mislead anyone (cough, cough). Yes, we know there were a lot of starving civilians and military troops throughout the war he started, but only the ungrateful wouldn't thank him because if it wasn't for Hitler, those soldiers wouldn't have been starving and without weapons in the first place. You're welcome.

Anyway, it's his money, and darn it, he earned it. If you wanted to do business in Germany, he and his cronies made it quite simple and easy — just make the "slush fund" checks out to Hitler or hand over cash in Gucci bags. All told, Hitler stole around 700 million reichsmarks from this "pay to play" arena. A minor pittance compared to his other means of wealth.

For Herr Looter, most of his wealth came from gold, jewelry, art, and currency. I'm talking billions and billions of dollars.

Here's a "laugh out loud" example of Hitler blatantly fucking over his constituents. Sometime in late 1934. the Nazi government bought six million copies of *Mein Kampf*, with all proceeds going to, of course, Hitler himself. This shit just writes itself. Can you imagine forcing the government to buy (I would assume at top dollar) six million copies of *Mein Shit*? C'mon, everyone can laugh at that.

I've seen Hitler's wealth described as anywhere from $5 billion to $300 billion in terms of late 1930s and 1940s dollars, when you include all of his massive estates, stolen artwork, automobiles, currency, gold, jewelry, etc., etc., etc. All 100% tax-deductible in a "socialist country." Yes, he was monetarily fucking the Germans too. Fortunately for him and to put all of the haters' minds at ease, he plainly didn't give a shit. So don't worry; no harm, no foul. It's just money.

Meanwhile, he continued to send German soldiers out to fight and die, and for what? More land for Hitler (yes), maybe another car (yes), more drugs (yes) — just fill in the blank.

How ironic that he constantly and consistently blames the Jews for all of Germany's financial woes and how they allegedly "controlled" all the finances (they didn't) in Germany, yet he became, by far, the worst pilfering leader in Germany and quite possibly, world history.

Did he EVER do anything that he claimed he was going to do? How can you people be so fucking gullible and blind?

Here's one you'll enjoy, and it sums up Hitler's concerns for Germany. Hitler licensed his face/likeness to the Nazi government. That's right — if his face or likeness was on anything for the government, he received a royalty…LOL. Now that is one of the most impressive narcissistic moves of all time. Every time Hitler stood up in front of his car during parades, he got paid.

"Hitler, would you mind giving the Nazi government some of that money, as your pictures are being forced to be put on public property, everywhere, and the government needs money?"

"No."

"Okay, thanks."

How much did he need? He had plenty of psychotic underlings who specifically catered to his every need. Furthermore, let's say if he wandered by your house and wanted it, poof, now it was his. Or, when he went into town to get his monthly Brazilian wax and mustache trimmed (preferring to use the same razor, of course) and he liked the business, he became the new owner. How about if he happened to walk into a local bakery, grabbed a few loaves of bread, spit on the person behind the counter to whom he was giving his bread order, and then had the person murdered? (He didn't need a reason.) Not a fucking thing you could do.

Yes, all that money he stole, and all those dead bodies he ordered, came from "his struggle." Who would have thought all these years later that there would be groups and organizations trying to keep his "bullshit ideologies" alive, even though it's clear he was a money-grubbing, sociopathic, narcissistic, insane, drug-addicted thief.

Art, Property, Valuables

Germany had organized looting throughout the country and wherever it reached in Europe. The plundering was carried out from 1933, beginning with the seizure of property of German Jews, until the end of World War II, particularly by military units known as the Kunstschutz, Einsatzgruppen, etc., although most of the plundering was acquired during the war.

In addition to gold, silver, and currency, cultural items of great significance were stolen, including paintings, ceramics, books, and religious treasures. I think we're almost at the millionth reason how full of shit Hitler and his butt buddies were. These douchebags thought so little of Jews, their customs, etc., so why did they feel the need to steal their belongings? Why would a German want a piece of artwork owned by a Jew? Wouldn't they find that reprehensible? How could a fine, upstanding Aryan woman want jewelry previously around the neck of a Jew? I don't get it. Didn't they read *Mein Kampf*?

Where do you start when trying to explain the largest looting achievement of all time? Let's start with property. Why didn't the Nazis blow up all the property and rebuild if the property was previously owned by a Jew? How could the Nazis possibly live in a place that a Jew formerly lived in? Where were the commitments from all these Nazis? The "master race" dimwits living in a former Jewish home or an apartment; how could that be? Stealing their jewelry and valuables, any and all currency, clothes, etc. Isn't it against everything the Nazis were teaching?

The Nazis, all of them, systematically trying to kill every Jew in Europe and the Soviet Union, were at the same time stealing all their property, art, artifacts, cash, coins, and so on without any justification in the theoretical mentality of how a Nazi is supposed to act as it relates to Jews.

The simple and obvious reason for their looting and not caring about items previously owned by Jews is that they were all full of shit liars. Hitler couldn't have been clearer on his thoughts about Jews and his attitude towards them, yet, when it came to valuables, he instructed concentration camps to pull out fucking gold teeth. Say it; it's okay — Hitler and the Nazis were all FULL OF SHIT.

These acts of thievery became the quickest way for him to become the wealthiest person in the world and the easiest way to fund the war. He had it down to an "art" form.

Not that Hitler or the Nazis gave a shit, but what about the massive amount of property that the few survivors had to come back to and find that their property was no longer theirs? Or a much larger number of Jews who owned property and never came back at all? Have all those families been compensated? How about all the cash and valuables that were stolen? We're talking hundreds and hundreds of billions of dollars stolen.

Hitler and Goering were by far the biggest thieves not only in World War II but in modern times and possibly of all time. Hitler will go down (sorry has gone down) as the biggest art, artifacts, sculptures, property, land, etc. thief in the history of the world. In my opinion, his thievery throughout WWII and the dollar value associated with it will last 1,000 years, or 988 more years than his Reich. Congrats?

Simply astonishing how much he and Goering stole.

Obviously, there were times in history when countries conquered lands and territories, such as Napoleon, Alexander, and Genghis Khan, while also accumulating incalculable amounts of money. But it wasn't under the bullshit guise that it was being done for the destruction of a specific race or this Volkisch, Weltanschauung, Lebensraum crap.

I certainly won't list all the art, artifacts, valuables, books, cash, property, etc., etc., etc., etc., etc., etc., etc., as that would take years, but I would guess in today's dollars, it would be a trillion dollars-plus that the Nazis stole. Currently, there's no consensus, and there will never be an accurate number, as there was no way they could have archived everything that was stolen, plus all the "off the books" theft. Again, it's quite tiring hearing the constant blaming of all the ills caused by the Jews…until Hitler wanted and needed their valuables.

Imagine if you were a soldier and your unit was in a battle with injuries and death all around, and you later find out it was all to capture and take a museum so Hitler and Goering could steal whatever was inside. I wonder if those soldiers felt contempt or if they were brainwashed enough to justify their actions.

Here are a few countries that were looted and have somewhat verified dollar amounts accounted for, but certainly not all. I'm not going to list all the countries, but those mentioned should give you an idea of the true definition of looting. This listing will also mention a few individuals who were the ringleaders of this outrageous amount of thievery.

Poland

According to the Polish Ministry of Foreign Affairs and the *Recovery of Cultural Goods*: "Thousands of art objects were looted, as the Nazis systematically carried out a plan of looting prepared even before the start of hostilities. Many facilities and 25 museums were destroyed." Let's continue. The *Gazeta Wyborcza* reported: "The total cost of German Nazi theft and destruction of Polish art is estimated at $20 billion, or an estimated 43% of Polish cultural heritage; over 516,000 individual art pieces were looted, including 2,800 paintings by European painters; 11,000 paintings by Polish painters, 1,400 sculptors, sculptures, 75,000 manuscripts; 25,000 maps; 90,000 books, including over 20,000 printed before 1800; and hundreds of thousands of other items of artistic and historical value."

The Polish Ministry of Foreign Affairs continued, "Germany still has quite a bit of Polish items looted during World War II. For decades there have been negotiations between Poland and Germany concerning the return of the looted Polish property."

Not that you haters give a shit, and obviously Hitler never did, but I wonder how many Germans, Polish military, and Polish civilians were murdered or wounded to capture this art? And again, where did the money go from the selling of this art? Do you think it might have gone to supplying food for people in the concentration camps? POWs? German soldiers on the front lines? German civilians?

According to Gideon Taylor, Director of Operations of the World Jewish Restitution Organization (WJRO): "Before World War II, 3.5 million Jews lived in Poland, making up 10% of the population; in Warsaw, the figure was estimated at about 1/3 of the then 1 million population. More than 90% of them were killed in the Holocaust, and their property was looted by German Nazis or nationalized by the postwar communist government," and "Heirless property taken over by the communist regime that ruled Poland until the end of the Cold War in 1989 had a combined value at $30 billion, according to the expert's commission by the Israeli government 14 years ago. They estimated that there were about 170,000 private properties held in Poland wrongfully seized from Jewish victims of the Holocaust and eventually nationalized by the communist government."

The estimates I've seen in Poland range from $30 billion to $300 billion. When you see a range like that, it reinforces that no one really knows the true vastness of the thievery. Regardless, it's a shit load of property STOLEN from the Jews.

Obviously, we will never know how much wealth was stolen from the Jews in total. How do you evaluate stolen property a year, ten years, or half a century later and put a value on it? There were probably some very low-priced communities back in the '30s and '40s that now could be the highest priced in the city and vice-versa.

This also includes gold, currency, art, etc., in the sense that so much of these were stolen by soldiers and civilians that still aren't accounted for.

The Germans, finally, did an internal study over three+ years, and here are their findings. Hans-Peter Ullman, a Cologne University Professor, states, "German Chancellors

Hitler's Nazi party actively worked to destroy Europe's Jews financially and financed 30% of the entire German war with their robbed money, according to researchers. "According to the daily mail, Nazi officials robbed 120 billion Reichmarks, over 12 billion pounds (today's U.S. dollar value $638,554,445,445) by looting and through confiscation laws," and "The figure has been revealed in a study by the German finance ministry to uncover its crimes while the Nazis were in power from 1933 to 1945."

Again, I want to highlight that this study was done by the German Finance Ministry. They would have more access than any individual or group to review and evaluate actual paperwork of all the studies that have been done.

According to Christine Kuller of Munich University, "Tax laws discriminated against Jews from 1934, while some who managed to leave Germany before the Holocaust had much of their wealth seized through an exit tax," and "Tax offices built hierarchies of bureaucrats who discovered dwellings and bank accounts and emptied them," and "Nazi officials seized and sold the property of Jews who left or were sent to extermination camps, both in Germany and in nations conquered during the second world war."

All that money, all that stolen wealth, and what did it get Germany? For all intents and purposes, the war was realistically over in early 1943. As Hitler and his psycho buddies were murdering Jews and other minorities, his actual policies wiped out Germany. For 12 years, Hitler and his merry band of thieves enriched themselves on the backs of unknowing German civilians and soldiers, and yet today, today, there are groups and organizations trying to emulate those selfish Nazi assholes. Why?

Well, it certainly helped pay for Hitler's drugs, Himmler's butt plugs, Goebbels rectum enhancement (his first two surgeries, they just couldn't get it small enough), Goering's knee pads, and just enough left over to extend the war long enough and ensure the Germans who elected him would get nothing.

The German citizens got 12 years of propaganda, terror, lies, and death. Too much death and too many lies. Hitler eliminated most of the Jews in Europe, and, unfortunately, there are ignorant Europeans trying to further Nazi lies still today.

It's important to note that this book applies to every hate group on the planet. I can't believe I have to state that, but if I knew the word "moron," "idiot," or "stupid" in every language, I'd type it out. This book is for anyone, anywhere, who tries to emulate anything about Hitler and Nazi ideologies, philosophies, propaganda, shitty mustaches, etcetera, if they act on it or not.

Also, regarding hate groups, I include anyone who is; antisemitic, racist, homophobic, religious, ethnic, disabled, etc., etc., etc.

Jews, in all the countries worldwide, have done nothing but enhance and advance the arts, politics, education, culture, economics, and overall, just great neighbors and citizens, no matter where we are.

Europe, as a continent, is not nearly as strong without the proud, long-lasting, vibrant Jewish communities that occupied every country there.

And you know what?

As more people really understand who Hitler truly was, we start associating him with you — those who participate in the hate. Why should we differentiate any hate group member from Hitler, the Nazi Party, and their actions? Their policies were all 100% about themselves, so by being in any of these groups, we already know your stance.

I just refuse to believe that you would want to bring your children up in a society without freedom and friends, as dictatorships always reward those who turn others in.

You hate groups one day may face a situation where your belongings are taken from you. Poof, gone. It may happen for no reason, just one day "out of the blue," gone. Gone, and you can't get any of it back. Do you advocate that or just when it happens to someone else?

Utterly disgusting, reprehensible, and more. How could you possibly support medical experiments on children? Being gassed in vans? Burning alive thousands upon thousands? Gas chambers, bullets, I could go on and on. My gosh, it's sickening, you're sickening.

Do you hate groups want to know the definition of real toughness? Then study those who made it out of those camps and lived their lives. Those are people you should admire and respect, and none of those great people ever did anything to you, your family, your parents, or your grandparents…NOTHING.

Germany

A few art dealers were commissioned by Hitler and Goering to sell roughly 16,000 paintings and sculptures from German museums from 1937 through 1938. Why, you ask, did they do this, and why wouldn't they just burn the art? I could go on a long diatribe about this question, but the answer doesn't require an explanation, as it's simply Hitler's ego and greed for money — a greed that caused the death of tens of millions for his personal gain. That's it. There's nothing "hiding behind door number 2."

Well, maybe that art wasn't burned so it could generate revenue for Germany's war effort… LOL. Yeah, right. Anyway, in late 1940, Goering, who, in fact, controlled the ERR (a Nazi Party organization dedicated to appropriating cultural property during World War 11), issued an order that effectively changed the mission of the ERR, mandating it to seize Jewish art collections and other objects.

According to Jonathan Petropoulos, author of *Art As Politics in the Third Reich,* Goering also commanded that the loot would first be divided between Hitler and himself. Hitler later ordered that all confiscated works of art were to be made directly available to him." Really, what took him so long?

Wait, what? So, the ERR was in charge of stealing, I mean looting, no, I mean repossessing of art, sculptures, etc., from Germany, France, Netherlands, Belgium, Poland, Lithuania, Latvia, Estonia, Greece, Italy, and some territories of the Soviet Union. Hitler, who was by now a billionaire on his way to becoming a multi-billionaire, dictated first where all of the valuable art was sent. And by sent, I mean sending the art to his palatial estates, tunnels, and underground storages.

Yeah, Hitler was all about "spreading his ideology," his backward ass ideology that intentionally enriched himself at the loss of his soldiers and civilians, who desperately needed food and equipment. Where do we sign up? What a sick psychotic dictator, but don't fret, he was quickly, and I mean really quickly, moving up the "wealthiest person in the world" list, which seems to be the only thing he could "hang his hat on." Also, and I don't expect you to give away any secrets, but which libraries and art galleries do you guys have your eyes on?

I'm sure most of Germany's soldiers and their relatives were comforted knowing how much money Hitler, Goering, Goebbels, etc., were profiting off spilled blood. Anyway, it was wartime, so how much time could Hitler and his henchmen spend on picking out art?

Petropoulos continued, "From the end of 1940 to the end of 1942, Goering traveled 20 times to Paris. (Paris was the first operating unit that acted like a hub for art from Western France, Belgium, and the Netherlands.)" Over that time,

Goering picked out 594 pieces for himself. Who knows how much Hitler received, thousands at a minimum? The rest were given to other subordinates.

In German-occupied countries, the ERR seized 21,903 art objects. Again, Goering traveled 20 times, 20 fucking times, in the middle of a war where he was head of all command of the Luftwaffe, to go steal art. It was bad enough the ass-kicking the Luftwaffe took throughout the war, and yet he was still out trying to collect stolen art. Another Nazi hero.

Russia

Where does one begin on the theft of Russian treasures? As of 2008, lost artworks of 14 museums, as well as bodies of the Russian State Archives and CPSV Archives, were cataloged in 15 volumes, all of which were made available online. They contain detailed information on 1,148,908 items of lost artworks.

The total number of lost items is unknown, so far, because cataloging work is ongoing for other damage to Russian museums. To summarize, I just picked out a few countries. Here are a bit more stolen items from Belgium and France. In artwork alone, France had over 100,000 pieces stolen by the Nazis. I don't think I can express enough about the overwhelming and outright theft from the Germans in WWII.

It just amazes me how much they stole in such a short period. These assholes would just walk into a museum or library with men ready to load empty trucks and proceeded to steal as much as they could. According to the *Jerusalem Post*, "Between August 1940 through February 1943, Nazi forces looted some 150 libraries across Belgium, stealing an estimated 250,000 to 300,000 books." I'm sure there was a heavily attended book-burning ceremony in Belgium that the Nazis put on, right? Nah, I'm sure those books were to be used in high schools and colleges throughout Germany, right?

During Germany's occupation of Belgium, Belgium was forced to pay nearly 2/3 of its national income equaling $5.7 billion. This, of course, was justified by Germany as they said it was a tax to pay for Germany's military occupation.

I'm sure there are a lot of you hate groups who've said, "Big deal, they're only paintings or miniature sculptures, etc." It's understandable when you've grown up thinking the greatest art you've seen is when taking a Rorschach test, but art has true value, both a market value and intrinsic value, for those who have kept certain art or any art in their families for years.

Now, this is just from eastern Europe alone, but according to R.L. Hadden, "The ERR are and of course the Wehrmacht visited (stole from) 375 archival institutions, 402 museums, 531 institutes and 957 libraries." Who knew Germans were so fond of the arts?

I've done a lot of research on this topic, and I haven't really found too many specifics from German-controlled countries regarding property theft. The number of stolen apartments, homes, and businesses is such a large number, but unfortunately, most of the cities and towns where all this thievery went on will not post their findings.

Can you imagine, right now, going into your dwelling and finding a couple of cops at your front door telling you that you have 20 minutes to collect your belongings, but adding, "Anything of value must stay?" From there, you go to the business you've built and find the locks have been changed, while you're watching through a window and seeing a few guys signing over your patents.

Or maybe, you're walking over to a family member's house for shelter. You take a few more steps and realize you're staring at one another as their house is now gone too.

That's how fast it was to lose everything. Eventually, though, you are rounded up and put in a ghetto where on average, a one-bedroom apartment needs to sleep 60. Again, what would your reaction be? Millions of Jews and a lot of non-Jews experienced this horror.

This didn't happen a thousand years ago; this was less than 100 years ago in a sophisticated country.

In the United States, our residences are our sanctuaries. We rest in our homes, we raise children, we laugh, we cry, and we have a tremendous number of laws to protect our dwellings. A home, condo, apartment, RV, boat, etc., gives us all something very special — comfort, security, and ownership. Look at our laws in the United States. My gosh, if someone tries to break in, vandalize, or commit arson, we can do virtually anything to repel them. If somebody breaks into our house in this country, and we shoot a bazooka at them, most of the time, a cop will just tell you, "Nice shot."

I don't know much about the laws in other countries regarding breaking and entering, but in this country, over 393 million guns are owned by citizens and a lot of laws to back those gun rights up. We can be and should be prepared for any encounter to repel any invader, legally.

Back to Germany. Say you've packed a suitcase of clothes and maybe a trinket, or a picture or two. Maybe you're married, and now you need to worry about your wife, of course, and a couple of kids. Are you starting to get the picture of what an absolute fucking nightmare scenario this was? Now imagine this happening to thousands of families and individuals at the same time.

According to Shannon Fogg, Professor of History at Missouri University of Science and Technology, "From 1942 to 1944, German occupation forces in France sealed off and systematically looted at least 38,000 "abandoned apartments" in Paris that were owned by Jews who had been forced to flee, or who had been deported to Nazi concentration camps."

What's that? Roughly 160,000 people were forced out, in ONLY one city. Just to put this in context of the thievery itself and before the 1942-1944 displacement of Jews, Fogg states, "Alfred Rosenberg, the mastermind of "Operation Furniture" (that's not a typo) wrote a letter to Hitler asking permission to strip uninhabited Jewish homes in Western Europe of their furnishings and personal effects."

Talk about a wasted letter. I mean, was Hitler going to say no…LOL. By now, Hitler was the founder and CEO of the Nazi Germany Ponzi scheme. By the way, some of Hitler's underlings and subordinates were getting a little frustrated because they felt they were only getting to choose from leftovers. (That's because it's true.) Now, they would never tell him that directly. However, Himmler kept bugging Hitler to allow him to suck Rosenberg's dick because of this certain duvet cover he knew Rosenberg would come across while in France. Anyway, Hitler said no, but Himmler asked him if it would still be okay if he could "blow" him without the duvet. The answer was "absolutely," and last I heard, that duvet looked gorgeous hanging in one of Hitler's chalets.

I do want to point out, regarding Rosenberg asking for "permission to strip uninhabited Jewish homes," this is officially the first joke I've heard from any Nazi Party member since I started writing this. Finally.

Anyway, Fogg wrote a substantive account of this grand theft, estimating the operation required 27,000 freight cars. Let me repeat that — 27,000 freight cars — and this was from 25,000 homes and apartments.

"The Germans literally took everything they found inside the apartments and homes," says Fogg. "Furniture, bedding, family photos, knickknacks, personal papers, rugs, light fixtures, and kitchen sinks."

Also, tricycles for Goebbels, used condoms for Himmler, stretch pants and nylon stockings for Goering, and money, gold, jewelry, and art for Hitler.

By mid-to-late 1942 and until they found Hitler's body smoldering like a flammable grease fire, you hate group members cared more about Nazis than Hitler did. However and during the same time, he definitely cared more about Hitler than you ever would.

Chapter 14: Holocaust Deniers and Hate Groups

"Terrorism is the best political weapon for nothing drives people harder than a fear of sudden death."
~ *Adolf Hitler*

So, you've gotten this far in the book. Hopefully, you are questioning your allegiance to a mass-murdering, drug-addled, thieving, lying mental case. If not, there's a good chance you may be psychopathic.

One topic that I rarely discuss or debate is the reality of the Holocaust. Why? By debating it with some idiot, other idiots might consider I'm defending it. Let's look at who didn't defend it at the time when the Jews were liberated from the camps.

How about everyone who was put on trial in Germany? How many of them said it never happened? How about every Allied soldier who liberated the camps, soldiers from multiple countries who saw first-hand accounts of the aftermaths? What about the large amounts of non-Jewish minorities that were in these camps together, who vouch for the massive murders of Jews and others? Lies right? 55,000 former Nazi guards, can you tell us how many of them said, "Nothing to see here?" The only thing former Nazi guards have said, and all 55,000 have said it, was simply, "We were ordered to do it." Give us some names that said it didn't happen, and stop trying to spin your perpetual wheels of ignorance and lies.

The problem for deniers is they can't find any of these people who were actually there denying it. Why would I debate with some racist who feels he (or she) "uncovered" the truth over hundreds of thousands of eyewitnesses?

I've been to Germany. You still can't bring up the Holocaust. The Germans still feel embarrassed and ashamed. They don't deny it. It's taught in their schools; the country has dedicated memorials and has paid billions and billions in reparations. Ya know, the place where it happened. However, you clowns have somehow concluded it was all a ruse and that it never happened.

You would have to be logically prejudiced or willfully ignorant to believe that the Holocaust never happened; hence, why I don't defend the argument. There is none.

After witnessing a concentration camp firsthand, Dwight D. Eisenhower immediately ordered all camps to be filmed "Lest someone ever deny what took place here." In most cities and villages where these camps were located, the citizens were rounded up and given a tour. Please read some of the literature or see their reactions from the camps they visited and point out the ones who said it didn't exist. Was Eisenhower in on this hoax? Were the soldiers who liberated these camps from various countries bamboozled into witnessing these staged events too?

Also, why deny it? Wouldn't the Holocaust be your crowning jewel of achievement? Shouldn't you be the biggest cheerleaders of the Holocaust and how it was pulled off? The greatest mass murder in history was done by your heroes, and some of you morons want to deny it. Why? Try visiting a Holocaust Museum. Read a bit of history. Watch a documentary.

As mentioned earlier, no one in Germany, including the

military, guards, civilians, and the government, denied the Holocaust happened. All the soldiers from the various countries who liberated concentration camps have never denied it. Again, Eisenhower was so pissed that he wanted documentation IMMEDIATELY so the world could see, on film, the unspeakable horrors. I'm extremely confident that Eisenhower NEVER expected that one day U.S. citizens would idolize Nazis in this country. Like, EVER.

At all the trials for Nazi war criminals, can you point out which individuals denied that the Holocaust ever happened? All the documentation of the deaths done individually at each camp was plainly written down by German guards. All the bodies dug up outside the crematoriums. All the footage, all the testimonies from survivors to liberators. No one has denied this except some really fucking stupid morons saying, "It never happened."

What proof, legitimate proof, do any of you "deniers" have that proves the Holocaust never happened? How about if I said, "I declare World War I never happened. I mean, I wasn't there, and I didn't know anyone who fought in World War I, so it couldn't have happened."

World War II. That was definitely a made-up war, started and filmed by Jews because they wanted their own country. Never happened.

See where I'm going here?

I've heard idiots talk about the Holocaust being filmed in Hollywood. If that's true, simply provide us some names of any of the directors of these films, actors, producers, and locations. Fun fact, "Yeah, we filmed a lot of those scenes in Hollywood." In order to ensure authenticity, we asked millions and millions of people to not eat for a couple of months."

By your esteemed logic, here are a couple more wars that didn't happen.

It Didn't Happen

Let's start with the Civil War. I, again, don't know anyone who was in the Civil War. Furthermore, I have searched and searched and cannot find anyone, anywhere, who was in any of the battles or can show me a picture or video with them in it. So, the Civil War never happened. Prove me wrong.

Vietnam War. Give me a break. The Jews filmed this "classic" war over two weeks in Napa Valley. It has taken a while for the Jews to gain some type of sympathy, so we rounded up a few thousand helicopters with New Age cinematography and were able to rent some tanks, bazookas, and planes. We added some fantastic editing and "Here you go." I wasn't in Vietnam, so it never happened.

Also, during filming, we received a lot of help from Santa Claus and Tinkerbell. They assisted in pre and postproduction. We were very fortunate to get the guy behind the curtain from The Wizard of Oz. He was fantastic.

Also, I wasn't at the birth of any of my friends. Guess what? They weren't born.

I mean, really, how can any of us confirm anything if we weren't there?

Look, honestly, at all those insane medical experiments done to children and adults alike, the yanking of teeth, the flaying of victims. If you are still sticking with "This is all made up," then you are a dangerous neo-Nazi. And by dangerous, I mean you're a fucking moron (which is dangerous).

I don't understand you cowards denying the Holocaust. Saying it didn't happen is like Hitler denying Rudolph Hess was a bad fluffer.

See No Evil, Hear No Evil

Here is another piece of information that Holocaust

deniers or any other hate group can attempt to deny.

Friedrich Kellner was a soldier for Germany in WWI who hated and opposed Hitler and the Nazis. While working as a justice inspector at a small courthouse, he wrote a diary to record his observations of the Nazi regime. Based on conversations, reading of newspapers, discussions with soldiers, etc., he described the various crimes of that regime. His diary is titled "Mein Widerstand," meaning "My Opposition." Kellner's diary is 861 pages with 676 individually dated entries.

According to David Casstevens of the *Fort Worth Star-Telegram*, "Kellner started writing his secret diary the day Germany invaded Poland to start WWII. He wanted the coming generations to know how easily young democracies could turn into dictatorships and how people were too willing to believe propaganda rather than resist tyranny and terrorism."

In Kellner's now famous diaries, he rarely wrote about his own personal situation, but rather Nazi policies, propaganda, the war, injustices in the court system, inhumane deeds, and the genocidal intentions of the Nazis. In all of this, he considered the German people as accomplices before and after the fact: first voting Hitler into power, and then acquiescing in his abuse of that power. Most Germans after the war would insist they knew nothing at all about the State-sponsored genocide of the Jews, yet very early in the war, Kellner recorded this in his diary, showing that word of atrocities reached the average citizens even in the small towns:

"A soldier on vacation here said he was an eyewitness to terrible atrocities in the occupied parts of Poland. He watched as naked Jewish men and women were placed in front of a long deep trench and, upon the order of the SS, were shot by Ukrainians in the back of their heads, and they fell into the ditch. Then the ditch was filled with dirt even as he could hear screams coming from people still alive in the ditch."

Kellner continues, "These inhumane atrocities were so terrible that some of the Ukrainians, who were used as tools, suffered nervous breakdowns. All the soldiers who had knowledge of these bestial actions of these Nazi sub-humans were of the opinion that the German people should be shaking in their shoes because of the coming retribution," and "There is no punishment that would be hard enough to be applied to these Nazi beasts. Of course, when the retribution comes, the innocent will have to suffer along with them. But because ninety-nine percent of the German population is guilty, directly or indirectly, for the present situation, we can only say that those who travel together will hang together."

Hate Groups

We live in a free country. I don't give a shit or not about your affection for Hitler and the Nazis; I really don't. As I've mentioned previously, as long as your meetings or rallies go no further than the laws that govern this country, knock yourselves out. If you want to hold weekly rallies, have a good time. If you attend daily *Mein Kampf* classes, enjoy. I do not care. Again, if it's legal, you should be able to flaunt your deep admiration for that sociopath wherever it's permitted. Just do it legally, meaning don't terrorize your fellow Americans, whatever their religion, creed, or culture.

Let's examine the qualifications for belonging to an "I Love Hitler" group. I assume you remember that he was only accepting purebloods? After all, he said, "The folkish philosophy of life must succeed in bringing about that nobler age in which men no longer are concerned with breeding dogs, horses, and cats, but in elevating man himself." Yes,

Hitler bred humans for perfection. Purebloods, so to speak. The pure Aryan race Is Not You.

How about we play a different game called "Spin the Genealogy Bottle."

How many of you racists had pure Aryan blood relatives who fought in the Civil War? I'll take a guess ... maybe ten percent, if that? You idiots should do a search on an Ancestry website and then build a tree all the way back to your 10X great-grandfathers and great-grandmothers. I bet your lineage ranges from less to much less than it does to being close to "pure." Somewhere, the DNA of one of Hitler's "foes" probably ended up in your family tree. If you are somehow connected to a homosexual, Jew, Jehovah's Witness, Black, Pole, Russian, Romani, or anyone with a disability ... guess what? You're disqualified. In Hitler's eyes, you are nothing but a mutt. You ain't pure. Hitler wouldn't have wanted to have anything to do with you and most likely categorized you in some area to work in a labor camp or murdered. And for the hundredth time, you are already disqualified because you live in the United States. Any name, face, or likeness cannot be used outside of Germany. If any German-based antisemitic, racist, homophobic, Nazi chapters wanted to sue your asses, they would have a very legitimate case.

There were 8,000 Jews who fought in the American Civil War and 225,000 American Jews who fought in WWI (the true pureblood). How many of your pure Aryan blood relatives fought in WWI? Hmm? Even less. Think about your "unworthiness" to be a Hitler acolyte. If he were alive, best case, you'd be somewhere making boots or canteens 18 hours a day and maybe given 300 calories of food before bedtime without heat. Oh, and don't worry, when you're dead in about three months, they'll have someone to replace you.

In fact, Jews settled in New Amsterdam on August 27, 1654, and quickly started setting up a synagogue, trading, and establishing property rights and the right to be a defense protector of the city. Jews have been servicing the military in this country for 350 years. That's 350 years, way before any of your recessive DNA genes were anywhere near our great country. If you truly want to show us your "Aryan" lineage, I suggest you take a test from an accredited DNA company and post the results online. I'm talking blind posting, meaning you'll post the results in real time on our Never Means NEVER Again website, and we can all view them together. I don't think most of you have the balls to do it, and furthermore, what's your game plan when you see that you're not a pureblood?

We live in a time when we don't need to leave our couches to verify information. This really fuels my frustration and anger because anyone can simply check to see if something is accurate, instantly, from a handheld device. We can research what shaped Judaism itself. We can take deep dives into events that highlight a plethora of dangerous lies and flat-out deceptions, myths, and misconceptions. If you've done any research and are still antisemitic, then I will add "excuse maker" and "lost cause" to your name.

When an entire people (like the Jews) have been falsely accused of something, anything, it falls to us to get the truth out. Let's explore how and why some are susceptible to misinformation. Most of it revolves around whom we trust.

When we're angry at a friend or family member, we, as human beings, respond in typical ways. Normally, it's an emotional response. We talk to that person and share our perspective, and they either accept it or they don't. Most of the time, by a large margin, we work it out, and we move on. Soon it's back to laughter and hanging out, and the original anger is forgotten. That's it.

There is almost always reconciliation with our influencers. These are the trusted people and organizations who help "mold" us throughout the years into becoming who we are. They "shape" the community around us. This applies to everyone regardless of their background, religious beliefs, education, relationships, and on and on and on.

Until it's broken up. When the trusted become untrustworthy or let down those who looked up to them, then it becomes a mad scramble for new leadership.

This is one of my analogies for why we have hate groups. Hitler himself, as I explained in a chapter above, fell for a hate group, then became its leader. Below I discuss how an insidious movement grew because the German people were so fucking desperate and ripe for a takeover. Therefore, a new influencer — Hitler — was perceived as a "savior" who promised to rescue them from their woes, but initially kept all the details to "how" he planned to do it. Of course, there had to be a villain for this narrative to work. The Jews were blamed. They still are today.

For all of you forward-thinking Phi Beta Kappas, there are very few totalitarian dictatorships in the world. All these brilliant dictators that you strive to emulate and want to bring to the U.S. because you are so enlightened and "misunderstood." I'm going to try and outline dictatorships as I don't think most of you understand what happens to us, the civilians, in these types of governments.

And make no mistake, Nazi Germany WAS run under a totalitarian dictatorship.

Dictatorships may have worked hundreds or thousands of years ago (I doubt it, but they may have) because, in dictatorships, 99% of all the people are extremely poor and kept poor. Those 99% never see an influx of new cash. With dictators, a lot of that money is used to pay for one thing and assured to always get paid first — their military. Revolutions, of course, can happen, but it makes little difference as they're usually followed up by another dictator. Rinse/Repeat.

Furthermore, dictatorships have no middle class. You're either connected to the top, or you're fucked. So, what outline do you guys have in order to get a dictator to power in this country? Once in power, how do you plan to feed the people, clothe, and oversee commerce and judicial systems, as the United States of America is already well past that? This country is very, very fortunate in many ways. One of, if not the biggest and fairest, way any government can be set up is, We Can Vote. In dictatorships, your main concerns are not to get tortured or starve to death.

What I don't understand is why you don't highlight your governmental plans to the citizens of this country. This is a large and diverse society, so there's got to be at least 50, maybe 60 people in this country who can't wait to vote for your groups. Maybe, 65.

In 2021, the outstanding Southern Poverty Law Center tracked 733 hate groups and 98 White nationalist groups in the United States. Overall, total membership numbers are not that large. However, unfortunately, they are growing.

In the U.S., when thinking about a group most associated with antisemitism and racism, the KKK comes to mind. They are but one of many various factions of hate groups, and currently, their groups have been involved in way too much backdoor "bitch fighting." This has led to a separation and formation of various other hate groups over the years. Also, it looks like a separation was influenced because somebody intentionally stole money.

Ironically, this is something you morons should have absolutely no problem with. Why? If we go by your ideology of Nazi-ism and see how Hitler was compensated and how he compensated himself, that money rightfully belongs to the head person of your organization. Only the head of your party is entitled to that money, just like the Nazi Party. Hitler simply took what Hitler wanted first, then left crumbs for others. Is there any logical reason your groups won't do the same? You want an Aryan ruling class based on Hitler's ideologies, so here you have it.

Initially, I was going to go over various hate groups and list their names, locations, who are in charge of their parties, their beliefs, and what they're trying to accomplish. As I started researching, it became obvious they all had basically the same wants and goals, so there was no need to individually separate them.

Again, the most prevalent group in people's minds is the KKK. I will briefly recap their history, but unfortunately, they are not even close to being the only hate group in this country. Remember, every hate group's platform is, in essence, the same, so feel free to substitute KKK for any group out there that wants to hurt us.

The KKK had things really rolling in the 1920s. They had almost four million members and were actively gaining political seats, which frankly is how it should be done and much more effective than a thousand of their rallies since. Even though they were founded in 1865, they went from being ignorant and racist against people of color and, over time, added Jews and Catholics to their oaths of hatred. Smart move as being just bigoted and racist towards Blacks was too small of a group for their targeted audience, and quickly, very quickly, they roughly quadrupled in size.

These "new and improved" racists fizzled out in the late 1920s and early 1930s, and it took them 30 or so years to find another batch of ignorant bottom-feeders to get a spike in new membership.

Membership went back up in the 60s and 70s, even though there was a lot of infighting, penetration of law enforcement, and members getting tired of wearing those same ugly, boring fucked-up robes and hats. The current KKK is a mere shell of its former self, we will monitor these groups, but with their current size, it will be minimal.

By the way, if you naively believe these dangerous hate groups are loosely organized and should not be taken seriously, you are wrong. There have been hate groups that filed for and received non-profit status. Eventually overturned, nonetheless, a very strong example that these people are lurking in the background of society and active on the internet.

I, Me, My Ramblings

I need to take a deep breath before I "roll out" this next section. Okay. I can't emphasize enough my goal of presenting every individual involved in hate groups with as much information and facts as possible. I don't think they're given the opportunity to read or hear information that refutes lies they deem as facts, and obviously, they aren't doing any research of their own. I hope people who need to read it do, and maybe it will help someone.

With that in mind, let's go over this again. To all of you and the groups I haven't mentioned, what are you trying to accomplish? Can you spell it out in terms any non-racist could understand? The fucking psycho Nazis may have had the strongest military in the world with virtually unlimited support and resources, yet they still ended up getting their asses kicked. Furthermore, they had a three-plus-year "head start" on rearmament, drafting, and training in all of Europe. By the end of the war, Hitler showed his millionth example of not giving a shit about anyone but himself by training German shepherds how to reload a Glock.

My point is, the Nazis had all of that going for them and still failed miserably. What could you possibly do to even get within one trillionth of their "accomplishments?"

In the end, the blueprint to get out of your hero's situation was suicide. I'm interested in knowing your commitment. Would you possibly kill yourself over anything those sociopaths endorsed? Are you a consistent Nazi wannabe, or are there some things you agree with and other issues you don't?

We are done with your antisemitic groups. You will no longer go after our women and children like cowards without recourse. Our elderly, families, friends, and synagogue communities are done. DONE. Why has no antisemitic group on the planet ever flown to Israel and had demonstrations? I mean, think about it. It's guaranteed worldwide television coverage, and from the "get-go," as soon as you arrive in Israel, you will quickly see there are Jews everywhere. Impossible to miss. You and your fellow members will have no need to look through your Commodore computers to find Jews to injure, as they'll be staring back at you as soon as you arrive. Of course, you and your buddies' "shelf life" would be around two minutes. But if you want to show your friends the hero in you, your true love and commitment to the Nazis, Israel is a country that's easy to get to, and hey, you might change some minds.

Also, to save money, avoid scheduling conflicts, etc., you will only have to book a one-way ticket. I'm quite confident that's all you'll need.

All right, please try and clear this up for me one more time. What examples could anyone give in a hate group about a Jew, Black, LGBTQ, handicapped, etc., etc., etc., that is "keeping them down" in the United States of America? Specifics, not theory. So, you Aryans want to continue a legacy of cowardice, weakness, intimidation, chaos, torture, unspeakable acts, etc. Okay, what's your endgame? What do you think life in Germany would be like had they won? You cling to a fallacy, a myth, of a society that most of you would have never excelled in. A society where you and your family would've been owned by the state, and your only thought would be of escape. Jews, Blacks, LBGTQ, and physically and mentally handicapped would not nor did not stop the real issue in Nazi Germany, and that issue was power. Hitler craved it, breathed it, and lived for it. Power, control, intimidation, and money. Lots and lots of money. EVERYTHING else was just noise.

All of you antisemites tarnish the "Greatest Generation." Every American who served in Europe, the Pacific, and Africa fought to maintain our freedom, fought for our allies, and fought so that Japan and every other nation understand: "No one comes into our house and pushes us around." For someone to believe in a totalitarian dictatorship with murder and power as the top agenda is reprehensible. You are a stain on our former soldiers' legacies.

These are not just Jews. These are Italians, Irish, Greek, Mexicans, and on and on and on. Hard workers, tough and fair, we look at Aryans and laugh. You are fortunate to live in the greatest country in the world (outside of Israel) and the wealthiest nation ever put on a map, yet all of you have joined an organization of hate and exclusion. Since Hitler and the Nazis accomplished nothing, it's not ironic that your organizations have zero achievements too. ZERO. Knowing that and 89 years later, there is still not one thing that you can point to as a hate group accomplishment. Yet, for some mysterious reason, you still don't seem to understand why. I'll help you out because 99.99% of the rest of the country isn't sitting around blaming others. Yeah, it's probably lower than 99.99%, but fuck it, I'm rambling.

We're way too busy trying to get ahead on our own. Instead of trying to work yourself out of hard situations, you're always taking the easy way out by blaming others. I'm confident enough to say, the real problem has always been and will continue to be YOU. Your hardships, issues, relationships, work, blame, whatever, when you actually break down all of your issues, you'll quickly see it's simply YOU.

Jews, for whatever reason, are rarely cast aside or thrown out of countries. Nope, we just end up being murdered. Have any of you lost family members to ethnic persecution or judgmental ideologies that some idiots use their own interpretations to define? What about harassment? There have been zero "back and forth" confrontations between hate groups and Jews because we don't do shit in response. That's ending.

You believe in fallacies that can easily be debunked. Your ridiculous statements, like Jews own all the banks, politicians, Hollywood, etc., are but just a few examples, and with a little amount of research, you will quickly find out it's just not true. As a percentage, yes, Jews have done very well in many fields, and there is no way we would ever apologize for that, but what you guys don't seem to be able to comprehend is no one gets a medical license following their own birth. It has to be earned.

We live in a country that has grown and thrived BECAUSE of our immigration policies. Would you like to know why you're getting passed up by minorities in the percentage of the U.S. population? Grab a calculator and let me know when you're ready… okay. It's pretty simple. You and the rest of white America are not having enough kids. If you want to scream about illegal immigration or immigration in this country currently, I agree; it's a fucking mess that needs to get cleaned up immediately. However, I have two words I will give you, which is the quickest and most logical advice to turn this around for you and your groups…more sex.

Why do you think what's in your mind justifies that you

are more American than any Jew, Black person, LGBTQ, Mexican, Iranian, Russian, pick a country, or any other minority IN THIS COUNTRY? You already know that Jews have been here for over 350 years, so saying "being here first" argument is irrelevant. What's your legitimate argument? Do you really, truly believe that immigration is holding you back? Have you ever looked at data that shows how better off the country is, and you individually are, BECAUSE of our legal immigration policies over the last two hundred-plus years?

If you want to blame strife through laws and politicians in a field that is highly, highly dominated by elderly White men and women, then maybe blame them. You all have taught yourself a belief that isn't there, so why stop now? Hitler's decisions were based on what Hitler wanted. Do you think that fuck went into any meetings asking for opinions? How many times from 1933-1945 do you think someone told Hitler "No?" His lackeys were also in a totalitarian dictatorship, and so they, too, ALWAYS said Yes. He never thought about the German people; he only wanted everyone to love and admire him. However, it was the power. Nothing drove him more than power.

Since this is your future, you really need to know. The power and the control of others were all he ever REALLY wanted. You could certainly put money as being near the top of his list, but it was always power first, and he knew in Nazi Germany, with power came easier and quicker ways to obtain a lot of money. Especially if you're on top. So, is it power that you groups are looking for? Because if that's it, good luck and get in line.

I think somewhere in the early 1940s, he actually forgot that he had citizens he needed to govern. *Mein Kampf,* the Enabling Act, murdering millions of civilians, imperialism, and looting — what the fuck did any of that have to do with helping German citizens? Do you think German citizens would have voted for that psycho in 1946? There's no question he fucked Germany too.

In his mind, power would give him the adoration of Germans and Austrians that he always wanted and needed. Initially, all he wanted was for German and Austrian citizens to plainly say, "Hitler did this for us," and "This couldn't have been done without Hitler," etc. For that psycho, that thought lasted in his head for probably a few months in 1933. After that and until he looked like an overcooked s'more, it was ONLY about him.

He didn't care at all about the rest of his staff, advisors, or anybody at some point. When his world-class narcissism took over in the mid-30s, there wasn't a decision made that wasn't all about him. None. I can't imagine what your meetings are like. I assume most of you can't wait for them. Do you guys have healthy debates on what charities to donate all your fundraising efforts to? What hospitals you'll visit next?

How many scientists are in these hate groups? Doctors? Physicists? World travelers? The reality is you guys have nowhere else to go. You need to blame someone for your inadequacies. It's always the Jews. What the fuck has a Jew ever done to you? You say we control banking. Give me a fucking break. What bank, what banks? Or is this just one of those "Rothschild" things?

Give me names. Tell me where all the funds go that suppress you and your family. What Jew-controlled bank has fucked over you and your family? Or the government? If Jews controlled a 100th of what you believe with your ridiculous accusations, you'd have been banned from your meetings, thrown in prison, or at the least fined for wearing swastikas outside of Germany.

I mean, how hard would it be for us to round up some

military guys and tell them we'll pay off their mortgages if they eliminate you from your mom's basement? Again, why don't you come out of the closet (relax, it's just an expression) and back more political candidates? How about you, a family member, a friend get degrees in banking, law, medicine, whatever, to change the system? There's got to be racist scientists out there, so why don't you ask them to come out and speak on your behalf? How about moving your meetings to "Main Street" throughout this nation in order to get more publicity? I just don't understand why you wouldn't want to maximize your exposure and highlight all your "wonderful" ideas and beliefs if that's what you all deeply believe in.

A 1,000-year Reich, yeah, not even fucking close. For Hitler, this was nothing more and nothing less than a one-time power-grab dictatorship. Rule of thumb, when murder, imprisoning, and torturing are a part of a political party, not only do they never last long, but the philosophy usually doesn't bounce around to other countries to be mimicked. Why, you ask? Well, how about totalitarian dictatorships screw their citizens over, crush their own economy, and nine times out of ten, they're dead before, or shortly after leaving office. Yay, when can we start?

I Have Some Questions

All right, I can do all the research I want, but my questions won't truly be answered until I get some questions answered directly from the decision-makers. I'm going to ask some questions and bounce around a bit, and I would like to see where your platforms are currently.

Are you thinking your grassroots "struggle" will somehow, someday, start catching onto the public, or do you plan on taking a different route? Have you picked out locations where you plan to build gulags and internment camps? Any idea yet on dates for disbanding our current government, Supreme Court, and local and state laws? When do you guys plan on releasing your manifestos and doctrines on a national scale? What are your plans for habeas corpus? What are your plans for city, county, state, and federal police? What are your syllabi for the roughly 27,000 high schools in the U.S.? What about the curriculum of the roughly 81,000 middle schools to first grade? Oops, subtract 45% of the high school and middle school numbers out, as they will be deported or worse. Where can we find these answers, or maybe you just haven't addressed those "small" topics yet?

I assume you also want to federalize all those Jewish-owned banks, farming, construction, automotive, medicine, etc. If so, what are your plans for that? What about payroll benefits? I assume these issues and many, many more will all come out, once in office. Will you offer health care or nationalize it?

At least we've seen this play out before in the U.S., which ended September 3, 1783, and that was with a king who wasn't a meth head. Well, I wasn't there, so maybe we defeated a king. Anyway, we, as a country, haven't looked back since.

I hope you're at least going to come out with a variety of new and updated Klan robes. Different colors, maybe holes cut out in the crotch or ass area? Accessories like leather whips and fraternity paddles? I mean, if I'm thinking these things, I assume you guys have already sent them out to various tailors.

Even if Hitler did care a little bit at the beginning about Germany (maybe), the drug-addicted, pornstache douche wouldn't even surrender as his own ashes were polluting Berlin. The fuck was clinically insane. Period. Everyone always looks for reasons, justifications, and excuses regarding Hitler. It's not that difficult, and no one needs to overthink it; he was INSANE. If you truly want to understand Hitler, go get a fucking book dealing with insane people and how they act, read it, acknowledge it, and move on.

Hundreds upon hundreds of thousands of people were decimated and cities leveled in the final few weeks of the war for one reason and one reason only — power. Even then, he just could not relinquish it. You Aryan wannabes whose love for Hitler seems boundless will eventually gain everything Hitler gained... nothing. Still don't believe me? Fine, ask the president of your hate group to list all of the group's accomplishments since its founding. Just hand him a paper straw wrapper and an oversized Sharpie to save time.

Isn't it stupid of you to admire a narcissistic power-hungry coward, who didn't and wouldn't surrender Berlin even as it was being reduced to rubble and the outcome had been decided? C'mon, the fucker was already reduced to kindling and was posthumously asking the Germans to continue to fight. Yep, real folk hero here, ladies and gentlemen. He really gave a shit about Germany and its citizens.

And again, why did he kill himself? He could have gone on trial and espoused all the wonderful, positive examples about Germany under Nazism and let the world hear his great forward-thinking ideologies. Why didn't he do that? He could have received worldwide attention, a "narcissistic orgasm" that he so desperately craved. It would have been televised, radio, print, movie reels, everywhere. Think how many people he could have spread his wisdom and ideology to. Why didn't he? We'll never know, but more importantly, why are you trying to continue his madness that he didn't want to?

Hopefully, by now, you're starting to understand why he didn't. He didn't because he was a sociopathic, murdering, money and power-hungry dictator and, as mentioned, certifiably insane. He took the cowardly way out just like all his fellow "yes-men" ended up doing too. Some by suicide, some by hanging, some by shootings but most by fleeing. Why didn't all those brave believers in Nazism stick around to regroup? Think about it, there have been Nazi groups worldwide since the end of WWII, yet the dickheads who founded, expanded, and were a part of it all hid, denied, and abandoned it five minutes after the war was over. Why?

We know how the U.S., Great Britain, and others let 95% or more of them go free and couldn't be bothered to bring them to trial, so why did they flee?

For all you antisemitic racists, how do you justify your heroes' "bailing," hiding, and denouncing everything you guys currently stand for? Do you offer excuses for their behavior? I mean, these are your guys; the Nazis are your people. Any clarification from each of your groups would suffice. Not many people "run" or denounce things they enjoy or love, so you could help my curiosity on this; thanks in advance.

The last time Goebbels saw Hitler, he told him that he was going to go on the radio and tell the people of Germany that Hitler was going to "die fighting with the troops" until the end. Right before the last of their millions of lies, and even though they would already be dead themselves, your heroes had countless more soldiers and civilians killed, which could have easily been avoided by simply surrendering Germany. Can any of you explain to me why they didn't?

Pathetic and cowardly. When I think of neo-Nazis, White supremacists, etc., that's one of the first things that comes to mind. Can someone, anyone, justify why Hitler and the Nazis allowed German men, women, elderly, children, and babies to die well after Nazi Germany had been defeated?

Well, it seems that during the first go around, this ideology didn't go so well. I mean, it led to the deaths in World War II of around 70 million people. The war basically wiped out all the Jews in Europe. It "petrified" a country full of German people who were so scared of their own neighbors turning them in for virtually any reason, that most of the citizens wouldn't leave the confines of their homes. Plus, they sent their kids off to war for a madman who ended up getting them killed and provided nothing for them anyway. I assume you Aryans already know this and are looking forward to living in these types of conditions. Or maybe, just maybe, you can do it better? Go back to bed; you can't.

Hate Group Q&A

I have covered a lot of articles, books, documentaries, etc., in trying to uncover as many facts as possible, to hopefully educate whoever reads this and to also try and dispel so many lies. I figure if I can show or highlight enough lies, hate group members may finally ask themselves, "What in the fuck am I doing?" and go out and do something productive.

So, I took a poll, and the voices won out. To clarify, no one knows I'm writing this book and who's gonna want to deal with any backlash from this anyway…LOL. So, the voices who wanted this Q&A are the ones in my head, and if you don't like either the questions or answers, bitch at them.

Before I start, I would like to thank myself for all of the great questions and phenomenal answers.

> **Question.** Why did it look like every time Hitler walked by someone, they would give that facial look like they just stepped in dog shit?

> **Answer.** Good question. Since no one is going to believe my answer, I ask you to look it up

when you're done reading. Anyway, it's no secret that Hitler had stomach issues. So, when his doctor was giving him his regular pills and injections, he just simply added a few more pills to help with his stomach.

Well, Rebecca Beamer and William Kennedy "went in deep" for a fascinating article from Grunge Magazine. One of Hitler's many illnesses was colitis and irritable bowel syndrome. Now, you can have various symptoms as a result of this illness; however, Herr FuckFace's symptoms "match with Dr. Schenk's writings on Hitler and would explain the Fuhrer's particularly repugnant reputation (in more ways than one)."

Hitler had chronic flatulence. Or, as they put it more bluntly, he had constant farting. Can you imagine all of his ass-kissing underlings having to deal with the second ugliest person on the planet (Himmler will never relinquish the top spot) constantly spitting on them, and now being constantly farted on too? I'm surprised he didn't get in front of this and have a national fart day to prove he was even the best at that. It also answers the age-old question, Why did Hitler always have a big pile of pig shit in his office? Simply to try and "counteract" his smell. Makes sense. What about all those lovers? My gosh, I hope they received fart medals or something,

Anyway, I could go on for days, but I hope that

answers your question. What a fantastic article written by those two. Have we gone over the Pulitzer Prize section yet?

Question. Was it true that Hitler was full of shit?

Answer. Yes, see question number 1.

Okay, someone mentioned Himmler. Do you have a question?
Yes, I do.

Question. You've mentioned Himmler's physical appearance a few times. Do you have anything besides your opinion to support your contention of his looks?

Answer. I have many, but I'll just use this coveted and respected polling company.

To start the new century and end in 1945, the world held a secret contest on appearance. There was a runoff for second place because such a clear-cut winner of the ugliest fucking person could NOT be topped. The inaugural winner was none other than Heinrich Himmler, a title he would not relinquish for 45 straight years, until he couldn't stand looking at himself anymore, and thankfully for all, he killed himself.

Question. Does it make sense on any level for hate groups to target Jews in this current climate?

Answer. I'm going to give you guys a piece of advice that is extremely unfortunate for me, and I hope "I can take it back" before it's too late. You and your groups are violating laws and morals to get rid of a race, the Jewish race, that's, quite frankly, already doing it for you. If you just wait it out, assimilation might just dissolve our religion in the United States within the next hundred years or less, and you guys will have to do nothing for it to happen. No jail, no probation, no "it's on your record," nada.

Furthermore, Jewish women have the lowest birth rate among all ethnicities in an already very small religion. Unfortunately for you guys, you're going to have to get off your asses and find another group that you feel fucks you over, and you can blame for all your excuses.

Question. Since all the top Nazis padded their resumes with monumental achievements they never earned, do you know their reputations as athletes?

Answer. C'mon, really, who asked that? Anyway, I knew someone, who knew someone, who knew someone who went out with a friend to play on a basketball court in the "mean streets" of Berlin. The story goes, "there were these three fucking dorks" wearing tube socks, headbands, and sunglasses, practicing underhand free throws.

Anyway, we obviously weren't going to pick

them up, but we noticed that one of the assholes continually circled the area where we had to walk through to get onto the courts. Well, we found out later that his name was Hitler and that he had a built-in "ass repellent," which smelled so bad and was so constant that no one dared to enter.

So, we had to pick them up. I said to that kid Hitler, "Don't guard them while facing each other. I only want your ass to face them while on defense, and you seem like you know what to do from there." Don't judge; I wanted to win.

I'll also say this, and if any of you were there, you would agree, but these were the three ugliest motherfuckers I had ever seen. I just wanted to point out how disgustingly ugly they were not just as individuals but also as a group. So, I felt we might actually have a chance to win as no one wanted to guard them.

Well, all three were of kindergarten height. One guy whose ass should have been insured. Another guy named Himmler was so ugly that the dogs at the dog park next door wouldn't allow him to hump them, and trust me, we watched him try. Now, my concern was, what am I going to do with the last one, Goebbels?

I was concerned about someone stepping on him. He was in his late teens, and I would guess he was around 3'4." I told him we could use him for special plays on offense, so I named him "step stool" as he would literally let us use his head to jump off of. I've never seen a bigger ass kisser than him. He even told us we could kick him in the nuts if we could find them. We couldn't.

After the game, which we lost in about five minutes, I asked them a few questions because they were not from this area. As I was talking to them, I quickly realized how fucking stupid all three were. I was starting to get frustrated not only from the loss, but they were constantly interrupting me. Finally, I shouted, "You three fucks couldn't run a turnstile," as they wouldn't shut up about running Germany one day. Yea, right, that's a fucking joke.

The only thing that may have been worse than their utterly unathletic and ugly appearance was that two kids who were playing in our game suffered broken ankles. Yep, that fart machine weirdo also showed an ability to spit like a garden hose and was turning the court into a skating rink. Hitler just wouldn't shut the fuck up while trying to coach in a game he knew nothing about.

These three goofy fucks and the many more you haters revere are people you would have never hung out with yourselves. Having these douchebags as your heroes tells 99.99999999999% of the world immediately who you are. They'll never need or want to talk or communicate with you as there's no need.

We already know you based on your association alone. Germany was definitely "down" after World War I, and yes, their economy and unemployment rate were bad for a few years, but to elect Hitler and get his awful murdering lackeys, and then listen to them blame everything on Jews, will go down as the greatest con job in the history of politics.

Question. Can a pussy shoot a gun?

Answer. Well, it seems like it. Robert Bauer, the asshole who murdered 11 innocent lives and injured six others at the Tree of Life Synagogue in Pittsburgh, certainly qualifies.

But, before I can make a complete ruling, I need to examine Robert's actions after his graduation from Harvard. Robert dropped out of high school; however, he quickly worked his way up to becoming a delivery driver for a bakery. I'd like to go further in-depth with his stellar bio, but that's it. My guess is if Jews or gays wouldn't have fucked him over so many times, he would have been a full-time physicist or worked in risk assessment at NASA. Somehow, this genius found the time to post various brilliant quotes like, "Diversity means chasing down the last White person." Yes, it does, Robert, yes it does.

Anyway, it's nice to have heroes, and certainly upstanding, hardworking geniuses like Robert Bauer are hard to find. With 11 antisemitic murders to his name, the only thing left for you guys to answer is, where do you intend to erect his statue?

I am still amazed that hate groups can look up to "martyrs" like Robert Bauer, Hitler, Himmler, Goebbels, and thousands of others with no accomplishments. Truly, the only consistent accolades they cared about were doing whatever, and I mean whatever, it took to please Hitler. THAT IS IT. If they (and thousands of others) had to make a decision, it was ALWAYS with the thought, "What would Hitler do?" By the way, how many people know if those three actually killed someone themselves?

After considering all facets of your question combined with the outcome, yes, a pussy can shoot a gun. Well, I hope that answers your question. I would like to add, on a personal note, that I looked at all the names of the people who were killed and injured in Pittsburgh and know they lived fruitful and happy lives. They all had their ups and downs, like most, but reading about them and seeing what they did with their lives and how they made something of themselves infuriates me, knowing a fucking ignorant, moronic, pussy coward murdered them for no cause. Antisemites must know that a response from us is justified, right? When you have one of your own psychotics, neophyte, murderer, kill unarmed and unaware Jews at a Saturday morning service, understand this will not be forgotten.

Now, you got me pissed off. Next question.

Question. You say Blacks, the LGBTQ community, the handicapped, etc., don't affect you, right? My question is, what do you mean by that, and why would the hate group community think the opposite?

Answer. As you know, I'm very open-minded, so without rushing into judgment, I decided I would do some of my own research to see where hate groups were gathering their data.

Here's what I did. I picked ten random days over a three-week period where I was going to do my natural, everyday "type" errands. HOWEVER, I focused on observing all the Black men, women, and children accused of always fucking over hate groups. I wrote down every negative incident only, from someone staring at me to being shot.

I did the same experimentation on the LGBTQ community, the handicapped, and a lot of other minority groups.

Here are my results. Zero. There were zero times that one person in any of these minority groups did one fucking thing that affected me. Not one. In the course of ten days, waiting with my pen and paper in hand, nothing. What's your data?

Yes, I know statistics of incarceration and one-parent homes plague the Black community, but those are minor talking points from hate groups. I focused only on individuals, and so I ask you, what has any minority of any group ever done to you that is keeping you down?

Question. Before Hitler's smoldering body started the first German forest fire, did he finally admit his faults and accept blame for Germany's defeat?

Answer. And in the end, in his last farewell, Hitler had his secretary type out a few of his last comments. Would you like to know the first thing your hero said? He blamed the Jews for Germany losing the war. Ha, ha, ha, ha, ha! Yes, there are people who actually put this douche on a pedestal. I'm not kidding; that's what he said. Ha, ha, ha. What are we now at, for example, 10,000, as to why no one can take any hate group seriously? He was fucking INSANE. If you're in a hate group, would you please explain Hitler's comment?

He also had Fegelein shot in the bunker two days before Hitler had himself turned into a campfire, and why? Two reasons. 1. Because he was Himmler's representative in the bunker. (Hitler was pissed with Himmler for contacting the U.S. for a surrender.) 2. Hitler was frustrated that he no longer had any veins left to "shoot up" his meth.

Question. Are Jews and other minority groups

worldwide being close-minded to all of the benefits regarding membership in a hate group?

Answer. Another great question. I've thought about it, and you know what, maybe we are. I mean, Hitler was so brave when it was his turn to face adversity head-on, that I guess it's inspiring enough to re-think my position. Maybe an esteemed and potential future hate group colleague can answer our questions.

Hitler wrote to others to "continue to fight" even after his death. I guess that's what you guys are trying to do currently, correct? Well, sell us on it. Let's hear it. I'm Jewish, so obviously, I'm not your target audience. But I'm open-minded. What ya got? Pitch me. Why do you love wanting to or being a Nazi? Now, this may also not go over too well with Blacks, Handicapped, LBGTQ, mentally handicapped, oranges, snow globes, etc., but fuck it. I want to hear it. Sell me, enlighten me, convince me.

This is the last question of this Q&A.

Question. This is a two-part question. If I wanted to visit Hitler's grave, is there funding available from my local or national hate group chapter? Also, do I need to make reservations or get tickets in advance, knowing the large daily attendance volume he must receive?

Answer. I cannot find an answer on funding for your exciting trip to visit your hero, but nothing is stopping you from canvasing your neighborhood for donations. Here is some information that should help you with prearranging reservations prior to your visit so you can make sure you have a reserved spot.

Today, if you want to go visit the site where Hitler's body once resembled a Bunsen burner, you will see one of the largest and heaviest monuments ever erected for a deceased former failed painter. It's been cordoned off and is officially a... parking garage. LOL. Well, it's nice to see such a reverent and historical site that allows people to walk all over it, dogs to shit on it, drunks to puke on it, and passersby to spit on it. Not sure whom we should thank for that, but thanks. If you're planning on making a pilgrimage to his final spot, plenty of parking is usually available.

I have a question. Are there any particular songs you guys sing around the machine that dispenses tickets? Do you fire up some meth or heroin as an ode to Hitler, then cite some Mein Kampf vignettes to pay homage while you're still parked, or do you get out of your cars?

Okay, stop bugging me. I'll take one more question.

Question. Since we all know Jesus was born Jewish, raised Jewish, and died Jewish, what do you think G-d's reaction to you will be, knowing you harmed or killed a Jew?

Answer. I don't know.

Well, thanks to all who participated in this Q&A session. I try not to brag or boast when I know I'm right about something, even though sometimes it's hard to stay humble.

However, I do want to point out that I've been telling people for years that Hitler was full of shit too. Now you know, he REALLY was.

Chapter 15: The Israeli-Palestinian Conflict

> *"We plan to eliminate the state of Israel and establish a purely Palestinian state. We will make life unbearable for Jews by psychological warfare and population explosion. We Palestinians will take over everything, including all of Jerusalem."*
> ~ Yasser Arafat

Personally, I've never really had a problem with the Palestinians or Palestinians who want land. I do, however, have a problem with any Palestinian who shoots Katusha rockets arbitrarily into Israel.

This is such a delicate issue, and contention arises quickly when this topic is discussed. I don't have the answer, but without a complete absorption of the territories or re-settlement of the territories, this conflict will continue. Furthermore, as you'll read below, there's very, very little area for Israeli expansion (that no one seems to understand) that would open up more land.

I rarely read about Israel's side of the story as most of the news slants towards the "underdog" Palestinians. I will lay out why it's extremely complex coming from a country that has always proven they would trade land for peace.

Israel's Size

I hear all the time that Israel is like the size of New Jersey, blah blah blah. Well, if half of New Jersey was a superfund site, then…bad example. Okay, how about if half of New Jersey was over a landfill? Fine, my point is that Israel is basically half the size of New Jersey, which is already a small state.

Population Density

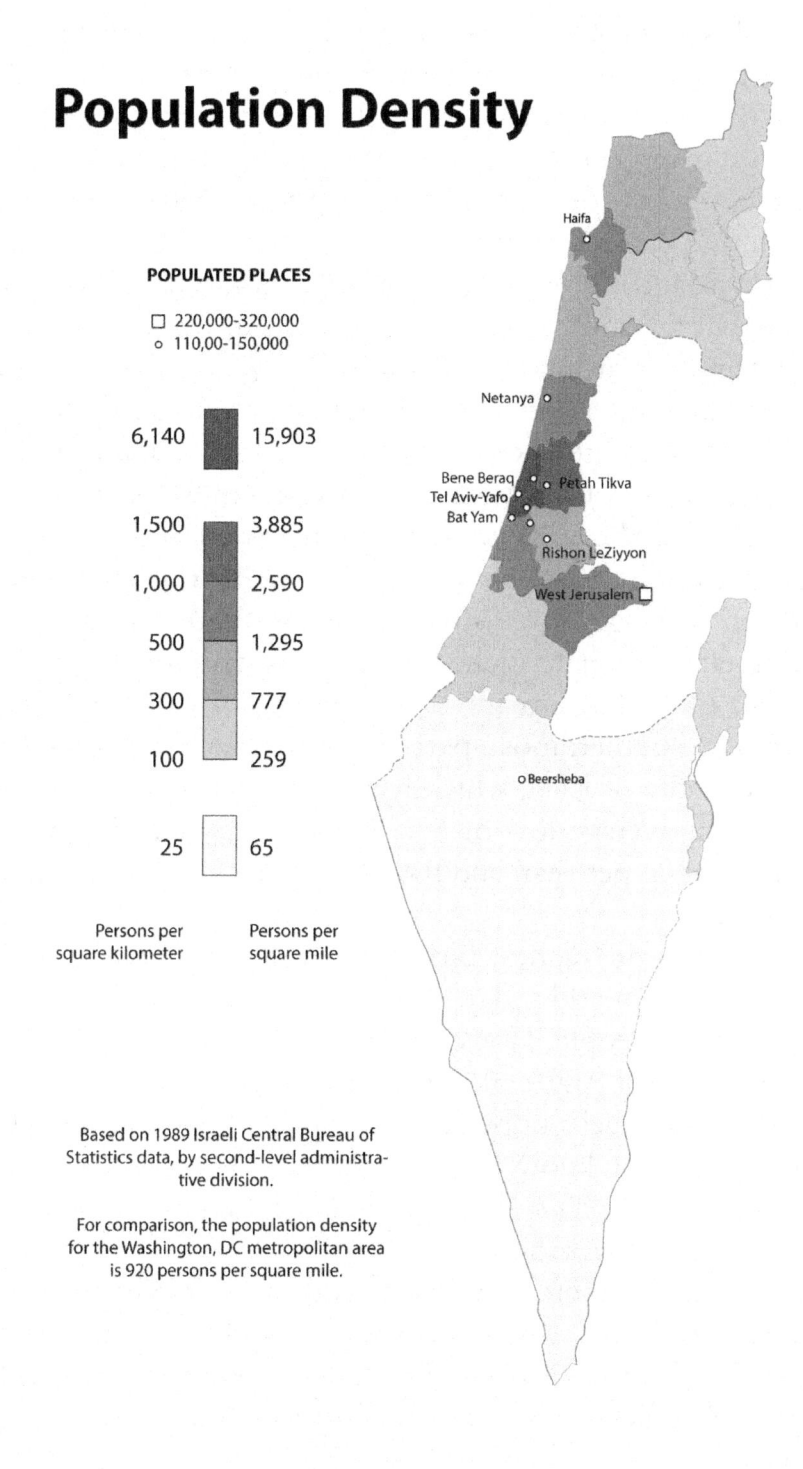

POPULATED PLACES

☐ 220,000-320,000
○ 110,00-150,000

Persons per square kilometer	Persons per square mile
6,140	15,903
1,500	3,885
1,000	2,590
500	1,295
300	777
100	259
25	65

Based on 1989 Israeli Central Bureau of Statistics data, by second-level administrative division.

For comparison, the population density for the Washington, DC metropolitan area is 920 persons per square mile.

I will show you a few things on the map to highlight, but there are very, very few citizens who live below this. Roughly 50% of Israel is virtually uninhabitable desert. The Negev desert...map. The Negev is home to only around 630,000 people, yet 55% of the land mass. Of those 630,000 people, roughly 25% are Bedouins. The largest city in the Negev is Ber Shiva, and it's located in the northernmost part. Dimona, located in the southeast, is a military town. It's a very rocky desert and has mainly impervious soil, meaning that it barely absorbs any water and almost instantly produces runoff.

There's very little vegetation and even fewer animals. To highlight this, let's look at the northernmost part of the Negev, Be'er Sheva, to the southernmost part of the country Eilat. Be'er Sheva has an average annual high of 78 degrees and an average low of 58 degrees, with an average precipitation of eight inches yearly. Furthermore, it rains an average of 41 days a year.

In the southernmost part of Israel lies the absolutely gorgeous city of Eilat, which has an average annual high of 87 and an average low of 67. The average precipitation in Eilat is 1 inch per year, and the average days of precipitation are 10.5.

Israel has the highest birth rate of any modern Western society in the world today. The current population is about nine million people. However, the birth rate is even higher amongst Israeli Arabs and Orthodox Jews.

By 2060, Israel's population is expected to be around 16 million, and you know whose birth rate is even higher? Yep, the Palestinians. They average four children per woman in the Palestinian territories.

My point is, there is no room and much less in the near future. Someday, when technology catches up to allow people in numbers to live in waterless nonporous dirt with very, very little area to generate electricity, then come on in.

But until then, you are not going to find too many takers to move to the Negev anytime soon. In the meantime, the next time you hear that Israel is roughly the same size, theoretically, practically, as New Jersey, I guess you will just have to know your audience and simply say…

The Beginning of a Mess

In 1947 after the United Nations partitioned the land, they gave Israel 50% to the Jews and the other 50% to the Arabs, with Jerusalem being controlled by international territory. Jewish leaders accepted it, but Arabs did not. In 1948 Britain withdrew, and Israel became a state, then immediately Israel was attacked by all its Arab neighbors. Dubbed the 1948 Arab-Israeli war, Israel was attacked by Jordan, Iraq, Syria, Egypt, and Lebanon.

Imagine you just escaped or were liberated from the indescribable hell of the Holocaust. You make your way to a country in a desert somehow, someway. You don't speak the language, and suddenly, you're fighting against five countries and the Palestinians who are already inside the country, plus, of course, fighting against the world press.

All right, pay attention: the war ended in the summer of 1949. After it was over, Israel now controlled two-thirds of the land, Jordan controlled the West Bank, and Egypt controlled Gaza. Most people don't know that Palestinians have been refugees for more than 70-plus years. They are scattered all over various Arab countries in the Middle East. They have no citizenship in any of those countries, and a lot of them are starting to flee to Europe and other non-Arab countries.

Anyway, this is the start of the West Bank and Gaza being used as a political tool for the Arab world to entice sympathizers, especially by Israel's Arab neighbors.

Also, at this time, a man by the name of Yasir Arafat

founded the Palestinian Liberation Organization.

Can we get a show of hands if you can tell me how many countries took in their own Palestinians from the West Bank and Gaza between 1948 to 1967? Let me know when you're ready. I can tell you that most weren't displaced or armed for the Six-Day War.

The Six-Day War of 1967

Israel is again attacked by five hostile countries, where they proceed to kick the shit out of them in six days. In that ass-kicking, they acquired the West Bank, Gaza, the Sinai, and the Golan Heights. In the history of warfare, I can think of no other countries that have taken more heat, ever, than Israel has for winning a war. Those countries attacked, got their asses kicked, Israel took the land, and immediately everybody put pressure on Israel to give it back. Why? Anyone can look at a map of the region and clearly understand that the advantages of that land are for Israel, so why on earth would they give it back, ESPECIALLY since they acquired it by defending themselves? It's called war, and Israel was attacked. Since that day, Israel has received only negative condemnation for having won a war they didn't start.

The Golan Heights will never be given back due to its strategic location. Israel took the Sinai and gave it back to Egypt for peace. They took the West Bank and Gaza and might have, just might have, given it back, if not been that guy Arafat and his organization. Oh, and that Arafat guy, he was head of a terrorist organization called Black September — the group responsible for murdering the innocent Israeli athletes at the 1972 Olympics. I wonder why those mean Israelis wouldn't give back land when this guy was in charge.

So, should Israel keep their current plan that protects our people and families, or should we leave the West Bank and

Gaza to those whose intentions are to drive us all into the sea? Should we give it back to the people whose own government, Hamas, is registered as a terrorist group throughout the world and will not recognize Israel as a country? Well, we know the media's answer, but what would you do?

Egypt

In this time, how many Palestinians do you think Jordan or Egypt has absorbed into their countries? How about if I told you that since 1978, Egypt has listed Palestinians in their country as foreigners? According to Workers' Liberty: "But since the legislation of 1978 which redefined Palestinians as foreigners, Palestinians are barred from working in the public sector. Private sector employers need to obtain work permits to employ Palestinians, and legislation restricts the number of foreigners in any company to 10%."

The site also states: "From 1978 onwards, Palestinians were also banned from attending public (state) schools, fees for university studies were introduced for Palestinians, and restrictions imposed on which university faculty they could attend (if they could afford to attend university at all)."

They can't own buildings or land either, and if Palestinians in Egypt can't provide educational enrollment, work permits, marriage to an Egyptian, a business relationship with an Egyptian, or a bank balance of $5,000, they can be deported. Really sounds like they give a shit.

Do any of you know the total population of Palestinians worldwide? It's around 14,000,000, with 5,300,000 in the West Bank and Gaza, and 7,000,000 in other Arab countries, with the balance scattered throughout the world. Why is it we NEVER hear about those seven million? Do those Palestinians not want their own land in the countries they reside? Do they hijack, terrorize, and shoot rockets into the countries that they're currently in? Why not? Are they so happy and treated with such respect that land for themselves in all of the other various countries is not needed? Well, we can see that in Egypt, they're treated like foreigners. Hmm...how could that be?

As you'll see, the Palestinians worldwide are treated like shit. This may shock most of you, but the Arab World treats Palestinians like shit and much worse than Israel. They are given no, none, zero citizenship in any Arab country. Anyone care to explain and defend that?

Israel is ALWAYS the "bad guy" to the world when it comes to any Palestinian issue or conflict, and yet, according to Officially, "The nearly two million Palestinian citizens of Israel (around 16% of whom self-define as Israeli Arabs rather than as Israeli Palestinians) enjoy a lot of the same equality with its Jewish citizens."

Look, it's not perfect and certainly not "Shangri La," but Israel, a country with a little over seven million Jews, has had to bear the cost financially and militarily for five million Palestinians in what I call the most expensive "babysitting service" in world history. This wide disparity in population is never brought up. Unless someone can tell the Israelis how they can have guaranteed security with no threats, I suggest you leave your "Monday morning quarterback" opinion to those dealing with this clusterfuck situation daily.

Are you starting to understand why it's a horrendous predicament that Israel is in? There's not an Arab, non-Arab, person anywhere in the world who wants this worked out more than Israel.

Israel allows free elections for the Palestinians who continue to elect Hamas in Gaza and Fatah in the West Bank. Both of those organizations have sworn for the destruction of Israel. If Israel was so heavy-handed, wouldn't they, I dunno, FIX the elections for whichever candidate they wanted, as most countries would do?

Jordan

The country's population is made up of 60% Palestinians. So, I'm sure they're given "carte-blanche" like all Jordanian citizens and have reached out their hands to welcome the Palestinians back from Israel. I say back as the Palestinians in the West Bank were Jordanian until they lost the 1967 war. So, in essence, and in fact, the Palestinians in the West Bank are Jordanian citizens.

From the Nakba, Amnesty International: "Palestinians of West Bank origin who were living in Jordan proper or residing in a third country generally maintained their Jordanian nationality. However, in the 2000s, Jordan arbitrarily canceled the national identity documents of thousands of these individuals. It revoked their Jordanian citizenship and gave them temporary travel documents that needed to be renewed after a certain period of time, usually ranging from two to five years. These temporary travel documents are not coupled with a national identification number, meaning their holders do not have access to the benefits of Jordanian benefits."

Maybe it's better for the people coming from Gaza. Nakba, Amnesty International also states: "Palestinian refugees who came to Jordan from the Gaza strip, many of whom had previously been forcibly displaced from their homes in what became Israel, were never given Jordanian citizenship and have consequently remained stateless. They had access to Egyptian travel documents during the period of Egypt's control over the Gaza strip between 1948 and 1967, but not Egyptian citizenship. When thousands of them escaped Gaza to Jordan after the 1967 war, the Jordanian authorities issued them temporary travel documents, which they and their offspring are still required to renew every two years in a bureaucratic procedure that involves the Ministry of Interior and the approval of the Prime Minister. Most of these Palestinian refugees reside in refugee camps in Jordan."

"While the temporary documents Palestinian refugees without citizenship are issued serve as identity cards, their lack of citizenship places them in an insecure position in Jordan."

"They lack access to welfare support for the poor."

"While they can access public schools and Universities, they have to do so as foreigners and thus pay double the tuition fees. They are not eligible for public health insurance, which allows Jordanian citizens access to free or low-cost medical consultations, medicine and hospitalization."

"They are barred from most positions of employment in the public sector and need work permits to obtain jobs in the private sector."

Well, well, well. Egypt and Jordan are two countries that reject the West Bank and Gaza as they clearly don't welcome them or provide any meaningful support. But the world keeps banging the drum of Israel's callousness by not giving them some of Israel's land.

Lebanon

This country has a terrible record with the Palestinians in the West Bank and Gaza. In a 2007 study, Amnesty International denounced the "appalling social and economic condition" of Palestinians in Lebanon. Another Arab country that wouldn't allow them citizenship. But wait, Lebanon is also led by another terrorist group, Hezbollah, that spouts the "world line" of condemnation against Israel for not giving Palestinians land.

Mudar Zahran, a Jordanian of Palestinian heritage, wrote: "Tendency to blame Israel for everything has provided Arab leaders with an excuse to deliberately ignore the human rights of the Palestinians in their countries." Nailed it.

Syria, Saudi Arabia, all of them. The Arab League has instructed its members to deny citizenship to original Palestinian Arab refugees (or their descendants) "to avoid dissolution of their identity and protect their right to return to their homeland."

Israel

Outside of "grandstanding" and "towing the line," every Arab country in the world doesn't give a shit about the Palestinians. They don't. Their plight, their want for land, NONE OF IT. They have never cared, and now that every Arab country has finally accepted that Israel is going nowhere, well, there's a reason we've all been hearing less and less about the Palestinian "plight" in the news and a bit more about Israel's massive commerce. This is nothing new for Israel as they have always wanted peace and to be friendly with EVERY country.

Not one member of the Arab league, NOT ONE, has granted West Bank or Gaza Palestinians citizenship. Do you know why? Because they don't want them. They don't give a shit. Most of their economies can't support them, so instead of figuring out a way to grant them citizenship or programs to help, they put it all on Israel.

Guess what? Israel is the ONLY country trying to help. Whether Israel initially wanted to or not, unlike the rest of the planet, at least Israel understands that they're THE only shot the Palestinians have. Also, can we get a show of hands from any Arab country that has sent Israel money, food, clothing, etc., to help the Palestinians in either the West Bank or Gaza?

That can't be true. It's Israel, those mean people in Israel? That has to be a lie, a made-up joke, and impossible. Why?

Because it's Israel, only Israel. Israel, Israel, Israel.

And please, it's insulting to everyone's intelligence when these Arab countries say, "They're doing it to put pressure on Israel." It's bullshit and has always been a big fat fucking lie.

Too many Palestinians have died from the "help" received, and that "help" has only delayed any real negotiations for the Palestinians to get, well, anything. That lie has worked for the last 40-50 years, but we now see through the façade, and more countries are seeing through that tired lie too.

Egypt and Jordan never wanted them, nor did any Arab country. NEVER. They all promoted to the world the "plight" of the Palestinians and how those bad Israelis were keeping them hostage. Seriously what have they actually done to help besides sending in weapons or using Palestinians' land for attacks on Israel? Oh, those attacks on Israel that have a 100% response rate from Israel and are killing innocent Palestinian citizens, not Iranian, Iraqi, etc., etc., etc., citizens. The reality, again, is Israel wasn't planning on taking that land, but it fell in their lap when they won the 1967 war AFTER THEY WERE ATTACKED.

All these neighboring states constantly speak up about the unfortunate situation of the Palestinians; you would think they would have done something, anything, to help out with their plight, right? Every Arab country has spoken out about the downtrodden and displaced Palestinians for years, and they have done…crickets. How many Palestinians have they truly helped? How much land has these Arab countries designated for Palestinians currently living in the West Bank or Gaza in their countries? They have a shitload more land than Israel. This question is open to any Arab country and individuals from anywhere in the world, but especially for those countries who are always bitching about Israel's treatment of the Palestinians.

Maybe instead of supplying the Palestinians with rockets and mortars, send over real estate agents or some Air BNB reps. If these countries and other Arab countries feel as strongly, as they say, this problem could be resolved quickly, like right now. This is something that should have been done years ago instead of every Arab country constantly and consistently fucking over the Palestinians. These countries should either help out or immediately shut the fuck up. I hope, someday soon, that all of these Arab countries will get together with Israel and put something in place. If they truly want to help, they can get this Palestinian situation fixed. One more time — Israel is the ONLY country that has done anything to help the Palestinians since the first day Palestinians were standing on Israel's land.

In 1987, the rise of the Intifada (the Palestinian resistance to the 1987 Israeli occupation of the West Bank and the Gaza Strip) was bad, very bad. It lasted a little over five years and nine months. Thousands killed, and the outcome? NOTHING but deaths and injuries. Arafat was allowed to go back to Gaza, and everyone celebrated. But it was another waste of people's lives and time. Per usual, NOTHING came of it.

During the second Intifada in 2000, Ariel Sharon visited a mosque, Palestinians were pissed, fighting broke out, and more senseless deaths occurred. This was obviously one of those excuses to fight — senseless, and nothing gained. Now class, from 1987 to 2005, how many of Israel's neighbors have taken in Palestinians? I mean, the Palestinians elected a terrorist organization in Hamas, and citizens around the world are always in disbelief because those "mean, nasty" Israelis just won't give them back the land they don't own.

Look, there's no need to overthink this. The land in the West Bank and Gaza is Israel's. Period. They won it in a war they didn't start, and it's been a pain in their ass ever since. The enormous amount of time, money, and manpower that Israel wastes trying to monitor, guard, and protect it is fucking ridiculous.

Let me repeat this again; Israel is guarding this land ONLY because the Palestinians have sent thousands upon thousands of unguided rockets, suicide bombers, and terrorism into Israel, and the Palestinians are governed by a known terrorist organization that will not recognize Israel's sovereignty. Would you just plainly give them your land under those circumstances? Of course not.

So, the next time you hear anyone from the Arab World or you see someone whining about the unfair treatment of the Palestinians by the Israelis, just ask them, "What is your country doing to help?" Besides complaining, not a fucking thing.

It's been over 50 years, 50 years that the Palestinians have been on Israel's land, and what do they have to show for it? What have all of those terrorist attacks led to? Currently, there are 165 nations worldwide that recognize Israel. The countries that Palestinians are listening to, how many countries recognize them? I just can't fathom why Palestinian leadership has never been interested in peace. Whatever the Palestinians have been doing is NOT, has NOT, and will NOT work. You don't need outside help.

Israel is so far ahead of the Middle East in education, technology, finance, and military... I could go on and on. Who wouldn't want them as a neighbor? Is all the bullshit really because we're Jewish? Give me a fucking break. I would think by now, most Palestinians have a pretty good idea about Judaism, and guess what? They're still there.

It's easy for people to bitch about, cry about, and write about the Israeli "mistreatment" of the "unarmed," "innocent" Palestinians, and per usual, always painting Israel as the bad guys. However, it's ironic because Israel has done more for the people of the West Bank and Gaza than all the other Arab countries combined, times ten, and unfortunately, that's not saying much. Worse, the world doesn't even know or appreciate it.

Why? Because 99.9% of the people go off headlines instead of researching the reality. It's bad and sad for all involved; however, the West Bank and Gaza are not, not, not, not, not the Palestinians' land, and no one, I repeat, NO ONE is coming after Israel to "set you free."

This also includes every and all settlement issues in Israel. Why? Because the settlements ARE ON ISRAEL'S LAND. PERIOD. The country of Israel can choose who can live there and who can't. PERIOD. So please, all of you douchebags who are always crying over the unfair treatment of the settlements, either invite them over to stay at your house or find a place in your neighborhood for them to live and pay their expenses. Then send me an email after a couple of years to see your progress. OR shut the fuck up and let Israel, AGAIN, figure out a way to do it on their own.

To the Palestinians, let our parents' generation be the last ones who fought these baseless and useless terrorist attacks and wars. Is there one person, just one, who thinks any Middle Eastern country, and especially Iran, gives a shit about you? If so, who? Examples? And I'm talking about helping the Palestinian people, not just the few top individuals in charge. By now, you must know that militarily there is nothing you nor anyone in the Middle East can do to prevent Israel from wiping whatever Middle Eastern country off the map if they wanted to. But that's not, nor has it been, Israel's position. Israel is tired of the bullshit too. They want peace with their neighbors. They want commerce with their neighbors, and they want to exchange embassies with their neighbors. They want what every other free nation wants.

And what's most frustrating to me is the Palestinians have BY FAR the best country possible for them to align with. Palestinians have been staring at their best possible outcome for freedom (yeah, I said it) since 1967, yet they continue with their thinking that they will someway, somehow get this land. In all the years and throughout all the attacks you've made on Israel and all the deaths and wounded the Palestinians have suffered, how much land have you taken? One, maybe two feet?

Have any of you asked yourselves why Israel has been able to make an "oasis in the desert" while the countries surrounding them remain third-world? I'm not asking this to brag or boast (maybe a little), but you should WANT to work with Israel as you share the same soil, and it's obvious they're doing something right. Shake hands and start putting food in your families' mouths. Let the world see the wisdom, brilliance, and fortitude of Anwar Sadat, whose name will last much longer than anyone the Palestinians have dealt with over the last 50 years.

There are more and more Arab countries wising up and working out plans for dealing with Israel, which I guarantee will be fruitful and profitable for each of those Arab countries.

My advice to the Palestinians is you need to wise up, stop being everyone's proxy, find negotiators who have your best interests in mind, find some politicians who are not on the world's terrorist list, recognize Israel as a country, and then let Israel know you're serious. What do you have to lose as none of your neighboring Arab countries' interests align with yours, and they're not going to help you anyway?

This is but one very, very small example of what Israel constantly has to deal with. There are many, many organizations of ignorance and moronic thought that Israel has to deal with, whether they want to or not? I just randomly picked out one group, the Democratic Socialists of America, from an article I read about their 2017 convention. This very far-left group is the largest socialist organization in the United States currently, with roughly 92,000 members.

At its 2017 convention, the 25,000-member Democratic Socialists of America (at the time), founded in 1982, supported Israel's right to exist for many years and proclaimed at this convention: "It's solid as it is with Palestinian civil societies struggle against (Israeli) apartheid, colonialism and military occupation." (Radosh, 2017).

The apartheid charge is designed to associate Israel, the Middle East's only democracy, with segregationist South Africa under White minority rule and Nazi Germany. After the anti-Israel resolution passed the convention with about 90% of the vote, the room erupted with chants of "From the river to the sea, Palestine will be free." (Riesman, 2018; Editorial Board, 2019).

The slogan called for the obliteration of the Jewish state, with Jews reduced to a powerless minority in an undemocratic Muslim-controlled nation, driven out entirely or annihilated.

So, I have a couple of comments and questions for the Democratic Socialists of America.

Let's go through your brilliant, open-minded, thoughtful, and caring comments about the plight of the Palestinians at the hands of the evil, heartless Jews. I'm going to jump around a bit, but let's start off with your comparison of the Palestinian situation to Nazi Germany.

I'm not exactly sure what dumb fucking idiot in your group made that statement. Not only is it patently false, but the wording and context are in such poor taste that I would say you now have 92,000 complete morons and dumbasses if they're singing along.

Is your group really okay comparing Israel to Nazi Germany? Just to be clear, you're saying Israel is systematically killing, raping, torturing, stealing, and watching family members die in front of them, starving to death, with no sanitation, no property, no heirlooms, no valuables, or warmth in the winters, to the citizens of the West Bank and Gaza? Do you have any evidence of these atrocities?

Is that what's going on with the Palestinians?

Is Israel invading Palestinian territories daily and taking their homes and possessions and sending them to death camps or leaving them in ghettos where sickness and disease are running rampant?

Is that what's going on with the Palestinians?

How about all the children? If they can't perform slave labor, no problem, killed. Hundreds of thousands and thousands of children were murdered. When did Israel start this practice?

Then you morons double down again in 2021. During the Gaza war, the DSA drew a parallel between Israel and Nazi Germany, condemning the Jewish state for committing a crime against humanity "against Arabs whom it confined in an open air prison." The DSA demanded that "all elected officials…support the Palestinian call to defund ethnic cleansing and fully boycott apartheid" (Democratic Socialists of America).

Shame on you, and fuck you. Six million Jews were murdered. Only a world-class ignorant, moronic, stupid fuck would make that comparison. That's NOT what's going on in the West Bank or Gaza. I have only read about your kind of stupid in books, and I really didn't think groups like this existed.

And if you were a part of the 25,000 at that convention or

currently a member of this "group," you should be embarrassed and ashamed.

Comparing Israel to Apartheid

When you say Apartheid based on verbiage under South African policies, it would be defined as "racial segregation between the ruling White minority and the Nonwhite majority."

Who leads your dumbass organization with 92,000 members? Not only is the word Apartheid factually incorrect regarding the Israelis, but your categorization of the Palestinians regarding Israel is patently false. On what planet is Israel the minority and the Palestinians the majority by ANY definition?

The word Apartheid was coined for South Africa but had to be defined by the mainstream as "a political system where people are clearly divided based on race, gender, class or other such factors." That's bullshit. They're divided because their land was "won" in a war the Palestinians lost. PERIOD. If the Palestinians wanted that war or not is irrelevant. I can tell you who did not want that war, Israel.

I'm sure your 92,000 members know that the Israeli-Palestinian issue didn't start last week. Israel has proven time and time and time again that it will give up land for peace. And by the way, is it Israel's fault that they had been attacked in three major wars and won? Furthermore, after being attacked and kicking the shit out of the four to five countries and, in the process, securing more land, why then does every country in the world bitch how the Israelis need to give it back? Where else has that happened?

How many of your 92,000 members live in Texas? By your brilliant logic, shouldn't we give that land that we fought for and won in Texas back to Mexico? What about California? Wouldn't you agree that it's rightfully Mexico's land? Have you called out Texas and California for their "Apartheid and Nazi-like" behavior, you twits? No one on the planet ever complains about land taken in a war except when it comes to Israel, as I've said many times, hoping somebody finally gets it.

If the race and gender class of the Israelis fired thousands and thousands of unguided rockets (like the Palestinians in the West Bank and Gaza) into the West Bank and Gaza, well, then you may be onto something. Between 2000 and 2013, the Palestinians shot 8,749 rockets and 5,047 mortar shells into Israel. As a guess, it's probably closer to 30 to 40,000 in total. Hey, assholes, what do you think that number would be if the Israelis weren't in the West Bank and Gaza trying to provide security for themselves?

Race, gender, class — which one best categorizes Israel being attacked by rockets arbitrarily (no guidance systems) of the "Katyusha" or "SAM" rocket class? Or maybe you'd prefer the Palestinians to go back to their old ways of suicide bombings? I know you don't care either way; just curious.

Show us the videos. I want to see the hundreds of bulldozers in the West Bank and Gaza covering up mass graves because there are too many dead bodies to bury individually. Show us the mass cremations in the West Bank and Gaza, the cremation of tens of thousands a day. Show us the raping of the malnourished, typhoid-ridden Palestinians. I could go on and on, but you guys have the intellectual honesty of a swamp rat, and if I insulted any rats, well, fuck them too.

Feel free to let me know your thoughts on this next issue. I'm quite sure that the leader of this brilliant "movement" is currently in Ramallah protecting children from missiles being arbitrarily sent in to kill and obliterate Palestinians and may not be able to respond until later. No problem; whenever you're done cleaning up rubble, asshole, it will be fine.

So, Israel has proven more than any other nation over the last hundred years that if peace is offered and it's without strings, they will capitulate. Even when attacked and defeating the opponent. As I'm sure all members of the "illustrious" Democratic Socialists of America are aware, the Palestinian government is run by nuns who were brought in to show multiple examples of how to live peacefully, respectively, and gallantly. Both in the Palestinian areas and with its neighbors.

That, or, maybe, just maybe... the Palestinian government is run by a terroristic organization that has said they will not recognize Israel as a state. Israel has made it very clear, it will not negotiate peace with Hamas or Fatah until they recognize Israel as a state. Before your next vote, let's look and see some history of this beloved and peaceful future neighbor with Israel.

Hamas won the 2016 Palestinian legislative election and became the de facto governing authority of the Gaza Strip following the 2007 battle of Gaza.

Hamas holds a majority in the parliament of the Palestinian National Authority. Canada, the European Union, Israel, Japan, the United Kingdom, and the United States of America have designated Hamas as a terrorist organization. All right, two quick questions for the Democratic Socialists of America.

> **Question 1.** As qualifications for membership, do you make sure your members have the inability to read, turn on a computer, or access any news outlets? If so, then that makes more sense.

> **Answer.** Since the founding of Hamas in 1987,

Israel and Hamas have engaged in several wars. In the 2006 Palestinian parliamentary elections, Hamas won a majority in the PNA parliament, defeating the PLO-affiliated Fatah party. After the election, the European Union, Russia, the United Nations, and the United States made future foreign assistance to the PNA (conditional) upon the PNA's commitment to nonviolence, recognition of the state of Israel, and acceptance of previous agreements.

Hamas rejected those conditions, which led the European Union, Russia, the United Nations, and the United States to suspend its foreign assistance program in Israel and impose economic sanctions on the Hamas (terrorist organization) lead administration. In 2007 when Hamas took over Gaza, in the battle of Gaza, Israel and Egypt imposed an economic blockade of the strip, because the Fatah was no longer providing security there.

Hamas has said countless times, "We will never recognize the state of Israel."

Question 2. Knowing that, can one of you please explain to me how Israel can negotiate with anyone from that government for peace? Hamas is the government, you nitwits. What would you have Israel do?

Answer. You people do know that the West Bank and Gaza are inside Israel's borders, right? On a clear day, if a rocket from the West Bank or Gaza is shot at the Israeli beaches, tens of thousands could be killed. Do you think Israel likes being in this position? They want peace. As mentioned, Israel has a proven track record that supports that. What fucking record do you and your member-"sheep" have to lecture others about a topic you clearly know nothing about? Have you ever thought that the Palestinians are pawns for larger Arab countries, like Iran, which is Hamas's largest form of aid and weapons? These countries don't want the West Bank and Gaza. Nope, they want Jerusalem, Tel Aviv, Haifa, and all of Israel.

Do you know the definition of Hamas in Hebrew? It literally means violence. Hamas's original charter (and trust me, it hasn't changed) is "committed to waging an armed struggle to destroy the state of Israel." So, I guess it's safe to assume that the Democratic Socialists of America would negotiate with a condemned terrorist organization whose main fulfillment is the destruction of Israel.

How about the other political party in the West Bank and Gaza, Fatah?

Fatah, formally called the Palestinian National Liberation Movement, is a Palestinian Nationalist Social Democratic political party and is the largest faction of the PLO. This was Yasir Arafat's party. Fatah, for many years, was widely recognized as a terrorist organization and used to have a decent number of militant groups. Currently, they have very little influence over the Palestinian people, and frankly, they had years and years to get it done and didn't.

It's an extremely complicated situation, and I think the Palestinian people are getting screwed, but it's definitely NOT by Israel. They are simply not being represented in their own best interests. Also, the Israelis are getting screwed when ignorant, moronic, dumbass organizations like DSA feel they have a platform to verbally coerce their own constituents, a group that needs others to tell them how to think. Who wouldn't want to join that fucking group?

Even though I'm sick of talking about your worthless group, I have one more question. Why is your organization calling for a "Boycott, Divestment and Sanctions" against Israel? That's just brilliant. Let's cut off the Palestinians' largest and basically only revenue stream, owes the most money to, supplies energy to, yada, yada, yada. This just confirms to me that you have dumbasses in your accounting departments, too. So you idiots want to eliminate the Palestinians' largest source of income to help the Palestinians? If the "esteemed" members of the DSA are willing to come out of their own pockets in a substantial way to help Israel help the Palestinians (millions upon millions upon millions), then and only then can you say you're truly helping.

This is the kind of ignorant, immature, dangerous horseshit Israel has to constantly deal with and Jews worldwide have to constantly defend against. I mean, you have a decent size left-wing group who has no fucking idea what they're talking about, yet they passed their "Palestinian plight" rhetoric with 90% of the vote. I have to admit, I'm looking forward to seeing what the topic is this year you'll be voting on while not having a fucking clue.

Of all the right-wing and left-wing groups I've reviewed, the Democratic Socialists of America could be the dumbest, most clueless, and most ignorant. Congratulations assholes. Comparing Israel to Nazi Germany…WOW.

Chapter 16: American Jewry

> *"A people that has produced such a disproportionate share of strikingly successful Americans has been strikingly unsuccessful in maintaining and reproducing itself."*
> ~ Bret Stephens

To my fellow Jews, I really don't know where to start, as I have so many thoughts on this topic. I will do my best to articulate this chapter so everyone can understand. I cannot highlight enough the importance of our American Jewry and where we are today. At our current pace, we are only a little less than two more generations away from having entire states with only one or two synagogues.

We are losing our religion and culture right in front of our eyes, and at such a rapid pace, yet, I still don't see anything being done about it. In my opinion, right now, we are at a "drastic threshold," and if we don't reverse this trend immediately, our religion and culture, as we know it in America, will basically be gone. The Jewish identity that was so clearly laid out for us will be a thing of the past.

There will be some areas where the Orthodox will have sizable numbers, so that's a positive. But Conservative and Reform will be so small that they will basically cease to exist. Am I being dramatic? By now, you know I provide facts. When you're done with this chapter, come back up and re-read the first two paragraphs again.

The only numbers on the rise for Jews in this country are, unfortunately, assimilation and apathy. As a race, I don't think we will ever be extinct in this country; however, at our current pace and by the end of the century, we will have virtually no presence in the United States, excluding Orthodox Jews.

Think about that. There are Jews alive today who may not step foot inside a temple.

This is a tough chapter to write. While I'm typing, for some reason, memories of my upbringing keep popping into my head. I'm thinking about my friends, my Jewish friends that I grew up with. How tight our friendships were. How sleeping over at a friend's house during a school week was allowed. Our BBYO trips where we were all so heavily involved. The guys and girls I grew up with at temple. How we all met at the synagogue at such a young age and saw each other two or three times a week all the way through early high school. We all knew each other's parents, brothers, sisters, and grandparents. A bond. A community. I assure you, as we got older, no one would have said something antisemitic to any of us, or it would have been a group ass whooping. We were a family.

Every Jew who reads this needs to fully understand where Judaism is heading in this country. I have a few suggestions, but the people involved in the vast number of Jewish organizations need to start immediately implementing ways to stop the slide of Judaism and quickly implement programs for growth, NOW. Hopefully, someone, anyone, who understands these words will make a commitment today to do whatever they can to grow Judaism in this country, NOW. Furthermore, if you are donating funds to any of the worthy Jewish organizations, you need to demand your money go toward our growth. You would think every Jewish organization in America would be "in front of this" issue because as their donor base shrinks, so do donations.

In May of 2021, the Pew Research Center did an extensive study on Jews in America. I looked through a lot of data and felt most comfortable with Pew's research. It's detailed and used by other groups and organizations. If someone could provide any legitimate evidence that refutes Pew's data, please provide it.

Trust me; no one is showing growth as it relates to Jews in this country unless you find a bullshit outlier or manipulated poll. If you're looking at any legitimate poll, they all show the only real growth in Judaism in the United States is an increase in Orthodox Judaism. Orthodox is by far the only sect in Judaism that is increasing.

Why is this? From Pew, "Orthodox women have on average 3.3 children while non-Orthodox are at 1.4 children average."

Here are their findings as it relates to American Jews overall, with my comments. From Pew: "There are roughly 7.5 million Jews who live in the United States. Of those 5.8 million are adult Jews with children making up slightly lower than 1.8 million. In that number, there are 4.2 million Jews who identify as Jewish by religion and 1.5 million or just over 25%, identify as a Jew of no religion. Furthermore, more than 40% of married Jews have a non-Jewish spouse, that number rises to 61% of Jews who were married in the past decade." Ouch.

Now, I've been around Jews my whole life, and I had no idea there were Jews who considered themselves a "Jew of no religion." I'm not mocking or disrespecting it; I was just naïve to it. In Pew's research, you are a "Jew of no religion" if you answered a question about your present religion by saying you were either atheist, agnostic, or had no religion in particular.

This number stings — 1.5 million Jews are in that

category. I had to reread those stats 20 times. I'm sure I'm going to get into some arguments with this, but by now, you know I don't care. Anyway, once I point out to them the birthrates of their category, well, we won't have a long discussion.

When you look below and see where I subtracted 1.5 million Jews from Pew's total population in the U.S., that's where my number came from.

Pew further states about children: "Currently there are 2.4 million children living in the U.S. in households with at least one Jewish adult. Of that number 400,000 children are being raised Jewish but not by religion. 200,000 being raised by Judaism and another religion and 600,000 are not being raised Jewish in any way." So, currently, half of all Jewish children are not being raised Jewish. That's a big fucking problem. No way to dance around or try to spin it. 2.4 million Jewish children in the U.S. is already a very low number in itself, but now 50% of that number is gone. How did that happen? Is someone talking to the parents or caregivers of these children? My gosh.

Taking nothing away from the excellent research from Pew, let me make their comments a bit easier to understand and provide the real numbers from their findings which represent the current Jewish population in the United States.

By my calculations from their data, there are currently 4.8 million Jews, in total, or .014% of the United States population, and rapidly declining.

Ladies and gentlemen, here's my recap of Pew's total number of Jews in the U.S.

- Currently, 7.5 million Jews are in the United States.
- 1.5 million Jewish adults — gone.
- 1.2 million Jewish children — gone.

So, again, there are currently 4.8 million Jews in the

United States.

Does that not bother any of you? Didn't our parents and grandparents show us many examples of our beloved, exceptional religion? Our bonded faith, traditions, and customs? We are not that far removed from the Holocaust. We are not that far removed from a few psychotic, hedonistic assholes who convinced an entire country of some 68 million people and people of Austria, Poland, Ukraine, Belarus, etc., etc., of the need for our elimination. Hitler and his top asshole buddies convinced so many that we, as Jews, were a people completely lowering the standards of everyone in Germany. Furthermore, because of our existence itself, we were the ones keeping all of the brilliant and downtrodden German citizens from their birthright to great achievements.

Here's one that I'm completely baffled by. From Pew: "Outside of the Jewish population, there are 2.8 million American adults who have a Jewish background. Meaning at least one Jewish parent or a Jewish upbringing. Most people in this category, 1.9 million, identify with another religion, but 700,000 have no religion and do not consider themselves Jewish in any way, and 200,000 Jews identify as Jewish and another religion too."

What? First off, I truly do not understand how this is even remotely possible. Secondly, that means there are roughly 58% more Jews, right now, that we should be approaching. They're Jews. Hello. My gosh, what a shocking statistic. We have such a low population "as is," and you're telling me there are 2.8 million we can start reaching out to today. WTF. There should be designated departments in every Jewish organization in this country focused just on retention and returning.

To recap, there are 4.3 million Jews right now (2.8 million with Jewish background but don't identify with Judaism and

1.5 million Jews of no religion) who can be approached about coming back into the Jewish Community today.

This is fucking nuts to me, ESPECIALLY in such a small, proud religion. Just to make sure we're all on the same page, here's how I see it. There are 4.8 million identified Jews and 4.3 million that aren't. Is the data wrong? No. Am I reading the numbers incorrectly? No. Is there a Jewish group I'm undercounting? No. Unfortunately, those are our current numbers.

To any of the 4.3 million, why? What needs to be done? What's the reason for leaving? You are wanted. You, too, bear the responsibility for the alarming decline of Judaism in this country, and we need your help, all your help. Believe me, I KNOW I'm repeating myself, but someone needs to explain to me how it's even remotely possible to have 4.8 million Jews in this country, with 2.8 million Jews who aren't even counted, 1.5 million Jews who are either atheist, agnostic, or have no religion in particular, and 1.2 million Jewish children who won't be raised Jewish. WTF. This has to be a bad joke. Is there another poll I missed?

We must NOW go "ALL-IN" and figure out what's needed to bring them back. I know I sound desperate, very desperate, because I am. Look, those are the numbers. Play with them all day if you'd like, but that's where we are. I will highlight again, Pew conducted a very thorough and time-consuming poll.

Just remember, our parents did a lot to ensure we went to Hebrew school, observed Jewish holidays, had strong attendance in Jewish youth groups, had Bar and Bat mitzvahs, and so on. Now, Judaism is slowly but surely being eliminated on our accord. Assimilation, laziness, apathy, lack of growth, lack of outreach, and misplaced funding for growth, in my opinion, are the main reasons, and we're doing nothing to "tackle it head-on." Nothing is stopping us but us. These are all self-inflicted and can be turned around if Jews will get involved and get interested. Unfortunately, it seems like most Jews in this country just don't really give a shit.

Shame on us. We are completely and utterly fucking up our responsibilities. We are not paying forward what was so beautifully given to us. Look, I am just as much at fault as anyone, and since we're so far past the blame game, it's time for all of us to be the solutions.

Growth, Growth, Growth

I am going to continue to harp on our need to focus on this one major, major, highly important issue — Jewish growth. The U.S. Jewish population is not only declining rapidly from the published stats but also declining as we break down the various Jewish sects. Orthodox Jews, who currently represent roughly 10% of the U.S. Jewish population, have a birthrate of over four per household, while the average number of non-Orthodox Jews is below the U.S. average at 1.7 children per household. Judy Maltz reported in the *Haaretz Newspaper* that currently, one in seven Jews are Orthodox Jews. Sometime around 2040, that number will be one in four and account for 23% of the total world Jewish population. It won't be long before Orthodox Jews are the largest Jewish sect in the U.S.

Personally, I have no problem with that at all. I am just highlighting another example of how Reform and Conservatives are losing vast amounts of Jews. Furthermore, I have not seen one data point showing either Reform or Conservative Jews leaving their synagogues for Orthodox synagogues, which dismisses any notion of Jews staying within the Jewish religion.

It is time for a Jewish revival, and I hope this book ignites the spark. I have no idea who or how many will read this, but if YOU have, well, then you have no excuse. You can't unread it. So, what are you going to do? What would be your suggestions? How are you/we going to help?

We can start by making phone calls and finding out where our donations are going. We need to make a concerted and immediate effort to donate to those organizations that are or will be implementing Jewish growth. Maybe you'll get on board with a couple of my suggestions, or maybe you have your own. I don't care, but action is needed. Hopefully, the Jewish organizations we support will have their own NEW ideas, as whatever they've been doing up till now is not working.

Groups like the ADL, Jewish Federation, Jewish Communal Funds, Hadassah, United Jewish Appeal, AIPAC, Jewish National Fund, American Jewish Committee, and many, many more are becoming a waste of time and money, in my opinion. Yes, they all do great things and contribute to various needs in our communities; however, if any of these and other Jewish Organizations are not setting aside a significant amount of funds and manpower actively focusing on Jewish growth, then personally, I wouldn't send them another donation until they do.

What are these organizations going to be doing in about 30 to 40 years? Protect whom? Defend whom? Represent whom? I am going to keep pounding our need to focus on one main issue, Jewish growth. Not tomorrow, not next week, NOW.

I am not picking on any specific Jewish organization, but here's their wake-up call. The large number and well-funded Jewish organizations are much better suited to come up with ideas, provide funding, and have a built-in network and platform for this critical need. They certainly have more than most who give a shit about this topic. Is there a reason why this issue should not be the MAIN focus, MAJOR focus, for EVERY Jewish organization in existence? And again, if they have been or are currently putting time and money towards Jewish growth, STOP! It isn't working.

Anyway, here are a few of my ideas to at least get started. I don't want to hear, "It's unrealistic," "It's not feasible," or "Well, we can't do it." Bullshit, and who gives a shit if it's not easy, as this is the position we put ourselves in. I hope others who have ideas will immediately start sharing what they deem are solutions too. This is what I would like to see implemented NOW.

Starting immediately, every Jew in every city needs to be granted immediate membership in the synagogue of their choosing. If someone cannot financially qualify, they will receive a vast reduction of membership price or all of it, which will be granted to the individual or family and paid by contributions from Jewish organizations.

Starting immediately, every Jew in every city needs to be granted immediate membership in their city's Jewish Community Center. If someone cannot financially qualify or afford it, either a vast reduction of membership price or all of it will be granted to the individual or family and paid by contributions from Jewish organizations.

Starting immediately, every Jew in every city needs to be able to visit Israel. If people or their families cannot financially qualify, they will receive a vast reduction or full payment through contributions from Jewish organizations. This includes airfare, accommodations, and some cash. Ages 13-18 in groups, age 18 and older in groups, or individually.

Same as above for Bar and Bat Mitzvahs.

Our Jewish organizations have done a fantastic job over the years in fundraising and receiving contributions. They have proven to us and the world their commitment to Jewish causes and consistently follow up in their actions. However, this is our biggest challenge, and they need to make it theirs. ALL of them need to re-focus their distribution of funding by either starting out with my suggestions or their own outside suggestions, etc. NOW.

If someone thinks I could help with fundraising, no problem, I'm in. Also, I will have a section on my website for fundraising, and 100% of the proceeds will go toward implementing my suggestions or other legitimate suggestions. I would prefer to partner up with one of our fantastic Jewish organizations and let them handle all of that, but if I can't find someone quickly, I'll do it myself. We don't have the time to fuck around on this issue anymore.

I would like for someone, anyone, to convince me that there are other issues more important than getting Jews into synagogues, Jewish Community Centers, Israel, BBYO, etc. There can be no more excuses. There is no higher priority for Jews or the Jewish organizations we fund than ensuring our existence in this country now and in the future.

It's fucking outrageous to me that there are Jews who are not members at various places I listed because they can't afford it. Isn't the Jewish Center where we Jews congregate for fun, activities, Jewish culture, and events? We are losing this battle, and someone or some organizations needs to step the fuck up and FOCUS on retention and outreach. How long until the J.C.C.s are simply called Community Centers?

I don't care how we do it. What formula makes the most sense? I've already supplied you with the Jewish statistics in this country, so if any of our esteemed organizations want to tell me what's more important than losing our Judaism in this country, I'm all ears.

Just know the important takeaway — our numbers are going down and not slowly. Let me be clear; I support every organization that deals with American Jews, Jews around the world, and Israel. We've been very, very fortunate that these organizations have been well funded and have had a lot of brilliant, hardworking men and women oversee and take part. Unfortunately, we have all overlooked our most important assignment.

I want to repeat myself for the hundredth time on this. Any donations that DO NOT highlight funding for stabilizing and Jewish growth, in my opinion, are wasted donations. There are only 4.8 million of us in the entire U.S. That's it. WE have to do this together as each of us shares the responsibility together. Assimilation alone in this country will quiet the doubters within the next 25 years. We will have no voice very soon, and an "all hands on deck approach" is severely needed. Right now, this is our only realistic option. WE have failed our religion, our families, this country, and all those who sacrificed everything in order for us to be here.

We, as Jews, know the value of our religion, customs, and culture. We know our Jewish communities. Growing up, we remember the relationships with our families and the love of Judaism, yet we're watching it disappear in front of us like it's this big fucking secret. It's pathetic, harmful, and a massive shame. We can reverse this, I know we can, but taking the adage of "Okay, we'll start tomorrow" won't cut it. What wouldn't you do for your parents? Grandparents? Friends and other family members who taught and showed us how to be good people? Tzedakah? How to be a Jew? Participating in holiday meals together? Marriages in synagogues?

By doing nothing, WE, "under our watch," are as to blame as the person who has left the religion. Yes, it's our fault, and we're doing nothing to reverse this awful trend. Two more generations at our current pace, then poof, gone. If you're ready, we can do this, but we need to start TODAY.

Chapter 17: Never Again MEANS Never Again

"We have no choice but to strike at the terrorist organizations wherever we can reach them. That is our obligation to ourselves and to peace. We shall fulfill that obligation undauntedly."
~ Golda Meir

I want to start out by reminding everyone that we, as Jews, made an oath of "NEVER AGAIN." I've laid my response out many times already, so what's yours? I will add a few more highlights to this very serious and extremely important topic, but I can't do it alone.

We either continue our current "do nothing" reactionary response to antisemitism, OR we get proactive, aggressive, and go on the offense against anyone who wants to harm Jews, our families, our synagogues, and more.

"Never Again" started with the ending of the Holocaust and the creation of Israel. What those Jews did in that land at that time has no words. Israel established and continues daily to enforce "Never Again" if they know they're going to face a lot of backlash or not.

Our parents and grandparents, who came to this country in droves from around the late 1800s until the 1950s, and in many cases not knowing the language, planted Jewish roots in this wonderful country and slowly made a voice for Jews that were here. Most of the Jewish organizations we know of today were started by, run by, and grown by them. It wasn't easy, but they already knew that. They made no excuses while growing our religion in this country and, when called on, enforced "Never Again."

What have we done? Because of our parents and grandparents, we have been afforded the ability and opportunity in this country to exceed on so many levels. The truly staggering number of achievements that we, as a very small minority, have achieved here was made possible by their sacrifices. So, when it finally became our turn to give the gifts we received to our children, what did we do? We simply hit the snooze button and went back to bed.

Their lack of religious opportunities from our abundance is being squandered by losing the only thing they really ever wanted us to continue. Do you think they'd be happy with us? Proud of us? What role in "Never Again" are we undertaking? What do you think our children are going to eventually write about us?

The book title *Never Again Means Never Again* is a reminder to Jews that we do NOT need to be held verbally or physically hostage to any individual or group, ever again. As a minority, we have an obligation to protect our own by any means necessary. Our law enforcement resources, including city, state, and all federal agencies that are made up of outstanding men and women, do not have nearly the time and manpower to ensure the safety of all Jews 24 hours a day.

Furthermore, there are plenty of laws that protect each and every citizen in the United States and also ensure we can defend ourselves. Those laws are pretty clear and concise. As citizens, we are given a lot of leeway to enforce those laws and protect ourselves.

In September 1972, Germany held the Olympic games in

Munich. As most know, 11 Israeli athletes and coaches were murdered by a terrorist group at the games. As you'll see, the incompetency level of Germany's actions and response was so horrifically shameful that I still have doubts about Germany's role.

Anyway, I'm using this event twofold:

1. Remind everyone of the event.
2. To highlight Israel's response.

A response, I might add, as an example to all Jews in this country on how WE should reply. A simple, justifiable response that we will indoctrinate and have as a new mindset.

Only 27 years after the Nazis murdered six million Jews. Only 27 years of Germany having to rebuild its society and dignity, and "come to grips" with the atrocities that spread throughout their nation. And yet, they somehow managed to "pull off" one of the largest blunders of the last 50 years. The words abhorrent, ignorant, and outrageous are compliments when you consider what took place at the Olympic games in Munich on September 5th and 6th, 1972, only 27 years after the Nazis were defeated. Five Israeli athletes and six coaches were murdered by the terrorist group known as Black September.

Now, maybe I'm missing something, but wouldn't you think, with the Olympic games being held in Germany at that time, that the one thing the Germans would absolutely do is to make sure NOTHING happened to the Jewish athletes and coaches "on their watch." I'm talking about precautions such as assigning multiple military units, if need be, to protect them at night and have armed security with each athlete throughout the day. At a minimum, security guards should have been watching their rooms 24/7 in case someone wanted to plant an incendiary device.

Anyway, Germany provided no security; the Israelis were put on the ground floor in a relatively isolated part of the Olympic Village. Do you know how the terrorist group Black September got into the athlete's village? They simply hopped a fucking fence, and not only did they hop a fence, but they also hopped it with another country's athletes who needed to get back to their rooms. Ho hum.

There were no armed personnel anywhere. *Der Spiegel* reported, and it's never been refuted, that German authorities were tipped off by an informant about the Palestinians planning an "incident," and the informant's information was credible enough that the German Foreign Ministry in Bonn sent the information to the Secret Service in Munich and told them to take "all possible security measures."

The German authorities did NOTHING. A contingent of Jews, on German soil, in front of the whole world... and they didn't think to ramp up security with a credible threat?

During the hostage negotiations, the Germans sent in 38 West German police officers, who, of course, had not a fucking clue how to respond to a terrorist plot. It was simply an absolute fucking boondoggle disgrace. Oh, and to really highlight the incompetency of this German "operation," the police didn't bother telling any camera crews who were filming on-site not to record. Sooooooo, the terrorists, who had televisions on in each room to see how the coverage was going, could see the positions of all the officers. Those guys must have been laughing their asses off.

The hostage negotiations were going nowhere. The terrorists conceded on five separate occasions to push back the time on negotiations. Now, the Germans agreed to supply a plane and transport all the terrorists and hostages to the airport in two helicopters. Guess what? The Germans had no intention of letting any member of Black September or the hostages leave on that plane. And by no intention, I mean...

So, the Germans brought in five snipers. Yes, five. There were eight terrorists, and in these types of hostage incidents, it's usually a ratio of three-to-five snipers attached to one terrorist. Meaning there should have been 24-40 snipers, NOT five. Furthermore, the five German "snipers" were also police officers, and none of them were trained snipers. Those five were picked because they shot "competitively on the weekends." What a complete cluster fuck.

Up until the helicopters landed at the airport, the German police thought there were only two to three terrorists. All that time, in all their negotiations and checking on the hostages, no one was able to pick out more than three terrorists? On the plane, there were 16 crew members, all armed German police officers. When the crew saw that there were eight terrorists, they abandoned the plane. In case you missed that last sentence, ALL 16 ARMED GERMAN POLICE OFFICERS ABANDONED THEIR "COVER" AND THE AIRPLANE WHEN THEY SAW EIGHT TERRORISTS.

Again, I don't think the Germans were in cahoots with the terrorists, but with the sheer ignorance and ineptitude, I wouldn't be shocked.

There's a lot more that happened at the airport and certainly in the aftermath of all of this, but in the end, 11 Israelis were dead. That's 11 intelligent, tough, stoic, and beautiful Israeli athletes, dead. The "world-class" incompetence of Germany led to a lot more countries developing antiterrorist units and the Olympics requiring changes to security, but it didn't need to be on the backs of 11 Jews.

Anyway, did Israel sit back and wait for another country to respond?

The tough, witty, Zionist beauty of Israel, Golda Meir, would not allow this massacre to go unpunished. On September 12, 1972, in her address to the Knesset about the response to the Munich attack, she said, "We have no choice but to strike at the terrorist organizations wherever we can reach them. That is our obligation to ourselves and to peace. We shall fulfill that obligation undauntedly." Yes, I agree, and Israel responded.

Golda's comments and Israel's response should *always* be our response. It may have taken years, but Israel eventually tracked down and killed all those suspected of planning or participating in the massacre. Israel also bombed ten PLO bases in Syria and Lebanon, killing 200 militants and 11 civilians.

My point is that Israel responded. Unfortunately, our response to antisemites in this country has been the opposite. It's pitiful and non-existent. That ends now, and the long-awaited mantra of "Never Again" will appear as our policy to defend any Jew that is being hunted.

I am speaking directly to you, us, the Jews who live in this country. If you're sick and tired of any antisemitic behavior and want to do something about it, maybe this is an outlet you will support. I'm not talking financially; I'm talking about standing with.

The ADL does a great job of reporting and documenting antisemitism, and from the ADL website, they "monitor, respond, educate advocate and speak out, about antisemitism," and they represent other minorities and inclusion. That's great, and we appreciate their diligent reporting. However...

The ADL, and every other Jewish group and organization in this country, does nothing to assist in the prevention of hate groups by NOT proactively and directly engaging the lunatics. My point is, no Jewish organizations allow or enable us to go on the offensive, so every response is reactionary. It's not working, and why should we always wait until after a Jew has been assaulted or injured to reply with a meager response? No laws need to be broken in order for us to "get in front of this," and surely, we are allowed to defend ourselves. At this time, we have no offensive capabilities.

Well, that's about to change.

If you've read through to this point, you understand and feel my passion for Judaism and why we no longer have to take shit from anyone. Especially from ignorant people that none of us have affected in any way. I'm done. We're done. All the contributions we've made in this country, and people still want us out or worse. Sorry, not happening. I was born and raised here, so fuck you, you leave. These people that want to harm and hurt us, I declare, they're fair game.

They need to be outed. We need to make sure their families, co-workers, neighbors, whomever, know which hate groups they belong to, where their meetings are, what type of underwear they wear under their robes, etc. I say we need to go after them, now. If any hate group members want to reciprocate and tell everyone I know that I'm Jewish, I accept. "Out me."

We have the resources and personnel, which will be much more powerful than all their groups combined if needed. I think we've spent enough time on defense and simply just "taking it." It's time.

I do want to highlight that we will not go after them as they do us, meaning we will not target their children, their elderly, or their innocents. Nope, just hate group members only.

We need to make sure that cowardly fuckheads like the pussy in Pittsburgh are dealt with before they try and hurt us. If they want to injure and intimidate the defenseless because we are Jews, then fuck it; let's finally get on the offensive side of the ball and go after them. By the way, I'm sure a lot of you anti-Semites "high-fived" or gave a "fist pump" upon hearing the news about that cocksucker in Pittsburgh. I am curious, did anything change in your life from the outcome of those murders? Can you tell me what benefits you or your groups received?

I'm giving notice to my fellow Jews and all hate groups, albeit on short notice, but you better get your shit together, as we are no longer going to sit idly by. You know we have the will and the means, so either stop now or good luck.

I've mentioned it a couple of times, but this will be the last. I have absolutely no problem with hate groups as a place to congregate, have meetings and legally gather. Obviously, I think hate groups are idiotic, stupid, ignorant, myopic, asinine, etc., especially since they include following a psychotic, sociopathic fucktard, but our laws are clear in this country, and if that's your thing, fine. Have a good time. You can talk about how every minority group is fucking you over and continue to blame, blame, blame. Knock yourselves out. I might even stop by and check it out myself.

BUT, the days of getting physical, defacing property, and intimidating Jews, will now be addressed, and aggressively. Some of these hate groups have been around for over 100 years. Please, again, list your accomplishments. What changes have been made because of your groups? Have you successfully kept out Jews, Blacks, homosexuals, or anyone from your neighborhoods?

I have launched a website that allows disagreements and dissension on a message board. We will also be able to talk sports, politics, anything, as long as it's civil. Hate groups and non-hate group members are encouraged to join. Anyone can post or stay, as long as they're respectful.

Imagine being part of a website where you can confront "your supposed enemy" directly. Imagine that. I think if you come in with an open mind, you'll be shocked to find we have more in common than you think.

We will always seek peace first because escalation between people with differences should be settled with words and respect…until it's not. Hate groups have done enough in the past to justify our responding years ago, but fortunately for them, we did nothing.

Our responses to all hate groups will be on a "need-to-know basis," and I won't reveal them. Anyway, if you deface our properties, we'll deface your homes. You throw bricks through our properties, fine, they'll be thrown into your homes. You try to burn down our properties, injure, or attack us…

This has been building and building and is 100% placed on you, the hate groups, the degenerates. For years we have been sitting back, trying to better our lives, our families' lives, and our friends' lives, while you've supported groups that are planning to harm us. There is just no way that even you guys could possibly argue with that.

We will just simply no longer accept being hunted for our religion and culture, especially by the most ignorant of our society.

If other minority groups want to help and you're sick and tired of their bullshit, too, well, our resources will be your resources.

As far as I'm concerned, this is, again, self-inflicted and inexcusable. If we're not going to do anything, then who on earth are we to blame? We are going to establish an agency to very aggressively go after anyone, anywhere, at any time, that wants to injure us because of our religious and cultural beliefs.

In this day and age, it's a much simpler environment to do this when all you need is electricity, a computer, and individuals ready to start "offensively" responding to others from the confines of…wherever the fuck they want.

We are starting to take a little bit too much shit again in a country that has given us much, and we've always tried to return the same. Isn't the retribution more than justified at this point? I'm sure the ADL is tired of writing all these articles, constantly highlighting these antisemitic incidents. The ADL reported 2,717 antisemitic incidents in 2021 and 2,026 in 2020. Soon, they will be able to highlight our stories. The "sit back and wait" or "sit back and hope" statute of limitations is up.

Yes, time's up for the Aryan, White supremacist cowards, and for diplomacy too. There are just too many racist leeches and governmental tit-suckers who contribute virtually nothing and are under the same laws and freedoms we are under, yet they target us with no recourse. Can we not defend ourselves? Should we not defend ourselves? If a group or mob has written charter rules and engages in private or public clear antisemitism, are we not allowed to help bring them to justice?

I just don't understand why we need to wait another minute to defend ourselves. If a mob has formed for some destruction, injury, or death to us, can't we immediately do something, or do we just have to wait and take it? I will answer that…NEVER AGAIN.

Herd mentality, mob mentality, or jack shit mentality is a daily fight in this country. The definition of those mentalities describes how people can be influenced by so-called "leaders" or their peers to adopt certain behaviors on a largely emotional, rather than rational basis. For thousands of years, we, as Jews, have eaten a "ton of shit" for basically no cause. Are we going to stay with the status quo, or are we going to let everyone know that Never Again is "open for business?" We have the resources, we have the will, and we have the justification. We'll start an open dialogue with any hate group or individual who wants to talk, but we'll talk once they dial our numbers first.

One consistent and extremely ignorant comment I hear from hate groups is always funny to me — a lot of you think you are more "American" than us. How does one convince themselves of that? What is the groundwork or rules to be more American than someone else?

Here's my rule, and I just have one regarding this topic, and it's the same as my asshole test. Ready? Are you a U.S. citizen, or are you not a U.S. citizen? There should be no hierarchy in your heads about citizenship, as it's pretty "cut and dry." Why you don't understand this very basic question and answer, I'll never understand. Stop trying the intimidation and threatening route. It's ineffective and pointless, and you've gained nothing from it.

If you want to make some real changes, go get people who align their views with yours elected. If you're not getting laws changed, you can burn a million crosses, but you will still have to pay a fine.

I'm still trying to figure out how many people I'll need, so we'll start out slowly and methodically until I'm satisfied, and then we'll focus on growth. If someone is interested and feels they have the know-how and resolve, I'd like to talk.

Individually or in a group, everyone wants peace and security, and that is universally accepted worldwide. One of the things I pride myself on is that I don't judge people. Anyone, no matter their race, religion, woke or un-woke status, Democrat or Republican affiliation, color, size, deficiencies, whatever — I do not judge them.

So, for us, going forward, there will be no more fucking around. No more of this "Let's see what happens, and we'll deal with it nicely, or passively, or not at all." Our passive responses do not work unless you consider 4,700 anti-Semitic incidences in the last two years alone acceptable.

Fuck that. No more responses with just "harsh" letters and identifying your groups to the media. Every Jew will be represented, and I'm looking forward to this new approach.

A Final Note To the Hate Groups

We are going to set up a Hate Group Hotline that we will not monitor. Just a simple phone number and email address of that nature. This is to help individuals who have questions or are just looking to get out of the hate groups and aren't sure how. We will have zero influence over any hate group individuals who want help. We will have zero listening abilities, conversations, or communications other than to get you information and help fund it. I will say this again. The United States of America has been a bastion of light since its inception. The Founding Fathers of this country set up a government and judicial laws so forward-thinking that they still exist today. Brilliant men. Those men fought a lot when writing up our government, constitution et al., but handshakes (or eventual handshakes) and maybe a beer or two would usually end the evening followed up by more bickering the next day.

My point is, we can have dissension in this country. We can have different opinions. We can have hate. We are afforded all of that by those men who wrote those documents a long time ago. However, misplaced hate always needs to be addressed, and violent hate that results in property damage, injury, terror, or death certainly deserves no place in our society.

One more time. No Jew is trying to fuck you over today, and no Jew is going to try and fuck you over tomorrow. No homosexual, no African American, no mentally or physically handicapped person, no other religion, nobody.

You have a 0.00000 chance of getting anyone deported or thrown out of this country, so what the fuck good is your group?

Look at this country, our country. Many people worldwide have benefited from something that came out of this country. In the overall "shelf life" of countries, we are still pretty young. However, a young country such as ours has produced some of, if not the most diverse, talented, and creative people the world has seen, and we are fortunate enough to call them fellow Americans.

Trying to emulate good people, ALL people, has been a standard for every culture and nation for thousands of years.

Here are some names I came up with while looking at various topics to find individuals who contributed something to this country. Why anyone would give a shit about their sexual preference, color, religion, disabilities, etc., is so asinine to me that even with my open mind, I cannot "see another side."

This list is but a very, very, very few, and you should find out who they were or are. Millions upon millions of American names could be listed — Dwight D. Eisenhower, Jesse Owens, J.P. Morgan, Abraham Lincoln, Thurgood Marshall, Muhammed Ali, Mae Jemison, Billie Holiday, Aretha Franklin, Toni Morrison, Henry Gerber, Serena Williams, Marsh P. Johnson, Harvey Milk, Billie Jean King, Sally Ride, Arlan Hamilton, Elvis Presley, Frank Sinatra, Pocahontas, Jack Nicklaus, and Thomas Edison.

What have any of your hate group members accomplished that's anywhere in the same stratosphere as these people and the tremendous more I could list? What possible scenario did you come up with to convince yourselves and allow you to think you are entitled to tell other Americans to leave this country? Or intimidate them? Injure them? Deface their property?

When you see someone in a car that you think you deserve, you don't. When you see some guy with a woman that you think should be with you, she doesn't. There aren't many groups or organizations that I can think of that waste more of their time to accomplish nothing, than hate groups.

If your groups really and truly want to help this country on issues that directly involve you, your family, and your friends, why don't you shift your energy over to the education and drug problems of this country? I assure you; those two issues alone have a million times more impact on you than any Jew or minority EVER will.

If you want to get involved and you think you have the necessary skills to help, please email me at author@neveragainmeans.com.

Anyway, I will say it again; I'm done with any antisemitic and racist organizations. DONE. I'm done with the ignorance, stupidity, and threats. We have the intelligence, manpower, and guts to go after ignorant groups, and we're coming. In the end, we all know your true reason, your ignorant reason, is because we are Jews. Yes. Yes, we are. We are proud, very proud, and extremely fortunate to call ourselves Jews.

We are a small religion, yet proud. For good or bad, we have memorials of our people in locations all around the world. We accept our past for both the good and the faults we've made. We love Israel and every country that helped make it happen. We embrace our customs and traditions and will never apologize for them. We respect. We have a long and beautiful history and are all bound to further and continue this beautiful, beautiful religion filled with nothing but good.

We understand, but we need to make sure that we remember and honor our past, while ensuring and protecting our future. Who are we if we don't? If we cannot protect our own, and if we do not respond, then antisemitic incidences will continue. That, unfortunately, is a proven FACT. As

Jews, we all share a common bond in many ways, but we always need to remember that letting our guard down, allowing people to disseminate lies on public forums, and doing structural and physical damage to us today, without a response or recourse, allows me to remind everyone: **Never Again MEANS Never Again.**

Resources

Introduction

Chavez, Nicole, Grinberg, Emanuella and McLaughlin, Eliott C. "Pittsburgh synagogue gunman said he wanted all Jews to die, criminal complaint says." *CNN, October 31, 2018.* https://www.cnn.com/2018/10/28/us/pittsburgh-synagogue-shooting/index.html. Retrieved October 3, 2022.

Chapter 1

Morris, Tim. "100 years after 'The war to end all wars,' we're still fighting." Nola.com, November 11, 2018. https://www.nola.com/nation_world/article_fdca27e7-2e0b-559a-8c7d-a7a21ca9aaf9.html. Retrieved October 3, 2022.

Chapter 4

Hitler, Adolf. Mein Kampf. lulu.com, February 25, 2020. https://www.barnesandnoble.com/w/mein-kampf-adolf-hitler/1100210044.

Epstein, Rob and Friedman, Jeffrey. Paragraph 175. 2000. (DVD format) https://www.amazon.com/Paragraph-175-Rupert-Everett/dp/B00005YUP1.

Tatchell, Peter. "The Nazi war on gay people: Survivors speak out." The Peter Tatchell Foundation, April 12, 2017. https://www.petertatchellfoundation.org/the-nazi-war-on-gay-people-survivors-speak-out. Retrieved

October 3, 2022.

Chapter 5

Morelock, Jerry D. "No, the 1919 Treaty of Versailles was not responsible for World War II." historynet.com, July 18, 2017. https://www.historynet.com/failed-peace-treaty-versailles-1919. Retrieved October 3, 2022.

"Peace Treaty of Versailles - Articles 231-247 and Annexes - Reparations." Brigham Young University. https://net.lib.byu.edu/~rdh7/wwi/versa/versa7.html. Retrieved October 3, 2022.

Chapter 6

Liddel, Guy. The Guy Liddell Diaries Vol I: 1939–1942: MI5's Director of Counter-Espionage in World War II, Routledge, New York, New York, 2005.

Chapter 7

Burns, Ken. "War Production." PBS. https://www.pbs.org/kenburns/the-war/war-production. Retrieved October 3, 2022.

Burns, Ken and Novick, Lynn. The War. 2007. https://kenburns.com/films/war. Retrieved October 3, 2022.

Cooke, Rachel. "High Hitler: how Nazi drug abuse steered the course of history." The Guardian, September 25, 2016. https://www.theguardian.com/books/2016/sep/25/blitzed-norman-ohler-adolf-hitler-nazi-drug-abuse-interview. Retrieved October 3, 2022.

Cornwell, John. "Hitler's Pope." Vanity Fair, October 29, 2013. https://www.vanityfair.com/style/1999/10/pope-pius-xii-199910. Retrieved October 3, 2022.

Fogg, Shannon 2017. Stealing Home: Looting, Restitution and Reconstructing Jewish Lives in France, 1942-1947. Oxford University Press, 2017.

Hadden, R.L. 2008. The Heringen Collection of the US Geological Survey Library, Reston, Virginia. Earth Sciences History, 27, no. 2: 248-249.

Loudis, Jessica. "The Third Reich Was Addicted to Drugs." The New Republic, March 6, 2017. https://newrepublic.com/article/141125/third-reich-addicted-drugs. Retrieved October 3, 2022.

Matelski, Dariusz Grzegorz. "Rewindykacja polskich dóbr kultury z NRD [Recovery of Polish cultural heritage from the GDR / Rückholung polnischer Kulturgüter aus der DDR / Извлечение польских культурных ценностей из ГДР]," Nadwarciański Rocznik Historyczno-Archiwalny, 2003, nr 10, s. 255-264. https://www.academia.edu. Retrieved October 3, 2022.

Petropoulos, Jonothan. Art As Politics in the Third Reich. University of North Carolina Press, 1990.

Redlich, Fritz. Hitler: Diagnosis of a Destructive Prophet. Oxford University Press, 1998.

Świata, Wiadomości ze. "Rosjanie oddają skradzione dzieła sztuki." Gazeta Wyborcza, October 14, 2007. https://wyborcza.pl/7,75399,4554829.html. Retrieved October 3, 2022.

Chapter 10

Cooper, Matthew. The Nazi War Against Soviet Partisans, Stein & Day Publishers, 1979.

Kitchens, Martin. The Third Reich: Charisma and Community. Routledge, New York, 2008.

SchubertFilm. "Mathi Schenks letzte Reise nach Polen." https://www.schubertfilm.de/filme-2000-2014/mathi-schenks-letzte-reise-nach-polen. Retrieved October 3,

2022.

Snyder, Timothy. Bloodlands: Europe Between Hitler and Stalin. Basic Books, 2010.

Chapter 11

Berenbaum, Michael. Witness to the Holocaust. William Morrow, 1997.

Chapter 12

Baron, Saskia, director. Science and the Swastika: The Deadly Experiment. IMDb, 2001. https://www.imdb.com/title/tt1809032/?ref_=ttpl_ql, Mar 26, 2001. Retrieved October 3, 2022.

Black, Edwin. War Against the Weak: Eugenics and America's Campaign to Create a Master Race. Dialog Press, 2012.

Costelloe, Keven. "Files Say Nazi Victims' Gold Teeth Yanked; Bodies Thrown into Bonfire." Associated Press, November 25, 1987. https://apnews.com/article/3624ff62d3b168ba2433ca2581ad8306. Retrieved October 3, 2022.

"Human Lampshade: A Holocaust Mystery." National Geographic, September 29, 2012. https://www.natgeotv.com/ca/human-lampshade-a-holocaust-mystery. Retrieved October 3, 2022.

Jacobson, Mark. The Lampshade: A Holocaust Detective Story from Buchenwald to New Orleans. Simon & Schuster, New York, New York, 2010.

JTA. "Lampshade made of Holocaust victim's skin sold for $26,800." The Times of Israel, August 5, 2014. https://www.timesofisrael.com/lampshade-made-of-holocaust-victims-skin-sold-for-26800. Retrieved October 3, 2022.

Maloney, Alison. "WAR 'WITCHES' Female Nazi guards tortured and killed thousands, beat naked women to death & 'made lampshades from human skin.'" The U.S. Sun, February 10, 2021. https://www.the-sun.com/news/2305735/female-nazi-camp-guards-lampshade-skin. Retrieved October 3, 2022.

Matalon Lagnado, Lucette and Cohn Dekel, Sheila. Children of the Flames: Dr. Josef Mengele and the Untold Story of the Twins of Auschwitz. Penguin Books, 1992.

Plath, Sylvia. "Lady Lazarus" from Collected Poems. HarperCollins, 1981. https://www.poetryfoundation.org/poems/49000/lady-lazarus. Retrieved October 3, 2022.

Santoro, Gene. "A Human Skin Lampshade Sparks a Journey into the Heart of the Holocaust." HistoryNet, September 30, 2010. https://www.historynet.com/a-human-skin-lampshade-sparks-a-journey-into-the-heart-of-the-holocaust. Retrieved October 3, 2022.

Chapter 13

Breidthardt, Annika. "Finance ministry served Nazi machine: historian." Reuters, November 9, 2010. https://www.reuters.com/article/us-germany-ministry-nazis-idUSTRE6A82HB20101109. Retrieved October 3, 2022.

BROTHERHOOD OF KLANS KNIGHTS OF THE KU KLUX KLAN INC. Bizopedia, updated February 23, 2016. https://www.bizapedia.com/oh/brotherhood-of-klans-knights-of-the-ku-klux-klan-inc.html. Retrieved October 3, 2022.

Harper, Jo. "Nationalized Jewish property: Warsaw's restitution problem." Deutsche Welle (DW), January 1,

2020. https://www.dw.com/en/nationalized-jewish-property-warsaws-restitution-problem/a-52156875. Retrieved October 3, 2022.

OSW (Center for Eastern Studies). "The role Nazi Germany's Ministry of Finance played in the Holocaust." November 17, 2010. https://www.osw.waw.pl/en/publikacje/analyses/2010-11-17/role-nazi-germanys-ministry-finance-played-holocaust. Retrieved October 3, 2022.

Petropoulos, Jonathan. Art As Politics in the Third Reich. The University of North Carolina Press, 1999.

Polish Ministry of Affairs. "Rewindykacja dobr kultury." Archived from the Wayback Machine. https://web.archive.org/web/20070821215332/http://www.msz.gov.pl/Rewindykacja,dobr,kultury,1775.html. Retrieved October 3, 2022.

Rosjanie oddają skradzione dzieła sztuki, Gazeta Wyborcza, October 14, 2007. https://wyborcza.pl/7,75399,4554829.html. Retrieved October 3, 2022.

VINnews. "Berlin, Germany – Report: Confiscated Jewish Wealth 'Helped Fund the Nazi War Effort.'" November 21, 2020. https://vinnews.com/2010/11/21/berlin-report-confiscated-jewish-wealth-helped-fund-the-nazi-war-effort. Retrieved October 3, 2022.

Chapter 14

Casstevens, David. "Spreading his message." Fort Worth Star-Telegram, June 5, 2007.

Ginsberg, Rachel. "Diary of Defiance." Mishpacha Jewish Family Weekly. June 8, 2021. https://mishpacha.com/diary-of-defiance. Retrieved October 3, 2022.

Kellner Diaries. "The Diaries of Frederick Kellner." https://kellner-diaries.digital. Retrieved October 3, 2022.

Kellner, Robert Scott. "The Diary of Frederick Kellner — Kellner Diary Entries." https://sites.google.com/site/friedrichkellnerdiary/kellner-diary-entries. Retrieved October 3, 2022.

Wikipedia. "Friedrich Kellner." October 1, 2022. https://en.wikipedia.org/wiki/Friedrich_Kellner. Retrieved October 3, 2022.

Chapter 15

Amnesty International. "Lebanon: Exiled and suffering: Palestinian refugees in Lebanon," October 2007. https://www.amnesty.org/en/documents/MDE18/010/2007/en. Retrieved October 3, 2022.

Nakba.amnesty.org. "Seventy+Years of Suffocation." https://nakba.amnesty.org/en/chapters/jordan. Retrieved October 3, 2022.

JTA. "Democratic Socialists of America passes BDS motion against Israel at convention." August 6, 2017. https://www.jta.org/2017/08/06/united-states/democratic-socialists-of-america-passes-bds-motion-against-israel-at-convention. Retrieved October 3, 2022.

Norwood, Stephen H. October 13, 2021. Institute for National Security Studies. *Antisemitism in the United States – collection of articles.*

Street, Dale. "The Palestinians in the world today." Workers' Liberty, September 14, 2021. https://www.workersliberty.org/story/2021-09-14/palestinians-world-today. Retrieved October 3, 2022.

Stephens, Bret. "Is There a Future for American Jews?" SAPIR Journal, Vol. 3, Autumn 2020.

Zahran, Mudar. "Demonizing Israel is bad for the Palestinians." The Jerusalem Post, August 1, 2010. Retrieved October 3, 2022.

Chapter 16

Maltz, Judy. "Nearly One in Four Jews Will Be ultra-Orthodox by 2040, New Study Says." Haaretz Newspaper, May 3, 2022.

Chapter 17

Ahern, Raphael. "Germany had a tip-off three weeks ahead of Munich Massacre." Der Spiegel, July 2012.

Made in the USA
Middletown, DE
28 October 2022